AGRICOLA
AND THE CONQUEST
OF THE NORTH

W.S. Hanson

B.T. Batsford Ltd London

© W. S. Hanson 1987
First published 1987
First published in paperback, with corrections 1991

Typeset by Progress Filmsetting
and printed in Great Britain by

Courier International Ltd
East Kilbride, Scotland

Published by B. T. Batsford Ltd
4 Fitzhardinge Street
London W1H 0AH

A CIP catalogue record for this book is
available from the British Library

ISBN 0 7134 5193 9

Contents

	Preface to the paperback edition	6
	Preface to the first edition	7
	Acknowledgements	9
	Illustrations	10
1.	Sources of evidence	13
2.	The Flavian connection	33
3.	Early campaigns	46
4.	Civil responsibilities	69
5.	From Tyne to Forth	84
6.	Total conquest	115
7.	The anatomy of withdrawal	143
8.	Assessment and reassessment	174
	Appendix: Emperors and governors	189
	Abbreviations	190
	Bibliography	190
	Index	205

Preface to the paperback edition

The paperback edition of this book has provided the opportunity to correct misprints and minor errors. I would like to thank reviewers and friends for drawing these to my attention. Within the constraints of a reprint it has not been possible to make more substantive changes. However, I am grateful to Batsford for permitting the insertion of some additional information at the beginning of the volume. Here the reader will find brief comment on recent discoveries and interpretations which affect the text, with bibliographical references. Attention is drawn to these comments at the appropriate place in the text by an asterisk. The bibliographical references can be found in the addenda to the bibliography, p. 204.

Addenda and Corrigenda
p. 54: Full analysis of the dating evidence from the primary levels of the fort at Caernarvon now supports a foundation date at the beginning of the governorship of Agricola (information from Dr J. Davies), though a slightly earlier date is not precluded. Pottery recovered from the recently discovered fort at Blennerhassett near Caermote suggests that its foundation may be similarly early (Evans and Scull 1990).

p. 61: Recent dendrochronological analysis has indicated a felling date of AD 72/73 for the timbers used in the construction of the Roman fort at Carlisle (information from Mr I. Caruana) and thus confirms that the fort was established as a result of the campaigns of Cerialis.

p. 121 and 153-7: Recent numismatic work (Hobley 1989) has indicated that the coins of AD 86 from various forts in northern Scotland provide more than just a *terminus post quem* for the withdrawal from that area. AD 86 and 87 were peak years in the supply to Britain of coins of the emperor Domitian. Thus the absence of coins of AD 87 indicates that occupation of the forts involved had ceased before their garrisons had received the later issue in their pay. Allowing time for transport of the coins to the province, this would suggest that the withdrawal had taken place by the middle of AD 88 at the very latest. Thus not only were Inchtuthil and the outer line of forts abandoned by this date, but so too were forts along the road line to the rear, such as Strageath (Frere and Wilkes 1989, 13), and those immediately south of the Forth-Clyde isthmus, such as Elginhaugh (Hanson and Yeoman 1988, 11). This leaves no time for the Gask installations to have served as a frontier during a phased withdrawal from the north. Moreover, since maintenance of such a controlled boundary makes little sense if a legionary fortress lay beyond it, occupation of the Gask frontier contemporary with the halt on the isthmus at the end of Agricola's fourth campaign seems the only reasonable alternative (Hanson 1991, 1765-7).

p. 167: Large scale excavation at Elginhaugh failed to confirm the existence of the anticipated native site beneath the Roman fort, though it did indicate that the area had been under pasture at the time of the Roman arrival (Hanson and Yeoman 1988, 10).

Glasgow, November 1990

Preface to the first edition

MY interest in Agricola was fostered at a relatively early age. Though as a schoolboy I struggled with the terseness of Tacitus' phraseology, the biography of his father-in-law left a lasting impression upon me. The subsequent development of my career in archaeology brought me back to Agricola: between 1974 and 1978 I excavated three sites with Agricolan connections and took up a post teaching Roman archaeology in a Scottish university.

Any work of synthesis depends largely upon the researches of others, as the length of the bibliography which accompanies it should indicate. I have tried to provide the correct attribution for ideas contained within these pages, but if any have not been credited to their rightful originators I apologise now. Throughout the writing of this book I was constantly reminded of the cyclical nature of our interpretations of the past. It will rapidly become apparent that I take a minimalist view of the achievements of Agricola. If the case is overstated, this should be seen as an attempt to redress the balance of the current consensus. Nonetheless, I am well aware that not only do my views reflect what is becoming the new orthodoxy, but that they are a return to the assessment of earlier generations of scholars, notably Collingwood (Collingwood and Myres 1936, 113–114) and Birley (1953, 10–19). I will not speculate on the reasons for such a process, but it does serve to emphasise that history is not static and is as much a reflection of the present as it is of the past.

The book is intended for that most difficult audience, the interested layman and the undergraduate student. I hope also that the work will be judged of some value by my academic colleagues, for throughout I have tried to present all the evidence upon which my interpretations are based. Though there are those who would affirm that archaeological and historical evidence are very different beasts and should be firmly segregated, I do not subscribe to such academic apartheid. The classical training of many established scholars who have studied the Roman period in Britain has tended to result in too much emphasis on the primacy of the written word: archaeology is sometimes even dismissed as concerned in the main only with the nature of objects and their manufacture (Salway 1981, 630). What is being made clear by the work of the younger generation, whose academic background has involved more archaeological study, is that archaeological evidence has at least as much to offer as the brief literary record to our understanding of the Roman period in Britain and that it can be used to write history.

The aim of the present work is to re-assess the role of Agricola in the conquest of Britain and to present a coherent account of that process formed from the various strands of evidence available. It is also intended to illustrate the way in which such a study is approached and to highlight its weaknesses as well as its strengths, for the picture will never be complete and will inevitably change as new information comes to light.

Glasgow, July 1986

Acknowledgements

This book has benefited greatly from the critical comments of Dr Lesley Macinnes, Mr G.S. Maxwell and Professor A.L.F. Rivet. My postgraduate students Duncan Campbell and Alan Leslie kindly read and commented on all or part of the text at an early stage. I thank them all, not least for not pulling any punches. Any errors that remain are entirely my responsibility. I commend Peter Kemmis Betty for his gentle chiding and forbearance.

I would like to thank all who kindly provided illustrative material: their contributions are acknowledged in the list of figures and plates which follows. Alan Leslie drew all of the maps and most of the other figures which accompany and enhance the text. To him I owe a considerable debt of gratitude.

Illustrations

FIGURES

To allow ease of comparability between sites of different types, wherever possible the line drawings which accompany this work have been prepared to standard scales. Thus military complexes and comparative plans of temporary camps are reproduced at 1:10000, while individual sites are illustrated at 1:4000, 1:2000 or 1:1000.

1 The British Isles according to Ptolemy *c.* AD 150 (by permission of the Controller of Her Majesty's Stationery Office : Crown copyright reserved)   24
2 Flavian forts in North Wales   52
3 Timber-built auxiliary fort at Pen Llystyn (after Hogg)   54
4 Pre-Agricolan penetration into north Britain   58
5 Cartimandua's capital at Stanwick (after Wheeler and Haselgrove)   59
6 Rey Cross temporary camp (after Richmond and McIntyre) 62
7 Roman forts at Dalswinton: (a) Bankfoot, (b) Bankhead (after St Joseph with additions) (by permission of Edinburgh University Press)   63
8 Flavian forts in northern England   66
9 Early Flavian fora at (a) Verulamium and (b) London (after Frere and Marsden)   75
10 Possible tribal territories and Flavian camps in Lowland Scotland   86
11 Large Flavian temporary camps at Dunning and Abernethy 88
12 Agricolan supply-base at Red House, Corbridge   89
13 Eildon Hill North: hillfort capital of the Selgovae and site of Roman watchtower (after R.C.A.H.M.S.) (by permission of Edinburgh University Press)   92
14 Agricolan forts at (a) Newstead and (b) Milton (after Richmond and Clarke)   98
15 Forts constructed between Agricola's third and fifth campaigns   100

16 Fort and camps at Castledykes (after R.C.A.H.M.S.) (by permission of Edinburgh University Press)   103
17 Agricolan *praesidia* across the Forth–Clyde isthmus   110
18 Tribal territories and possible Agricolan temporary camps in north-east Scotland   118
19 Forts and camps at Ardoch (after St Joseph)   122
20 Comparative plans of Stracathro-type camps north of the Forth–Clyde isthmus   124
21 Comparative plans of large temporary camps of putative Agricolan date north of the Mounth   132
22 Flavian forts north of the Forth–Clyde isthmus   144
23 Incomplete legionary fortress at Inchtuthil (after Richmond) (by permission of Edinburgh University Press)   147
24 Plan of the auxiliary fort at Fendoch (after Richmond and McIntyre)   150
25 The Gask frontier   154
26 Comparative plans of Gask frontier towers and fortlets   155
27 Flavian forts in Scotland occupied after *c.* AD 90   159
28 First-century Roman artefacts from native sites in Scotland 172

PLATES (*Between pages 82 and 83*)

1 Denarius of AD 84 which supposedly commemorates the victory at Mons Graupius (courtesy of The American Numismatic Society, New York)
2 Weaponry from Llyn Cerrig Bach, Anglesey (by permission of The National Museum of Wales)
3 Chariot and horse gear from Llyn Cerrig Bach, Anglesey (by permission of The National Museum of Wales)
4 Lead waterpipe from the legionary fortress at Chester inscribed IMP. VESP. VIIII T. IMP. VII COS. CN. IULIO AGRICOLA LEG. AUG. PR. PR. (by permission of the Grosvenor Museum, Chester)
5 Lead pig from Chester inscribed (top) IMP. VESP. AUG. V T. IMP. III (SIDE) DECEANGL. (by permission of the Grosvenor Museum, Chester)
6 Horse and chariot fittings from the Melsonby hoard, Stanwick (by permission of the British Museum)
7 One possible restoration of the Agricolan dedicatory inscription from the forum at Verulamium (by permission of the Verulamium Museum)
8 Walls Hill native fort from the air
9 Roman fort at Birrens from the air showing as crop marks the

additional complexity of its defences (Cambridge University Collection: copyright reserved)

10   Roman fort and annexe at Easter Happrew from the air (Royal Commission on Ancient Monuments, Scotland)

11   The two-period Roman fort with annexes at Dalswinton (Bankhead) from the air (Royal Commission on Ancient Monuments, Scotland)

12   Stracathro-type camp and adjacent Roman fort at Dalginross from the air (Royal Commission on Ancient Monuments, Scotland)

13   The hill of Bennachie from above the site of the camp at Durno (Cambridge University Collection: copyright reserved)

14   Iron Age carnyx (war trumpet) from Deskford, Banffshire (by permission of the Royal Museum of Scotland)

15   Roman fort and Stracathro-type camps at Malling from the air (Royal Commission on Ancient Monuments, Scotland)

16   The Sma' glen from the watchtower by Fendoch Roman fort

17   The Roman fort and Stracathro-type camp at Inverquharity (Royal Commission on Ancient Monuments, Scotland)

18   *Asses* of AD 86 from Inchtuthil (a and b) above better preserved copies of similar types (c and d) (Hunterian Museum, Glasgow)

19   The line of the Gask ridge from the west with the watchtower at Muir o'Fauld in the foreground (G.D.B. Jones)

20   The wall trenches of two timber-built barracks at Elginhaugh showing only one period of construction (by permission of Historic Buildings and Monuments, Scottish Development Department: Crown copyright)

21   Part of the timber gateway of the Roman fort at Carlisle burnt after partial demolition

22   Severed heads on display outside a Roman camp on Trajan's Column

23   Part of the Flavian temporary camp at Dun and adjacent native settlement revealed as crop marks from the air (Royal Commission on Ancient Monuments, Scotland)

TABLES

1   Temporary camps in Scotland with Stracathro-type gateways   125
2   So-called 30-acre (12-ha) temporary camps   127
3   Putative large Agricolan camps north of the Mounth   134
4   The Gask frontier   156

· 1 ·

SOURCES OF EVIDENCE

THE Roman period in Britain falls into a halfway category between prehistory and history: what the French or Dutch would call proto-history, that is a period when such written sources as exist are all external to the area involved. Although the existence of the island of Britain was known to the Greeks as early as the fourth century BC, we do not begin to hear anything about its inhabitants from classical writers until the time of Julius Caesar. Before this our knowledge of Britain is entirely derived from archaeological data: we have no indigenous literary tradition upon which to call. The invasion and resulting conquest of Britain, beginning in the reign of the emperor Claudius, inevitably increased the number of references to the island by classical writers, but the information remains brief and is of uneven coverage. The incidental writings, the inscriptions on pottery, stone or metal, known collectively as epigraphy, whether official dedications or simply graffiti, serve to augment our purely historical sources and provide within them the only written records produced by the indigenous inhabitants. But we are still largely dependent upon archaeology to broaden our understanding and put flesh on the bare bones.

The process of integrating the quite disparate types of evidence available to form a corporate whole is often a difficult one, but the challenge holds its own attraction, and the end result can often be far more informative than the sum of its constituent parts. The first forty years after the invasion, and in particular the last seven of those, provide an excellent example of this process. We have archaeological evidence of wide distribution and high quality; rather poorer epigraphic data; but one of the fullest written accounts for any period of the Roman occupation in the works of Tacitus, best exemplified in his *de vita Iulii Agricolae*, the biography of Gnaeus Julius Agricola, governor of Britain from AD 77–83 (see Chapter 2 for discussion of the date of his appointment).

THE WRITTEN RECORD

Yesterday is history, as will today be when tomorrow dawns, though we rarely think of it as such. But how do we know what happened in the past? How do we know what happened in the world last week? A simple question with a simple answer: we watch the news or documentary programmes on the television, or listen to them on the radio, or we read daily papers, weekly papers or news magazines. It does not take long to realise that the picture we receive is not always consistent. Inevitably the various news media approach the subject in different ways, but even within a single branch it will come as no great surprise to find the same story reported differently in, for example, the *Guardian* or *Time* magazine as opposed to the *Daily Telegraph* or *National Review*, and different again in the *Morning Star* or in *Village Voice*. Of course, we all have differing opinions, different political stances, and these will be reflected in our news media to varying degrees, so that several interpretations of why events occurred or what results may stem from them are possible. This assumes that the facts, the actual events themselves, are fully and precisely known. But are they? How do we *know* that the facts are correct? The television camera may record events which can be shown to us later, but what did the cameraman miss, or the film editor decide to omit? Even eye-witness accounts have their limitations. The middle of a battle is not necessarily the best place to judge who is winning that battle, let alone the war. The police estimate of the number of protesters present at a political rally or march rarely coincides with that of the organisers; but which figure would be included in the history of that political movement should it ever come to be written?

What has all this to do with ancient history? It is to remind us of three basic principles which must be applied in all our dealings with written sources of evidence for the past. Firstly, where did the author get his facts from: is he likely to have had access to accurate and reliable source material upon which we can depend, or at the other extreme is he dealing with hearsay padded out with his imagination? Secondly, is there any likelihood of bias in his account which would colour his judgement and interpretation of events, or prompt him to omit some information or include more dubious material in order to bolster the case that he wishes to get across to the reader? Finally, we must recognise that there are few, if any, absolute truths in history. One man's truth is another man's propaganda.

For the period of the Roman occupation of Britain, the surviving literary references are, to say the least, meagre (Mann and Penman

1977). In some ways this simplifies matters, for we lack the multiplicity of often apparently conflicting accounts which confront the modern historian. The dangerous result, however, is the tendency to accept almost without question what remains as the literal truth either because there is nothing to gainsay it, or simply out of a desire to maximise the surviving information. This tendency is particularly marked in the case of Tacitus, by common consent the greatest of Roman historians. Reference to the chapters dealing with the period of the conquest in any one of the numerous books about Roman Britain will show how much they depend upon the brief narrative account that he provides, supplemented occasionally by brief passages from Suetonius or Cassius Dio. The fact that Tacitus is such a useful, indeed often the only, source of information for the first forty years of the Roman occupation, should not exclude him from the same level of critical assessment accorded to any other written record.

First of all, what sources of information were available to Tacitus? On the positive side, he was himself a senator and progressed through the various stages of a military and political career in the latter part of the first century AD, leading eventually to higher office as governor of the province of Asia. He seems to have earned a reputation as an orator, and is praised as such by the Younger Pliny in several of his published letters (*Ep.* 2, 1; 2, 11). While not necessarily one of the leading men of his day, he was sufficiently experienced to understand well how the system worked, and had the contacts to ensure that if necessary he could talk to the right people. In effect he was an insider. Again, Pliny illustrates the point in a letter to Tacitus replying to a request for information about the death of Pliny's uncle in the famous eruption of Vesuvius which buried Pompeii and Herculaneum in AD 79 (*Ep.* 6, 16).

Tacitus' historical writings, published between AD 98 and *c.*115/ 120, provide an account of the empire from the reign of Tiberius to that of Domitian (AD 14–96), though not all the books survive in full. He started his own political career in the mid 70s AD and so was writing contemporary, or near contemporary, history for much of his work. He could have consulted people directly or indirectly involved in events about which he was writing. The most obvious example is Agricola himself, Tacitus' father-in-law, though since the biography of Agricola was written several years after the death of its subject, we cannot be certain that it had been planned sufficiently far in advance to make this possible. Indeed, Tacitus himself makes clear that he had not seen his father-in-law for four years prior to his demise (*Ag.* 45). For earlier periods, however, Tacitus would have had to rely upon written accounts. For the relationship between the emperor and the Senate he would have had access to the *acta senatus* (records of Senate business) (Talbert 1984, 326–34), the Hansard or Congressional Record of its day, or the *acta diurna* (daily news-sheet). But for activities in the provinces, which are our main concern here, he would have had to call upon earlier published memoirs or histories. Precisely what sources Tacitus used has been a matter of much scholarly debate, but it is clear that he relied to a greater extent on the writings of earlier historians than would be acceptable within modern historical methodology, and was much less rigorous in assembling and assessing all available data (Syme 1958, chs. 16, 22 and 23; Martin 1981, chs. 8–9).

At this juncture it is worth emphasising the different between history as written today and as written in the classical world. Ideally, the modern historian would marshal all the evidence available, consulting primary documents wherever possible, applying his critical judgement in the process to weigh the different strands in turn in order to produce a reasoned narrative upon which informed assessment of cause and effect might be based (e.g. Carr 1961, 22–4). Classical historians were less concerned with establishing an accurate record of events and more concerned with passing moral judgements on the past as a lesson to the present. In Tacitus' own words:

> My conception of the first duty of the historian is to ensure that merit (*virtutes*) shall not lack its record and to hold out the reprobation of posterity to evil words and deeds. (*Annals* 3, 65)

This is a theme even more strongly echoed in the introduction to his biography of Agricola (*Ag.* 11), where the term *virtus* (merit or excellence) occurs four times in the first paragraph.

In the classical world history had much in common with oratory. Accordingly, style and presentation were at least as important as content. No one who has read him in the original would disagree that Tacitus' style is both original and memorable. Again this is a topic much loved of classical scholars (e.g. Martin 1981, ch. 10 with bibliography), but it concerns us here only in terms of the effect that it had upon the accuracy of his narrative. The very brevity of his writing, the pithy, punchy prose which was so popular with his contemporaries, can result in obscurity of thought and expression which makes his work difficult to translate (for examples in the *Agricola*, see Ogilvie and Richmond 1967, 31). Wellesley quotes a few examples where our understanding of events would have benefited much from an additional phrase of explanation (1969a, 69–70). The concern for fine writing or speaking as such may result in description which owes more to literary or oratorical style than to the events under consideration. The close similarity between Tacitus' description of the rout of the enemy at Mons Graupius (*Ag.* 37, 2–3) and Sallust's account of the battle against Jugurtha (*Jugurtha* 101, 11) has long been known (Ogilvie and Richmond 1967, 23–5). More recently, Woodman has drawn attention to Tacitus' tendency towards self-imitation where poorly documented events are given substance by imitation of better known ones recorded elsewhere in his work (1979). Although such borrowings can only be demonstrated in a limited number of cases, it does call into question the validity of trying to tie down Tacitus' description of battle scenes too closely when his account is rather generalised (below, pp. 129–30).

Similar problems arise with his use of invented speeches. Even where we know, or can infer, that some address would probably have taken place, it is often highly unlikely that Tacitus would have had access to any record of it. Perhaps the best example of this for our present purposes is the lengthy speech of Calgacus before the battle of Mons Graupius (*Ag.* 30–2). Some such address may have taken place, but, even if it did, there is no way that Tacitus could have know what was said. The speech is entirely his own work. Even where he could have known exactly what was said, this principle still seems to hold true. The one surviving example of an actual speech by the emperor Claudius, originally given to the Senate and subsequently inscribed on a bronze tablet in Lyons (*CIL* XIII, 1688), may be compared with the Tacitean version (*Annals* 11, 24). There can be no doubt that Tacitus had read the speech, for certain points of the argument are borrowed, but they appear in different order, with others added or omitted. The end result is Tacitus speaking, not Claudius. Presumably Tacitus could have consulted Agricola about how he addressed his troops before the battle of Mons Graupius, but the substance of that speech as written by Tacitus is derived largely from examples in Livy (Ogilvie and Richmond 1967, 265). That the speeches have no real historical value is well accepted, but this propensity for invention should be borne in mind when considering Tacitus' reputation for veracity in general (Wellesley 1954).

Rather more dangerous is his use of rumour and innuendo, the former often in the form of reported speech. For example, several times he alludes to the possible poisoning of Germanicus by Piso (*Annals* 2, 69; 71 and 73), yet subsequently reports the charge unfounded (*Annals* 3, 14). A similar 'rumour' is reported concerning Domitian's possible involvement in the death of Agricola, though this time the allegation is not refuted. (*Ag.* 43). Given the moralising tone of classical history, it will come as no surprise to find that Tacitus often took a particular stance against certain individuals. Thereafter, no matter what their actions, these were shown in an unfavourable light, either by casting aspersions as to the motivation or by the simple process of balancing any creditable behaviour with something discreditable. The cumulative effect of this procedure is both damning and distorting. The classic example is Tacitus' treatment of the emperor Tiberius who is categorised throughout as a cruel, hypocritical despot, a view to which few classical historians today would give unqualified acceptance (Seager 1972, 260–2). Because Tiberius, and subsequently Domitian, are seen by Tacitus as tyrants, he ascribes to them all the behavioural traits typical of such rulers, and so the characterisation becomes self-fulfilling.

Elsewhere we may observe the same form of bias in reverse. Certain individuals are taken by Tacitus as exemplars of his ideal of *virtus* (merit or excellence), notably Corbulo, Germanicus and, of course, his own father-in-law, Agricola (Dorey 1969b, 9–10). A full assessment of Agricola's character, abilities and achievements should best be left for the final chapter of the present work, but there can be no doubt that Tacitus takes every opportunity to cast him in a favourable light. In effect, he becomes a stock character: typecast as the good man and great general, who succeeds despite the hostility of yet another stock character, the tyrannical ruler exemplified in Domitian (Ogilvie and Richmond 1967, 19–20). Tacitus is quite specific as to the purpose of the *Agricola*:

> This book, which sets out to honour my father-in-law Agricola, will be commended, or at least pardoned, for the loyal affection to which it bears witness (*Ag.* 3)

As Ogilvie and Richmond note (1967, 15), it is Agricola who is almost always the subject of sentences and almost every event is used to highlight his character and achievements. Thus, in addition to the strong contrast drawn with the tyrant Domitian, the role of Agricola's predecessors as govenor of Britain, some of whom were very illustrious men, is consistently played down (below, pp 39, 50), while his successor, though alluded to, is not named. If our only source of evidence for the activities of Vettius Bolanus while governor of Britain (AD 69–71) had been the *Agricola* (8 and 16), our impression would have been of general inactivity in the face of military indiscipline. Fortunately we have Tacitus' own later account in the *Histories* (3, 45), although Bolanus is not mentioned by name, and the testimony of the poet Statius (*Silvae* 5, 2, 140–9). These make clear that Bolanus was involved in a fairly major upheaval amongst the Brigantes, the rescue of Queen Cartimandua and the construction of garrison posts, probably in northern England.

Classicists have long argued over the precise literary genre into which the *Agricola* fits, whether it should be classed as history, biography or even funerary oration (Goodyear 1970, 4–5). It has elements of all three, but its general eulogistic tone sets it apart from any strictly hsitorical study and thus we must take even greater care when asseessing the judgements contained therein. To accept verbatim Tacitus' assessment of the character and achievements of his own father-in-law, to whom he was quite obviously devoted, seems little short of naivety.

There is, however, slightly more to the *Agricola* even that a laudatory historical biography, an act of *pietas* (dutiful respect) which was so highly regarded in the Roman world. It has as an underlying theme a very specific contemporary political purpose (Syme 1958, 215–16; Goodyear 1970, 6–7 *contra* Ogilvie and Richmond 1967, 17–19). We have already seen that Tacitus strongly characterised Domitian as a tyrant, an assessment less obviously ill-founded than his similar judgement of Tiberius, yet both the author and his father-in-law had advanced their careers during the reign of that very tyrant. There is no reason to believe that Tacitus had subsequently come under any direct attack, but inevitably those who have suffered at the hands of an oppressive regime will tend to resent those who served and prospered under it (Dorey 1969b, 4). Thus he seems to have felt obliged to justify his own actions both to his contemporaries and to posterity; to explain why neither he nor Agricola had opposed Domitian. Accordingly, Tacitus' political creed is clearly expressed:

> Let it be clear to those who insist on admiring disobedience that even under bad emperors men can be great, and that a decent regard for authority, if backed by industry and energy, can reach that peak of distinction which most men attain only by following a perilous course, winning fame, without benefiting their country, by an ostentatious self-martyrdom (*Ag.* 42)

It is inevitable that maintenance of this theme would further colour Tacitus' interpretation of events and result in even greater polarisation between excellence and infamy as personified by Agricola and Domitian.

But what of Tacitus as a souce of purely factual information? Here his reputation is high: often his factual accuracy is praised and the testimony of archaeology quoted by way of support (e.g. Ogilvie and Richmond 1967, 18–19; Dorey 1969b, 7). Large parts of the following chapters will be concerned with exactly this question in some detail, but it is nonetheless worthwhile to make some general observations and quote some specific examples. Our first difficulty, however, is to disentangle the factual core from the presentation and interpretation of it. As Miller has taken pains to emphasise, 'apparently obvious content may be subtly affected by the form in which it is cast' (1969, 99). Indeed, Tacitus is a prime example of the maxim: what matters is not what you say, but how you say it. Our second problem is to allow for circular arguments when archaeological evidence is used to support Tacitus. This is not a criticism of him, but of the way in which he tends to be used, or perhaps misused, by modern scholars. For example, the foundation of virtually all the first-century Roman forts in northern England is attributed to Agricola (Frere 1978, 123–5) and consequently they are taken to support Tacitus' assertion that his father-in-law was responsible for the total subjugation of that area (Ogilvie and Richmond 1967, 55–7). Yet the majority of these sites are dated only by reference back to Tacitus (*Ag.* 20; *cf.* Frere 1978, 125 note 5), and independent assessment of the archaeological evidence suggests that a growing number originated in an earlier or later context (below, pp 63–5, 161–2). It is salutary to note that none of the sites quoted by Dorey (1969b, 7) as supporting evidence for Agricola's supposed skill in selecting fort sites (*Ag.* 22, 2) can now be claimed unequivocally as Agricolan foundations (below, pp 143–9). Finally, and perhaps most fundamentally, Tacitus is often the only source for a particular piece of information and it may well be impossible either to confirm his statement or contradict him. In such circumstances it should be recognised that acceptance of what he says is an act of faith.

It is not the intention here to try to discredit Tacitus totally as a source of information or to suggest that he deliberately falsified the underlying facts, though such a view does have its supporters (Urban 1971), even if he often misrepresented them. But obviously he was human and, therefore, could make mistakes. Syme lists a number of inaccuracies gleaned from *Annals* 13–16, which he uses to support the argument that this section was never revised (1958,

746–8). A more specific example relating to Britain is the discord between Queen Cartimandua of the Brigantes and her husband Venutius. This figures twice in the pages of Tacitus (*Annals* 12, 40; *Histories* 3, 45), but the two accounts are placed in quite widely separated chronological contexts. There has been considerable academic debate over the years as to whether these two accounts should be accepted as distinct events, but there is now a strong case for suggesting that Tacitus made a fairly major error of duplication (Hanson and Campbell 1986).

We may also point to occasional minor errors. The best known is the reference to the Brigantes which occurs in Calgacus' speech before the battle of Mons Graupius. They are named as responsible for a revolt led by a woman, involving the burning of a Roman colony and the storming of a camp (*Ag.* 31). There can be no doubt that this must refer to the Boudican revolt and the destruction of Colchester, events which took place while Agricola was serving in the province as a legionary tribune. Yet this brief reference is in error on two points. Firstly, in the fuller account in the *Annals* (14, 33), Tacitus not only makes no mention of a camp being attacked, but states that the rebels actually avoided military posts; secondly, it is quite certain that the Brigantes under Queen Cartimandua were not involved in the rebellion, for she took an avowedly pro-Roman stance, as her handing over of the fugitive Caratacus to the Roman authorities should serve to illustrate (*Annals* 12, 36). Tacitus has simply confused Cartimandua and the Brigantes with Boudica and the Iceni. Recently a similar confusion of tribal names has been suggested in the context of an earlier revolt amongst the Iceni (Rivet 1983).

These examples may seem relatively trivial slips, but they do highlight a notorious Tacitean failing: a consistent lack of concern for specific names of peoples and places on the outer fringes of the Empire. The whole of the *Agricola* contains only fourteen geographical names relating to Britain: five tribes (Ordovices, Silures, Brigantes, Boresti and the inhabitants of Caledonia), four islands (Mona, Thule, Orcades and Hibernia), three rivers (Clota, Bodotria and Taus), one harbour (Portus Trucculensis) and one hill (Mons Graupius). Of these the harbour, hill and one tribe, the Boresti, still remain unlocated. It is customary, by way of explanation, to point out that the readership for whom Tacitus was writing, upper class Romans, mostly knew little about outlying provinces and would undoubtedly have been bored by the use of too many strange sounding names. Certainly at one point, when writing about Spain,

Pliny the Elder deliberately limits the number of tribal names that he mentions (*Nat. Hist.* 3, 3, 28), but elsewhere he lists them at length. Burn takes the apologia for Tacitus one stage further and suggests that this deficiency in the *Agricola* was a reflection of the different literary style required for biography: had the relevant parts of the *Histories* survived, the geographical picture would have been much fuller (Burn 1969, 35–7). Clearly there is no way that this can be proved, or disproved, but the references to Britain in the surviving sections of both *Annals* and *Histories* do not vastly increase the geographical haul. In fact, they add three more tribes (Iceni, Trinovantes and Deceangli), three further rivers (Tamesa, Trisantona and Sabrina) and three towns (Camulodunum, Londinium and Verulamium), of which one tribal name and one river name are garbled (for conveniently assembled references see Rivet and Smith 1979, 93–8). It is hardly surprising, therefore, that one eminent scholar has been prompted to ask 'how much did Tacitus know, or indeed care, about Britain in general and about its political geography in particular?' (Rivet 1983, 204). The answer would appear to be not very much!

So far it has been assumed throughout that what we read is, in fact, exactly what Tacitus wrote. There is, however, one further possible source of confusion, the reliability of the Latin text. The fact that not all of Tacitus' works have survived to the present day has been alluded to several times. The reasons for this are enshrined within the method of their transmission. No original Tacitean manuscript survives. The number of copies of the original, probably on papyrus rolls, would have been quite small. Those that survived the end of the Roman Empire, possibly already only second generation copies of the original, passed into the hands of the learned classes of the so-called Dark Ages, the clergy. Here they were copied and recopied until eventually they were rediscovered and put into print in the fifteenth century (Reynolds and Wilson 1974). The present text of the *Agricola*, for example, is based upon a mid-ninth-century manuscript augmented by fifteenth-century derivatives (Ogilvie and Richmond 1967, 85–90). The process of repeated copying, particularly by scribes ignorant of the significance of their text, inevitably resulted in errors. Words, or even lines, may be omitted or mistakenly transcribed. Marginal remarks by some reader or earlier copyist may become incorporated in the body of the text. It will come as no surprise, therefore, that all surviving manuscripts differ to some degree. Many of the problems have been ironed out by the judicious comparison of different manuscripts, combined with the application of a detailed understanding of the Latin language. Occasionally, however, difficulties remain and scholarly emendations are necessary to make sense of the Latin. Names can be particularly troublesome: reference to the Deceangli has been deduced from the manuscript reading *inde Cangos* (*Annals* 12, 32), while recognition of the name of the river Trent comes from an emendation of *castris Antonam* to *cis Trisantonam* by Bradley (*Annals* 12, 31). Fortunately, the text of Tacitus is generally reckoned to be sound and such problems are comparatively few.

To sum up, when Tacitus is compared with other classical historians his superiority in terms of style and authenticity becomes rapidly apparent. He is readable, informative and stimulating. Tacitus' writings display an analytical approach with which we are sympathetic even when we judge them by the standards of modern history. It is undoubtedly for these reasons that classicists tend to leap to his defence at the first sign of any criticism. But the biases within his writings are undeniable, and their effect upon not only the interpretation of events but the very manner in which the facts are revealed should always temper our assessment. Despite the indirect connection through Agricola, Britain remained to Tacitus one of the remoter provinces of the Roman Empire which he had not visited and for which the source material for his writings would have been very limited. Wellesley is perhaps right to question how important geographical exactitude was in the context in which Tacitus was writing (1969a, 66), but this particular lack of precision leaves the uneasy feeling that on occasions the overall narrative may have suffered similarly.

Before turning our attention to other forms of evidence, one further important literary source should be mentioned, though it can hardly be classified as literature. The *Geography* of Ptolemy was written towards the middle of the second century AD in Alexandria, the centre of learning of the Greek-speaking half of the empire. It consists of a list of place names, including geographical features, giving their latitude and longitude and occasional explanatory comments, many of the names being grouped according to tribal areas. Though published in the second century, it makes no mention of the Antonine Wall and appears to have been based on an earlier work by Marinus of Tyre which, unfortunately, has not survived. Marinus was writing around the end of the first century AD and is likely to have got his information for north Britain as a result of its annexation by the Flavian governors some years earlier. Ptolemy is, then, a useful, if indirect, source of information on tribes and places which were brought into close contact with Rome during the governorship of Agricola and his predecessors. There is a strong possibility that one of his major sources was a Roman military map of the area, for detailed mapping by Ptolemy ceases at the Moray Firth, which probably marked the limit of penetration by Agricola's forces (Rivet and Smith 1979, 116). Unfortunately, for no obvious reason, though perhaps simply to comply with received wisdom of the day (Tierney 1959), the whole of Scotland is misplaced in relation to the rest of Britain (fig 1). This makes it extremely difficult to make precise identifications of features that appear. Various attempts have been made to correct the error, the most recent and most convincing

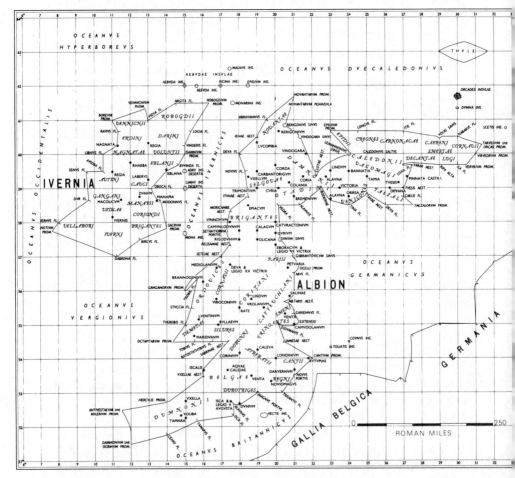

1 The British Isles according to Ptolemy c. AD 150 (by permission of the Controller of Her Majesty's Stationery Office: Crown copyright reserved)

study being that by Rivet and Smith (1979, ch. 3). Nonetheless, the identification of archaeological sites with Ptolemy's place names must remain speculative, for we cannot even be sure of the status of the places. Rivet and Smith suggest that they are likely to have been Roman settlements. In the north this should mean forts or camps, but the naming of sites in Ireland, even though derived by Ptolemy from a different source (*Geog.* 1), raises the possibility that some native places were included. Furthermore, the process of aerial photographic discovery continues to add new Flavian military sites to the map of Scotland and thus provides further alternative identifications (e.g. Maxwell 1984).

EPIGRAPHY

We are extremely fortunate that the Romans were in the habit of recording official acts on stone, or some other permanent medium, a number of which have survived. The bulk of these are conveniently assembled for Britain in one volume (Collingwood and Wright 1965), though further discovery by accident or by archaeological work continues to augment this corpus. Records of official buildings, religious dedications and tombstones are the main categories of inscription, of which the first are perhaps the most useful for our present purposes. Although they do not always record what has been constructed, for this would have been evident from the location of the inscription on the structure concerned, or why, they usually refer to the reigning emperor and the governor responsible, so that the work can often be dated quite accurately (Collingwood and Richmond 1969, 199–203). Accordingly, inscriptions can provide unimpeachable evidence of building activity in a particular place at a particular time.

The study of inscriptions is a rather specialised branch of ancient history, for they can often be difficult to read and interpret. The text is usually much abbreviated. It may be considerably worn and, if the stone has been broken or reused subsequently, may not be complete. Epigraphists have first to decipher what survives, attempt to restore missing sections and expand abbreviated forms before they may present a full reading and translation of the text. With a large and fragmentary inscription the process is rather akin to doing a jigsaw from which a large number of pieces is missing, but without reference to the crib. Fortunately, official inscriptions are consistently formulaic so that full restorations may often be made with relative confidence from surprisingly little surviving text. On the other hand, it must be remembered that these are restorations, and discovery of further fragments or even careful re-examination of an older stone may result in quite significant changes. Most celebrated in recent years has been the re-reading of the text of a building inscription from Chichester dedicated to Tiberius Claudius Cogidubnus, a client or friendly king. The long accepted reading had Cogidubnus as a Roman legate, an official administrative post of considerable status and a unique honour for a native monarch, but the stone is now seen to refer to him only as a 'great king' (Bogaers 1979). Even when complete the abbreviated format can cause difficulties of interpretation. Another famous inscription dredged from the Tyne at Newcastle has long been taken to refer to the arrival of troops from Germany in the mid-second century AD (*R.I.B.* 1322), but a recent re-interpretation suggests that it commemorates exactly the opposite, a conclusion with considerable historical implications (Wilkes 1985).

For the Flavian period in Britain, however, we are extremely poorly served by epigraphy. Despite the large number of military sites which were constructed during the seven years of Agricola's governorship, only one, the legionary fortress at Chester, has produced any inscriptions on which he is named, and these are restricted to several lead waterpipes (pl 4). The absence of further epigraphic records should not be taken to cast doubt on the magnitude of the fort building programme instigated during Agricola's governorship, but simply to reflect the impermanence of the building materials employed in forts at this date. Almost without exception their ramparts were constructed of turf blocks and their gateways and internal buildings of timber (Hanson 1982). In these circumstances, the records of completed tasks would almost certainly have been of wood also, with correspondingly less chance of their survival. The only known stone inscription which mentions Agricola is from the forum at Verulamium (pl 7), and that is heavily restored from a number of small fragments (Frere 1983b, 69–72).

ARCHAEOLOGY

It is not the intention here to outline in detail the methods by which archaeologists obtain their information: the topic is already adequately covered in a number of general books (e.g. Barker 1977; Greene 1983). It is important, however, to discuss some of the advantages and limitations of archaeology and the ways in which archaeological material is utilised, particularly in the treatment of an historical period. Archaeology is the study of man's past activities based upon the material remains which he leaves behind: the structures he built, the artefacts he made, the rubbish he abandoned. It might be thought, therefore, that the evidence produced is more objective than that derived from historical sources. In a limited sense this is true: the artefacts in museums and the monuments in the landscape are concrete and tangible keys to the past. But they are subject to bias in terms of their differential survival and discovery, and, of course, in the way in which they are interpreted by archaeologists. The survival of an archaeological site in the landscape depends entirely upon the subsequent treatment of the land. Any modern human activity which disturbs the ground may cause some damage to a site according to the depth and extent of the disturbance. Thus urban development, road construction, afforestation and, most important of all, ploughing are all responsible for the destruction of archaeological sites. Since such activity is not equally intensive in either regional or local terms, there is bound to be differential survival of evidence. Thus the densely populated south and east has lost more of its archaeology than the relatively more sparsely occupied north and west; more sites have been destroyed in lowland areas favourable to agriculture than on poorer land in upland areas.

This bias in favour of more marginal land is balanced to some extent by alternative specialised methods of site discovery. Extant sites, even where the remains are slight, usually reveal themselves to the experienced eye as patterns of humps and bumps on the ground surface. Even where no such traces are visible there may still be evidence surviving beneath the surface, for destruction by the plough is a very gradual process. The structures that lie hidden beneath the ploughsoil, enclosure ditches long ago silted up, pits and even the foundations of buildings, may still be revealed to an observer in an aeroplane and recorded on film (Wilson 1983). Colour differences in a recently ploughed field, where a thin slice of what lies buried below has been brought to the surface by the action of the plough (soil marks), or differential crop growth reflecting the differential availability of moisture retained in the soil (crop marks), may make patterns which betray the presence of an unsuspected archaeological site (e.g. pls 10–12). In fact, aerial photography, particularly of crop marks, is by far the most important single method of archaeological site discovery. Its widespread application since the 1940s has revolutionised our understanding of the past and brought about the realisation that in many regions virtually the whole landscape is an archaeological site, since the density of remains is far greater than previously suspected and the number known continues to grow. To give some relevant quantification, between the second edition of the

Ordnance Survey map of Roman Britain in 1928 and the fourth in 1978, the number of permanent Roman military establishments known in Britain north of Hadrian's Wall almost trebled, most of the increase being the result of aerial reconnaissance (Frere and St Joseph 1983, 88); while amost ninety per cent of the temporary camps known in Scotland have been discovered from the air. Even though this technique has made tremendous impact, it too has its limitations, since not all areas are favourable to the production of cropmarks because of regional or local variations in geology, climate or agricultural practices.

Since the discovery of new sites continues unabated, with the possible exception of certain very limited areas which have been intensively surveyed over several decades, it should be apparent that not only do we not possess the totality of the evidence, in terms of site distribution, but we have no certain idea what percentage of that total we do have, even for the relatively predictable activities of the Roman army. Clearly this presents major problems when attempting to identify the areas in which Roman campaigning took place, or the extent to which consolidation in the form of fort building was achieved. We are, for example, as much concerned with gaps in the distribution of forts as with concentrations of them, for the former could reflect areas which either were not controlled by Rome, or whose population was pro-Roman in outlook and did not require the presence of garrison troops. There are notable gaps in the distribution of forts in the eastern and western Lowlands of Scotland, yet these must be differently interpreted in the light of the different levels of archaeological fieldwork in the two areas (below, pp 91, 106–7).

It would not be enough to know even the total distribution of Roman forts and camps in any particular area; we must also know their date more precisely if we are to understand the changes and fluctuations in their occupation over time. Morphology alone will usually permit the ready recognition of Roman military works, typified by their rectilinear form with rounded corners (pls 10-12), but to place them more precisely within that period we require dating evidence. This comes normally in the form of artefacts, the most obvious of which are coins. Though not marked with a date in the way of modern coinage, Roman coins are at least attributable to the reign of a particular emperor on the basis of the portrait on the obverse. Frequently they are assignable to a shorter timespan according to the number and type of honorific titles which are attributed to the emperor, titles whose dates of award we know from historical or epigraphic sources. But it is not enough simply to record the presence of coins of a particular date as indicative of occupation of the site at that time, for this fails to take into account the length of time which the coin might have been in circulation before being lost; for silver coins in particular this might be quite considerable. It is, for example, not uncommon to find quite a high percentage of Republican silver coins in hoards deposited as late as the reign of Trajan, indicating that they had remained in circulation for over a century (Reece 1974, 84–5), though such a lengthy period of use is usually reflected in the amount of wear on the coin. The larger the number of coins recovered from any particular site, however, the better the chances of determining the periods of occupation on statistical grounds (Casey 1974a; Collis 1974, 178–81).

In most periods of archaeological study, however, and the Roman period is no exception, it is pottery which provides our major means of dating simply because it survives in the ground so well. Clay, once baked, is virtually indestructible, yet the pot which it forms is fragile and has a relatively short life span. Combine these two characteristics with the limited restrictions that the physical properties of clay impose upon the potter's own creative instincts, and it is easy to see why we have an excellent medium for typological study. The shape of different forms of pottery develops through time so that a relative sequence or type series may be identified. Absolute date brackets may be attached to elements of this sequence when examples are discovered in archaeological contexts firmly dated either by coin evidence or more usually by a restricted historical association (Gillam 1970, 2 and appendix 1). Even greater precision is possible with samian, the fine red-gloss tableware imported from Gaul. This was mass-produced and quite frequently stamped with a potter's name. It has been possible, therefore, to refine the absolute dating process even further and attribute particular pots to the working life of a particular potter (Hartley 1969, 235–6). The end result is a dating method much envied by prehistorians, but even so the precision is not such as to enable us to distinguish between forts founded under successive governors, let alone those established in successive years. Indeed, the dangers of circular reasoning must again be borne in mind. The historical context which provides an absolute date for much Flavian pottery in Britain is, of course, the historically attested fort-building programme of Agricola in the north!

There is a further chronological problem: the extent to which pottery could have survived in use after its generally accepted life span (Hanson 1980a, 61–2), a principle already familiar in relation to coins. Pottery, as already noted, usually had a relatively short life span because of its fragile nature, but is not so accurately datable to begin with, so we must allow for the possibility that certain forms could have been in use somewhat longer than is normally accepted. Sometimes this can be clearly demonstrated, as for example at Camelon on the Forth–Clyde isthmus where excavations have recovered several examples of *terra nigra* and Lyons Ware (Maxfield 1980, 77), fine imported pottery normally attributed to the pre-Flavian period (Greene 1979, 17 and 142). Yet on historical grounds a fort this far north ought not to have been occupied before *c.* AD 79 at the earliest.

Our dating evidence may derive from fieldwalking after ploughing or disturbance during modern building operations, which may bring to light pottery or other datable artefacts. But controlled archaeological excavation is necessary to recover evidence of phases within the life of a fort, many of which show signs of several periods of use during the different Roman occupations of the area. Human occupation of a site for a period of time results in disturbance of soil and accumulation or deposition of material. The digging of ditches, pits or post-holes, the construction of earthen ramparts or stone walls, all have readily identifiable effects. Where these processes continue for a long time, where pits are filled and fresh ones dug, buildings demolished and new ones erected, it is possible to reconstruct the sequence of events. Applying the principle of stratification from geology, it is readily apparent that of two successive floor levels, walls, pits or post-holes, the lower must be earlier in date. By the consistent observation of such relationships, activities on the site can be put into relative chronological order. Approximate dates may then be attributed according to the datable artefacts recovered from each layer, taking care to apply the commonsense rule, known as *terminus post quem*, that the deposit must be later in date than the latest dated artefact that it contains. The more abundant the dating evidence, the more likely it is that the *terminus post quem* date will coincide with the real date. It remains a salutary lesson, however, that after forty-six seasons of excavation spread over more than half a century, the discovery of one piece of samian pottery in a construction trench of the earliest phase of occupation at Corbridge indicated that the fort could not have been built by Agricola as had previously been thought and resulted in the search for, and eventual discovery of, the Agricolan base almost three-quarters of a mile (1.2km) away to the west (Hanson *et al.* 1979, 1–5).

Many fort sites in Scotland can be dated with some precision because they have been subject to investigation by the spade and usually produce datable finds. It should be emphasised, though, that many of the excavations took place in the early decades of this century when archaeological techniques were less refined. This factor and the consistent strategy of sampling only limited areas can present problems of interpretation, particularly when dealing with the earliest structures present. In a fort occupied on a number of occasions, as many in Scotland were, the first buildings will be sealed beneath and possibly damaged by later activity, thus making their decipherment all the more difficult. The more numerous temporary works, the sites of brief habitation by armies on campaign, are less complex to excavate but rarely provide any dating evidence, as indeed we might expect from the very limited nature of their use: they were not occupied long enough for sufficient datable rubbish to accumulate.

These difficulties, which obscure our perception and provide fuel for the different interpretations of events, pale into insignificance when compared with those attending the study of the archaeological evidence for the indigenous inhabitants at the time of the Roman conquest of the north. All of the problems already outlined are multiplied ten-fold. We have only a general idea of the types and distribution of contemporary native settlements, largely because of the difficulty in attributing dates. Pre-Roman Iron Age pottery in north Britain tends to be of poor quality and chronologically undiagnostic (but see Cool 1982 for a more optimistic view), while carbon-14 dating of organic remains will provide a date only to within two centuries at best. To rely for dating upon the presence of Roman pottery or other artefacts, which is frequently the case, immediately raises questions of how such material reached the site, and might well exclude from consideration sites of contemporary occupation which were unable to obtain Roman material for political or economic reasons. It is hardly surprising, therefore, that consideration of the native population by modern authors examining the period of the Roman occupation has tended to be relegated to an introductory or background chapter.

CONCLUSION

Comparison between our understanding of the archaeology of purely Roman sites and of contemporary native settlements serves to illustrate the advantages of 'historical' archaeology. Most important is the greater chronological precision made possible by being able to tie the typological dating methods applied to artefactual material, which provide only relative dates, into an absolute chronology based on epigraphic or literary evidence. Without this process we would have little hope of accomplishing the sort of detailed studies which make Britain one of the best understood provinces of the Roman Empire despite being one of the most remote. Nonetheless, much of the above chapter has been couched in rather negative terms emphasising the problems and difficulties encountered when using ancient literary sources or epigraphic and archaeological evidence. This was quite deliberate in an attempt to encourage critical appraisal of the evidence and an awareness that what follows is merely one possible interpretation of events.

· 2 ·

THE FLAVIAN
CONNECTION

THE full title of the man we refer to as Agricola was Gnaeus Julius
Luci filius Aniensis Agricola Foro Julii, indicating not only his family
name (Julius) and forename (Gnaeus), but his father's forename
(Lucius), his place of origin (Forum Julii) and his voting tribe
(Aniensis). The sixth element of the full nomenclature of a Roman
citizen, the *cognomen* or personal name (Agricola), originated as a
nickname but became formalised as Roman citizenship expanded.
Since there was only a limited number of forenames and family
names, the elements in everyday usage, it became a practical
necessity to be able to distinguish one Gnaeus Julius from another,
much as the way that the Welsh are reputed to differentiate one
Evans or Jones from another by reference to their job or some other
personal characteristic. Agricola means farmer, the name perhaps
reflecting the agricultural interests of his father, who had written a
manual on viticulture which earned the praise of Columella in his
own systematic treatise on agriculture (1, 1, 14). The family name,
Julius, perhaps indicates enfranchisement by Julius Caesar, who was
probably responsible for founding Forum Julii (Fréjus) as a colony
for his legionary veterans some 90 years before Agricola was born
(Février 1973, 18–19), for in such circumstances it was common to
adopt the name of the person responsible for the grant of citizenship.
This in turn would suggest that the family was originally of local
origin, probably members of the landed aristocracy. The name of
Agricola's mother, Procilla, is distinctively Gaulish and may well
betray similar roots for her side of the family.

Thus, although Agricola could perhaps trace his Roman ancestry
back only some four generations, by the time of his birth on 13 June
AD 40 his family had become well established Roman provincials
(*Ag.* 4). Both his grandfathers had been equestrians and had served
successfully in the imperial service, each attaining the rank of
procurator. Both his uncle and his father, Julius Graecinus, had
advanced further up the social scale and achieved senatorial rank, the
former reaching at least the rank of quaestor (*A.E.* 1946, 94), the

latter rising as far as the praetorship before falling foul of the emperor Gaius (Caligula) who had him put to death shortly after his son's birth for refusing to prosecute a fellow senator. As a result, Agricola was brought up by his mother. Of his childhood we know little except that he was educated in the old Greek colony of Massilia, modern Marseilles, where he flirted briefly with the study of philosophy, a pursuit apparently deemed inappropriate for a future Roman senator (*Ag.* 4).

Though entry into the Senate was at the discretion of the emperor, as the son of a senator Agricola would have expected to progress through the imperial service at least as far as his father. Prior to formal entry at the age of twenty-four or thereabouts, aspiring candidates were obliged to serve as one of the vigintivirate, the committee of twenty, made up of four boards of minor magistrates in Rome. Agricola will have been no exception, though Tacitus fails to mention the post. He does indicate, however, that at the age of nineteen Agricola served as the senior military tribune (*tribunus laticlavius*) in one of the British legions under the governor Suetonius Paullinus. Again this was quite normal, though not all future senators progressed from the vigintivirate to a legionary post (Birley 1981, 8–9). Most translators have taken Tacitus to imply that Agricola was specially selected by the governor to serve on his headquarters staff (e.g. Ogilvie and Richmond 1967, 145), but it has recently been pointed out that the relevant phrase may mean no more than that Agricola was given his commission as military tribune by Paullinus (Dobson 1980, 1; Birley 1981, 74). Such selection was normally in the hands of the governor, but the system operated by a process of personal contacts and recommendations (Dobson 1979, 193). Thus Agricola's appointment indicates no more than that he was reasonably well connected. Indeed, Agricola may well have been favoured by Seneca, one of Nero's two chief advisors and a dominant figure in Rome at the time, who seems to have had some admiration for Graecinus, Agricola's father (Birley 1981, 73–4).

We are not informed in which legion Agricola served, but he was certainly in Britain in AD 60 during the Boudican revolt, the major rebellion which shocked the province and seriously set back its development. Tacitus does not record any direct personal involvement by Agricola but succeeds in praising him either by implication or by the use of vague generalities:

> The campaign, of course, was conducted under the direction and leadership of another – the commander to whom belonged the

decisive success and the credit for recovering Britain. Yet everything combined to give the young Agricola fresh skills, experience and ambition. (*Ag.*5)

Taken literally there is nothing in this passage to indicate that Agricola played any part in putting down the Boudican revolt – indeed, one might argue that the very absence of any such specific reference is a strong argument that he did not, otherwise Tacitus would undoubtedly have elaborated on the affair. Nonetheless, it is a credit to Tacitus' skill as a writer that it leaves the reader with the impression that Agricola had been involved, but was too modest to speak of it.

On his return to Rome Agricola married Domitia Decidiana, who shortly bore him a son. On his election to the quaestorship, a magistracy with financial responsibilities, he gained formal entry into the senate. He was then allocated by lot to assist Salvius Otho Titianus, the brother of the later short-lived emperor Otho, whose governorship of Asia is dated to AD 63–4. Each proconsular governor was accompanied to his province in the summer, when he took up office, by his allotted quaestor, although elections for the latter office took place at the end of the previous year (Mommsen 1952, 258). Thus Agricola must have been elected in December AD 62 at the age of twenty-two, though he would have been twenty-three by the time that he took up this post. This is marginally too young to enter the Senate, but the *ius liberorum* granted candidates for office one year's remission from the age qualification for each child born to them. It is often assumed that Agricola was elected in AD 63 (Ogilvie and Richmond 1967, 149 and 317), but this would imply service under successive governors which is justified neither by known practice nor by the testimony of Tacitus. Of Agricola's activities in Asia we know nothing except that he returned uncorrupted either by the wealth of the province or the greed of his superior (*Ag.* 6). There is no reason to doubt Agricola's honesty, though it seems strange to modern ears that it should be referred to as such a virtue.

The next formal office to which Agricola might reasonably aspire was that of praetor, a judicial post, which he could expect to attain some five years after his quaestorship. Meanwhile there were various posts for which he was eligible. After an interval of one year he served as *tribunus plebis* (tribune of the people), but according to Tacitus his year of office was as uneventful as the year of inactivity which preceded it. By this time the duties of the post were largely ornamental rather than functional. After perhaps another year, and certainly no later than AD 68, Agricola was elected to the praetorship. At the age of twenty-seven or twenty-eight he was perhaps two years younger than the legal minimum for this office, but there is no need to see him as especially favoured. The birth of his second child during his quaestorship, the daughter who subsequently became Tacitus' wife, secured a further year's remission from the formal age qualification, even though his first child had since died. This magistracy too involved no serious activity, since no judicial duties had fallen to his lot, other than the normal organisation of public games. Election as praetor carried with it an obligation to finance some such public spectacle and many men took the opportunity to promote their popularity with the people of Rome by lavish expenditure. Tacitus does not miss the chance to praise Agricola for his moderation in steering a middle course between economy and excess, while still winning popular approval (*Ag.* 6).

After the praetorship a whole range of posts potentially became available. Most numerous of these were the legionary commands, the governorships of various minor provinces and the role of assistant (*legatus*) to governors of senatorial provinces. With some twenty-five legionary legateships, lasting an average of three years, and a maximum by the end of the first century of only eighteen praetors elected each year, it is a matter of simple arithmetic that around fifty per cent of the praetors would subsequently have been required to serve as legionary commanders (Birley 1981, 15–17). In fact, Agricola took up none of these posts yet, but immediately after his year of office was appointed by the new emperor Galba to investigate the misappropriation of temple treasures which had occurred during the later years of Nero's reign.

So far Agricola's political career had been notably uneventful. He had reached the praetorship, the minimum level to which he aspired as the son of a praetor, at the normal age, taking into account the two years' remission for his two children. Nothing had occurred which would have marked him out as special in any way: he had not, for example, received imperial backing for his candidacy for any of the elective magistracies, a sure sign of favour. He had carried out his limited duties honestly, conscientiously and competently, and subsequently had been given a suitable, if undemanding, task by the emperor.

The events of the following year heralded a dramatic change in the course of Agricola's career. Galba's accession to the imperial throne on the death of Nero was not without opposition. Counter claims were soon made, first by Vitellius, with the support of the legions on the Rhine, and then by Otho in Rome, backed by the Praetorian guard who murdered Galba in January AD 69. The stage was now set for civil war with the Empire as the prize. Where Agricola's sympathies lay at this time is uncertain. He had established potential links with the Othonian cause early in his career: he had served as quaestor in Asia under Otho's brother and as military tribune in Britain under Suetonius Paullinus, who had become one of Otho's generals. But in March or perhaps early April of that year Agricola's mother was killed and her estate in the territory of the Intimilii in northern Italy plundered by men of Otho's fleet which had been ravaging the Ligurian coast. While *en route* from Rome to pay his last respects to his mother, Agricola heard that there was a fourth contender, Vespasian, commander of the armies in Judaea, and immediately espoused his cause (*Ag.* 7). Close examination of the chronology indicates that Agricola must have been one of the first to join the Flavians (Birley 1975, 139–40). Vespasian was not publicly claimed as emperor until 1 July in Alexandria, yet Agricola's mother was probably killed in March. Certainly her death cannot have occurred later than early April, since the raiding by Otho's fleet took place before the unsuccessful battle of Bedriacum against Vitellius on 14 April, shortly after which Otho committed suicide. Thus, either Agricola was inexplicably tardy in leaving Rome to attend to his mother's affairs and, indeed, must have missed her funeral by over three months (Ogilvie and Richmond 1967, 153), or he was approached by the Flavian party long before the public declaration of Vespasian's intent. Certainly preparations for the coup had been under way for some time and may well predate the suicide of Otho (Chilver 1957, 34; Wellesley 1975, 114–21). Potential long-standing connections between Agricola and the Flavian family have been postulated to explain his early involvement. The procurator of Gallia Narbonensis at the time, Valerius Paulinus, was a close friend of Vespasian and an early activist for the Flavian cause; as a native of Forum Julii, he would almost certainly have been well known to Agricola (Birley 1975, 139–40; Dobson 1980, 2). Petillius Cerialis, who was probably Vespasian's son-in-law, may also have known Agricola since both had served in Britain during the Boudican revolt, quite possibly in the same legion (Dobson 1980, 2). Less certain is the suggestion that Vespasian's son Titus might have been one of Agricola's colleagues while both were serving as military tribunes in Britain (Birley 1975, 140; 1981, 75). There is no doubt that Titus did spend part of his tribunate in the province (Suetonius *Titus* 4, 1) and that he was of similar age to Agricola, but the evidence seems to be against their service being contemporary (Jones 1984, 14–16).

We do not know how Agricola demonstrated his early allegiance but he was presumably soon active in the Flavian cause. Birley has suggested that his appointment to enrol recruits on their behalf may have been made as early as the summer of AD 69 (1975, 149 note 11; 1981, 76), but it is difficult to reconcile this with the clear statement by Tacitus that this mission was instigated by Mucianus, Vespasian's right-hand man, who did not arrive in Rome until after the death of Vitellius in December of that year (Dobson 1980, 3). The work was undertaken enthusiastically and conscientiously and shortly thereafter Agricola was given the command of *legio XX Valeria Victrix* in Britain, probably then stationed at Wroxeter (Frere 1978, 108). Since the appointment was again made by Mucianus it must date from the first half of AD 70 before Vespasian arrived in Rome. This was a clear sign of Agricola's political reliability in the eyes of the Flavian's, for the XXth had been slow to take up the oath of allegiance to Vespasian. Moreover, its previous commander, Roscius Coelius, is portrayed by Tacitus as something of a troublemaker (*Hist.* 1, 60), although his subsequent elevation to the consulship under Titus would suggest that he had not shown overt opposition to the Flavian cause. There is no need to assume that Agricola's appointment was in any way a reflection of particular military ability demonstrated ten years earlier while he was serving in Britain. Service as a military tribune seems to have counted little when appointments to legionary commands were being made (Dobson 1979, 193–4) and, as already noted above (p 36), the chances of any ex-praetor obtaining such a post were reasonably high. It was, however, something of a reward for Agricola's proven loyalty, for appointment soon after the praetorship – in his case the gap was two years – was a mark of favour (Dobson 1980, 3).

The governor of Britain at the time was Vettius Bolanus. Though appointed by Vitellius he had not been particularly active in his support and was allowed to continue as governor. Indeed, his subsequent career, promotion to the rank of patrician, the Roman nobility, and appointment to the governorship of Asia, hardly implies disfavour towards a supporter of an opposing faction (Birley 1981, 65). It was during the early part of his governorship that the political arrangements on the northern frontier broke down and Queen Cartimandua had to be rescued by Roman troops (Tacitus, *Hist.* 3, 45). This action was over by the time of Agricola's arrival in the province, though the problem in the north was not resolved. Bolanus' replacement by Petillius Cerialis and the arrival of a new legion, *II Adiutrix*, to replace *XIV Gemina* sent to serve on the Rhine was the signal for a new forward policy.

Cerialis' task was to punish the Brigantes for the insurrection and explusion of Cartimandua, and to bring their territory formally within the Roman province of Britannia. There is no doubt that he campaigned widely in their territory, but Tacitus, our only source, seems less than favourably inclined towards him (Birley 1973), and this makes more difficult any reasoned assessment of his activities:

> Petillius Cerialis at once struck terror into the hearts of the enemy by attacking the state of the Brigantes, which is said to be the most numerous in the whole province. After a series of battles – some of them by no means bloodless – he had overrun, if not actually conquered, the major part of their territory. (*Ag.* 17)

At first glance Tacitus is most complimentary. He is crediting Cerialis with successful action against one of the most populous tribes in Britain. But by skilful choice of expression he manages to imply less than total victory and makes no mention of Venutius, elsewhere hailed as the greatest British general since Caratacus (*Annals* 12, 40), whose defeat Cerialis' actions must have encompassed. Archaeological evidence, however, is beginning to hint at the depth of penetration into Brigantian territory and the extent of consolidation by fort building (below, pp 60–5). Agricola was personally involved in these campaigns and commanded detachments or larger forces at various times, but Tacitus provides no specific examples of actions in which he participated. Instead he relies upon vague generalisations and references to Agricola's modesty to give the impression that he played a major part:

> Yet Agricola never sought to glorify himself by boasting of his achievements. As a subordinate, he attributed the success of his operations to their originator, his general. Thus by his outstanding obedience and his modesty in telling of his deeds he won distinction without arousing jealousy. (*Ag.* 8)

Since the next governor of Britain, Julius Frontinus, is not mentioned in the account of Agricola's legionary command, we must assume that Agricola had left Britain by early in AD 74 at the latest, for Cerialis had been replaced and was back in Rome by May of that year when he was honoured with a second consulship (*CIL* XVI, 20). Further rewards came Agricola's way also. Along with other supporters of the Flavian cause he was promoted to the rank of patrician by the emperor, a position in society of some standing and a signal honour heralding further speedy advancement. He was then made governor of the minor imperial province of Aquitania in central and western Gaul, next door to his home province of Gallia Narbonesis. This was a purely administrative post as the province held no army, but it marked him out as destined for further rapid promotion and an early consulship. Provincial governorships were the most prestigious posts men of praetorian status could aspire to and their tenure was a mark of imperial favour (Campbell 1975, 16). Again Tacitus provides little hard information concerning Agricola's activities, but gives a generally favourable assessment of his role: he is praised for his dispensing of justice with mercy, his strict honesty, and his avoidance of intrigue and rivalry (*Ag.* 9). Much of his time here would have been spent travelling around the province holding judicial sessions in the main urban centres, though we have no independent record of his governorship. After less than three years he was recalled to Rome with the immediate prospect of a consulship (*Ag.* 9), probably therefore late in AD 76.

It is generally assumed that Agricola became consul some time in AD 77 at the age of thirty-six or thirty-seven. This was some five or six years below the usual minimum age of forty-two, though he had served the recognised minimum of two posts after the praetorship. As we have seen, there was nothing in his early career or, indeed, in the performance of his subsequent duties, which would have justified further rapid promotion on the basis of outstanding merit. Certainly there is no need to see him as a specially selected *vir militaris* (military man), if such a category actually existed (Campbell 1975 *contra* Syme 1958, 655–6). His accelerated progress is directly atrributable to his Flavian connections, the early consulship being justified on the basis of his newly acquired rank as a patrician (Morris 1964, 333). Had he been patrician by birth, he could have expected to attain the supreme magistracy in his early thirties. It was during his consulship that Agricola betrothed his daughter to Tacitus. Though aged only thirteen at the time, she was not too young for marriage by Roman standards (Balsdon 1962, 173), and the ceremony took place after Agricola's term of office had expired. Immediately afterwards he was further honoured with a pontificate, a place in the college of priests of which the emperor was always head, and appointed to govern Britain, arriving there in the middle of the summer.

It had long been customary to set Agricola's arrival in the province in AD 78, by counting back from AD 84, the presumed date of his seventh and final campaigning season. The crucial evidence upon which this assumption is based is the contrast which Tacitus draws between the reaction of the Roman populace to Agricola's victory over the Caledonians at Mons Graupius and their attitude to Domitian's recent triumph to celebrate his 'sham' victory in Germany (*Ag.* 39). Clearly this means that news of Agricola's success reached Rome after Domitian's triumphal celebrations which marked the end of his war against the Chatti. Domitian's triumph is thought to have taken place late in AD 83, for the *congiarium* (distribution of money to the populace) which accompanied it was made early in AD 84, the same year in which numerous coins bear the new title Germanicus. It is argued, therefore, that the battle of Mons Graupius cannot have occurred before AD 84 (Syme 1958, 22; Ogilvie and Richmond 1967, 318-9).

This conclusion is not justified when the chronology is considered more carefully (Birley 1976). The precise date of Domitian's victory over the Chatti is not recorded, but, even though the subsequent triumph is likely to have taken place almost immediately he returned to Rome, the *congiarium* need not have been paid out until some time later, as occurred after Claudius' celebration of his British victory of AD 43. Moreover, Domitian may not have assumed the title of Germanicus until later still, perhaps egged on by flatterers, since there was no ready precedent for assuming such an honorary title commemorating a victory (Birley 1976, 13; 1981, 78). In fact, the title is attested on a coin minted late in AD 83 (Holder 1977), which suggests that the victory must have occurred earlier that year than has previously been thought. Mons Graupius, on the other hand, clearly took place at the very end of the campaigning season, since we are told that there was no time left for further operations (*Ag.* 38). Tacitus then emphasises the deliberately slow march to winter quarters while the fleet sailed back to its base around the north of Britain. Since all these events were reported to Domitian, it must have been well into October by the time Agricola set about composing his dispatch. Thereafter a courier had to carry it to one of the channel ports and thence to Rome. If we take the average daily distance which might have been achieved using the *cursus publicus* (see below, p 43), the 1000 mile (1600 km) journey would have taken twenty-two days. Greater speed was possible: the news of Nero's death passed from Rome to Spain, a distance overland of some 330 miles (530 km) in less than thirty-six hours (Plutarch *Galba* 7), while news of the mutiny of the IV and XXII legions was brought from Mainz to Rome, a distance of some 800 miles (1280 km) in nine days (Tacitus *Hist.* 1, 18 and 55). These, however, were exceptional events with far reaching political import and considerable potential impact across the whole Empire. News of Agricola's victory in Britain hardly falls into the same category and such efforts would not have been justified. Moreover, travelling conditions would have become less favourable as winter approached and the nights began to draw in, so that the journey to Rome is likely to have taken at least a month. It is unlikely, therefore, that Domitian could have been aware of Agricola's victory much before the end of November. That this information reached him after his own German victory-celebrations does not, therefore, require the battle of Mons Graupius to be dated to AD 84. On the contrary, the force of Tacitus' contrast would have been all the more marked if the two events had followed very closely upon one another in the latter half of AD 83.

Two other pieces of evidence are sometimes marshalled to support the dating of Mons Graupius to AD 84 and must, therefore, be considered here. The first involves a coin of Domitian, dated to AD 84, on the reverse of which there is an unusual motif depicting a cavalry trooper riding down a barbarian while another foe lies dead nearby (pl 1). The victory here commemorated is thought by some to have been Mons Graupius (Kraay 1960, 109–13), but the imperial titles on the obverse will not allow such a link to be made. After the original declaration as *imperator* on ascending the throne, a Roman emperor received subsequent acclamations after major victories and the number of times this occurred became part of his official title. On this coin Domitian is styled *Imperator VII*. If Mons Graupius had taken place late in AD 84, Domitian's seventh imperial acclamation could not possibly refer to it for that title is already attested on a diploma from Carnuntum in Austria at the very beginning of September that year (*CIL* XVI, 30), far too early for news of Agricola's success even to have reached Rome, let alone the Danube frontier.

The second argument concerns an auxiliary unit serving in Britain, a cohort of Usipi, which mutinied, commandeered three ships and in its flight accidentally circumnavigated Britain. According to Tacitus this occurred in the summer of Agricola's sixth and penultimate campaign (*Ag.* 28) which, it has been argued, must be dated no earlier than AD 83 since the territory of the Usipi, an area in western Germany adjacent to the Dutch border, was not annexed until that date (Anderson 1920, 159). But the territory of this tribe lay so close to the Rhine, which had been the Roman frontier until AD 83, that recruitment may well have occurred before formal annexation, as it did with the Frisii further north. Moreover, Cassius Dio attributes these same events to the reign of Titus (66, 20) who died in AD 81. It could be argued that he is simply presenting a garbled and erroneous version of Tacitus' account, but he does provide some additional information, so that his chronology should not be dismissed out of hand (Urban 1971, 30–4).

None of the above arguments requires that the start of Agricola's governorship should be delayed until the summer of AD 78, particularly since Tacitus gives the impression that it immediately followed his consulship (*Ag.* 9). If this came in AD 77, as is generally assumed, the question that must first be answered is whether or not such a timetable is feasible. Clearly Agricola would have had to have held the consulship early in the year, yet we know from the *fasti* (list of magistrates) that in AD 77 the ordinary consuls (*consules ordinarii*), who took up office on 1 January, were the emperor Vespasian and his elder son Titus (Degrassi 1950, 22). However, from as early as 5 BC it had become standard for the consuls to resign half way through the year and be replaced in order to increase the number of men who, as ex-consuls, were eligible for higher office. The year continued to be named after the first two. Unfortunately the names of their replacements, known as suffect consuls (*consules suffecti*), were not recorded in such a systematic way. Succeeding emperors sometimes reduced the period of office of suffect consuls, though usually maintaining the six-month tenure of ordinary consuls. After the accession of the Flavian dynasty, however, the period of office of both types of consul was quite frequently reduced to as little as two months, though the involvement of members of the imperial family often upset the pattern. We do not know when in AD 77 Vespasian and Titus demitted office, though Domitian is attested as consul, apparently alongside his father, on a papyrus dated to early June or July of that year (Degrassi 1950, 22) and it has been suggested that his tenure began as early as mid-January or February (Gallivan 1981, 214). If the dating of this papyrus can be relied upon, for such documents are perhaps more prone to error than inscriptions on the matter of formal titles, Agricola could not have begun his consulship before June. Even allowing for the shortest possible tenure, he could not, therefore, have left Rome before early August. It has been estimated that an average daily distance which might be travelled using the official postal service (*cursus publicus*) would be around 46 miles (75 km), though the ordinary traveller along Roman roads might not have expected to achieve much more than 28 miles (45 km) (Chevallier 1976, 194). Agricola was setting out on imperial business and therefore entitled to use the facilities of the *cursus publicus*, but even if we allow a faster than average figure for the 1000 mile (1600 km) journey, he could hardly have taken much less than three weeks to reach Britain. Exactly what Tacitus meant by the expression midsummer (*media aestate*) is debateable (Ogilvie and Richmond 1967, 318). There is no reason to believe that he was using the phrase with any greater precision than it might be used in everyday conversation, but even so, since the Roman summer was normally considered to run from mid-May to mid-August, it is difficult to accept that what Tacitus had in mind was a date in late August.

We appear to be facing a dilemma. After detailed examination of the chronological relationship between Agricola's major victory and Domitian's triumph in Germany, it would appear best to place the former late in AD 83 and consequently see the beginning of Agricola's governorship in AD 77. On the other hand the *fasti* would seem to indicate that he could not have held the consulship sufficiently early in AD 77 to have reached Britain by midsummer. There is, however, a possible solution. Agricola was recalled from his governorship of Aquitania after less than three years in office with the *immediate* prospect of a consulship (*Ag.* 9). He may thus have taken up office not early in AD 77, but late in AD 76 (Campbell 1986): not at the very end of the year, for the office-bearers for the last two months are recorded, but perhaps in September–October.

One problem remains unsolved, the timing of Agricola's arrival in Britain. Exactly when the governor was supposed to take up office in his province is uncertain. Because of potential transport problems midsummer has been suggested as the most convenient season for both incoming and outgoing staff (Talbert 1984, 498), but this would have seriously hampered any campaigning in the year of the changeover so that, if there was a standard time of year, late spring would seem to be a more sensible suggestion. Agricola, on the other hand, certainly reached Britain in the middle of the campaigning season, but Tacitus' phraseology – it was *already* midsummer (*media iam aestate*) – would seem to imply that he arrived rather later than was normal (Ogilvie and Richmond 1967, 208). This has in the past been variously explained. Had his consular term been completed at the end of April, it would certainly have been late June, if not early July, before he could have reached Britain (Furneaux and Anderson 1922, 167). More recently special personal circumstances have been postulated: his departure perhaps being delayed in order to allow his daughter's marriage ceremony to take place in late June, a more propitious time of year (Birley 1981, 79). Both of these explanations, however, assume that he held the consulship in the same year that he took up post in Britain, which now seems unlikely. The solution may be no more complicated than the vagaries of long-distance travel in the ancient world.

· 3 ·

EARLY CAMPAIGNS

ANGLESEY AND THE ORDOVICES

On his arrival in the province as governor, Agricola was immediately faced with a crisis. The Ordovices had almost wiped out a cavalry unit operating in their territory and the further escalation of hostilities was a possibility. The Ordovices, whose name may mean 'hammer fighters' (Rivet and Smith 1979, 434), seem to have gained something of a reputation amongst modern writers as opponents of Rome (Hogg 1966, 30; Salway 1981, 584). In fact, this seems to have been somewhat exaggerated. The one previous appearance of the tribe in the pages of Tacitus was in AD 49 when Caratacus, who spearheaded the early armed resistance to Rome, transferred the war to their territory from that of the Silures in the face of a Roman attack (*Annals* 12, 33). Other than that they are not heard of again. The presence of garrisons in their territory through the Roman period, the main reason for stigmatising them as a continuing thorn in the side of Rome, seems more likely to be explained by the need to control the exploitation of mineral resources in that area (Hanson 1986b). Moreover, it is arguable that the portion of central Wales concerned does not even fall within their territory.

This raises the question of the location of the tribe and, thus, of Agricola's first military operation as governor. According to Ptolemy the Ordovices held lands below the Brigantes and the Parisi, and to the west of the Cornovii (*Geog.* 2, 3, 11), but there has been considerable debate about whether or not they should be seen to extend over both west central and north-west Wales. The two places, Mediolanum and Branogenium, attributed to them by Ptolemy do not help us greatly. The coordinates he gives would seem to place them in North Wales (fig 1), but the suggested identifications, Whitchurch and Leintwardine, lie too far to the east and should probably be attributed to the Cornovii (Rivet and Smith 1979, 121 and 143). Two factors do, however, point to the north-west as the focus of insurrection at this time. Firstly, Agricola extended the operation, apparently on the spur of the moment, into

Anglesey (*Ag.* 18). This would hardly have been justified or even feasible if the primary action had taken place somewhere on the upper reaches of the river Severn (*contra* Jarrett and Mann 1968, 168). Secondly, the only Roman forts which on archaeological grounds might reasonably be dated late enough to be credited to Agricola are located in the north-west (see below). Despite doubts that Anglesey should be included in Ordovican territory (Jarrett and Mann 1968, 170), the similarities between the later prehistoric and Romano–British settlement types on the island and the adjacent mainland are so great as to make this a strong possibility. The other named group in the vicinity, the Gangani, may represent a tribal element incorporated within an Ordovican federation, such as is suggested for the Brigantes (below, p 57), or perhaps, since the tribe also appears in Ireland, the name was accidentially transferred to Wales by Ptolemy because of the way in which it was written across his original map source (Rivet and Smith 1979, 365).

Our knowledge of the Ordovices is relatively rudimentary, particularly in west central Wales where there are very few sites known to belong in the later Iron Age or Romano–British period. Many more are known in the north-west, but even here the pattern is far from complete, reflecting the survival of stone-built settlements on lower-grade modern pasture land which has been subject to less intensive ploughing in the immediate past. In contrast, the better soils are largely devoid of evidence because sites which undoubtedly would have been situated there were destroyed long ago by ploughing, but are not now recorded from the air as cropmarks because of the modern predominance of pasture, itself the consequence of the generally high rainfall in the area. Moreover, it can be extremely difficult to date the sites which are known because they do not yield native pottery and few carbon-14 dates have been obtained. Often the only dating evidence recorded has been Roman pottery, which has resulted in some highly dubious interpretations of the effect of the Roman arrival in the area (below, p 83).

Hillforts, one of the characteristic settlement forms of the Iron Age, are well represented in the north-west, though only half as common here as elsewhere in Wales. They show considerable variation in size with several over 15 acres (6 ha), but most under 2 acres (0.8 h) in area (Davies 1980b, 21). Combined with the multiplicity of smaller stone-built homesteads, whose origins most probably lie in the pre-Roman period (Davies 1980b, 133–5; Lloyd Jones 1984, 47), this may indicate some hierarchical social organisation and at least rudimentary political centralisation. Though excavations at such sites often suggest a rather limited, even primitive, level of material culture, this is perhaps to be explained by the greater use of leather, wood and other perishable materials and is in any case contradicted by the discovery of two metalwork hoards which exhibit considerable wealth. Most famous of these is that from Llyn Cerrig Bach in Anglesey which comprises a range of fine metalwork including weapons, as well as horse and chariot gear (Fox 1946) (pls 2 and 3), though the only other evidence of what might be termed a warrior aristocracy is a single inhumation containing a sword of late La Tène type, also from Anglesey (Lynch 1970, 248).

Though the Ordovices are often categorised as pastoralists, a description which has been wrongly taken to carry with it implications of a nomadic and perhaps more politically decentralised lifestyle, there is growing archaeological evidence that the local agricultural base was broader. Field lynchets reflecting arable cultivation are quite frequently found in association with stone-built homesteads; quernstones are common finds, and the pollen and seed remains identified in modern excavation are beginning to furnish solid testimony for the practice of arable farming (Davies 1980b, 16).

A stable community with appreciable territorial ties, such as the Ordovices would now seem to have been, should not have presented major problems to the Roman army. It was standard practice to devastate the countryside when on campaign in order to force the inhabitants to stand and fight. Once they had made such a commitment their fate was sealed, for the Roman army was supreme in open battle. In any case it is far from certain that all elements of the tribe were opposed to Rome. One 11-acre (4.4-ha) hillfort in Caernarvonshire, Braich-y-Ddinas, may have continued in occupation well into the second century AD, for abundant Roman finds are known from the site, including coins (Davies 1980b, 360–71). It seems unlikely that hostile elements would have been allowed to continue to hold a site which could have been defended against Rome. Even towns founded under Roman auspices were not allowed to surround themselves with defensive walls without specific permission.

We might reasonably suggest, therefore, that only a part of the tribe was involved in this uprising, and should not overestimate the magnitude of the problem just because Tacitus makes much of the situation. Indeed, it seems not to have been too unusual for such problems to arise when control of the province was changing hands, particularly if the new governor's arrival was delayed for any reason. Tacitus records Ostorius Scapula facing similar circumstances on his

arrival to take up office in AD 47 (*Annals* 13, 13). If the reactions of
the new governor were being put to the test, then Agricola passed.
His response was rapid. Although he had to organise the campaign
immediately upon his arrival in the province, and contend with the
dispersal of his troops and the lateness of the season, Agricola had the
advantage of general familiarity with the area, for he had served as
legate of *legio XX*, stationed probably at nearby Wroxeter, as
recently as four years earlier.

Once Agricola was in the field, the Ordovices appear not to have
presented any serious threat and he took the opportunity to attack
the island of Anglesey. Tacitus makes clear that this was unpremedi-
tated and that the necessary preparations, particularly the provision
of ships to ferry troops across the Menai Strait, had not been made
(*Ag.* 18). Picked auxiliary troops, probably Batavians who were
famous for such skills, swam the strait and launched a surprise
attack. Others may have crossed on foot at low tide near Caernarvon
(Ogilvie and Richmond 1967, 211). The element of surprise seems to
have been sufficient to win the day. The enemy sued for peace and
surrendered the island. The venture might well have been criticised
as foolhardy, perhaps Agricola overstretching himself on his first
fully independent command, but Tacitus skilfully turns the episode
to advantage using it to praise Agricola's courage and resourceful-
ness. One may doubt, however, whether Agricola did lead his
troops into battle personally, for the description is a stock rhetorical
convention applied to 'brave' generals and need not be taken literally
(*cf.* Caesar *de Bello Gallico* 1, 25, 1; Sallust *Catiline* 59, 1).

Tacitus makes much of Agricola's modesty in decrying the whole
enterprise as no more than an action to control an already defeated
tribe:

> Yet he did not use his success to glorify himself. He would not
> represent his action as a campaign of conquest, when, as he said,
> he had merely kept a defeated tribe under control. He did not even
> use laurel-wreathed dispatches to announce his achievement. But
> his very reluctance to admit his title to fame won him even greater
> fame. (*Ag.* 18)

Is there any reason to doubt Agricola's own assessment? The Roman
army had been campaigning in North Wales on and off since early in
the governorship of Ostorius Scapula (AD 47–52). It was hardly
uncharted territory. Nor was Anglesey. Roman interest in that island
goes back certainly to AD 60 when Suetonius Paullinus fought a
bloody battle there and established a garrison, only to be recalled by

the Boudican rebellion in his rear (Tacitus, *Annals* 14, 30). Agricola may even have accompanied him, for he had been serving as a military tribune in Britain at that time. Though his involvement is attested only with the Deceangli to the east, a similar recall to deal with a revolt in his rear may well have prevented Ostorius Scapula from reaching Anglesey in AD 48 (Tacitus, *Annals* 12, 32). The considerable Roman interest in the island has been explained by reference to the Druids, who have been seen as orchestrating the early British opposition to Rome (Webster 1978, 86–9). According to Caesar the Druids came to Britain for training (*de Bello Gallico* 6, 13) and Tacitus mentions their presence on Anglesey (*Annals* 14, 30) where the widespread origins and rich contents of the Llyn Cerrig Bach hoard have been taken as indicative of their wide influence (Fox 1946, 70). Though clearly of some religious significance, the hoard fits into a series of offerings in watery contexts well known across northern Europe and need have no specific connection with the Druids, while Tacitus' reference to them noted above is the only one in the whole of his surviving writings on Britain (Todd 1981, 255–6). Thus, such a major political role for these shadowy religious figures is now less popular, and more prosaic factors may have influenced Roman strategy. The island, with one of the largest fertile areas and some of the most favourable climatic conditions in North Wales, may rightly be regarded as the local granary, and thus the key to control of the area. In addition it contained mineral resources, notably copper, whose exploitation is more often a factor influencing Roman conquests than is usually admitted.

Nor was pre-Agricolan involvement in North Wales limited to that some seventeen years earlier. That a cavalry unit was active in Ordovician territory at the time of Agricola's arrival in the province suggests that his immediate predecessor, Julius Frontinus, had also been operating well to the north. He was a man of considerable military ability, amongst his other talents, who would undoubtedly have recognised the necessity of attempting the total conquest of Wales if at all possible. That Tacitus gives him credit only for the subjugation of the Silures is probably as much to avoid letting any of Agricola's actions be overshadowed by those of his predecessors as it is an accurate reflection of Frontinus' achievements. That these received any credit whatsoever is almost certainly because of Frontinus' influential position in Rome at the time the *Agricola* was published.

The process by which Rome gained military control of an area was a well-established one. The first object was to defeat the enemy, preferably in open battle where Roman arms were supreme. This might take some time depending on the nature of the opposition and the local geography, both political and topographical. A mobile enemy without fixed assets was difficult to pin down, especially in heavily wooded or mountainous terrain where guerilla warfare could be brought into play. It was perhaps partly for this reason that it had taken so long to overcome the Silures in southern and central Wales. Once the enemy had been defeated, or had capitulated, Roman control was exercised either by formal agreements involving the taking of hostages, or, if annexation was thought desirable, by the imposition of forts both to control the inhabitants and protect them from external aggression. Thus it was not a piecemeal advance akin to trench warfare, but the accumulation of territory tribe by tribe. The account provided by Tacitus does not make it absolutely clear whether the cavalry unit attacked by the Ordovices was actually in garrison in their territory, though this would be the natural interpretation of their presence in that area at that time. If so, it implies that the above process was already well into its second stage, the consolidation of all Ordovican territory by the construction of forts. This gains some support from the archaeological evidence, although the precise attribution of early forts to the governorship of Frontinus rather than Agricola is difficult and prone to circular reasoning based on an assessment of the historical probabilities. Though happy to see most of the forts established in southern and central Wales as originating under Frontinus, modern scholars (e.g. Davies 1980a, 261 and figs. 17.3 and 17.4) feel obliged by Tacitus' account to leave a good deal to Agricola.

But on the basis of the archaeological evidence alone almost all of the forts in North Wales could as easily be foundations of Frontinus as of Agricola (fig 2). Many of the sites have not provided artefactual evidence which is sufficiently abundant or diagnostic to indicate a foundation date more precise than Flavian (i.e. c. AD 70–95); for example the forts at Caerhun (Reynolds 1938), Tomen-y-Mur (Jarrett 1964, 173) and Pen Llywn (A.W. 1983, 32), the putative fort at Rhuddlan (A.W. 1983, 36) and the fortlets at Brithdir (White 1978, 44 and 54) and Erglodd (Davies 1980c, 724 and 727). Indeed, the excavator of the putative fort at Aberffraw in Anglesey could not provide a more accurate assessment of date than first century and did not exclude the possibility of association with the historically attested activities of Suetonius Paullinus (White 1980, 339). Occasional accidental finds may clarify the situation. Caer Gai and Pennal have provided examples of particularly distinctive fine-glazed ware vessels

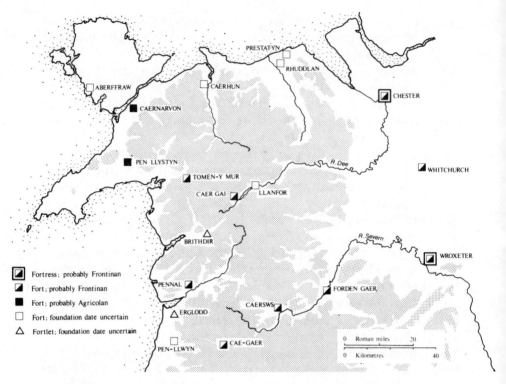

2 Flavian forts in North Wales

imported from Gaul; in both cases they were found outside the fort, the former associated with a burial (Boon and Brewer 1982). Material of this category, which has been studied in some detail, is normally found in pre-Flavian contexts (Greene 1979, 99–100) and may, therefore, suggest an occupation beginning early in the Flavian period, perhaps in the governorship of Frontinus. The fort at Tomen-y-Mur, which is closely linked both geographically and morphologically with these two sites (Davies 1980a, 261 and note 20), is thus likely to be contemporary.

One site where Agricola's involvement is securely attested is the legionary fortress at Chester, for it is the only military establishment to have produced any epigraphic record of him. But it is difficult to accept that the fortress, actually located in Cornovian territory, was founded by him. The interpretation of the evidence is quite complicated. On the one hand it has been noted that the three inscriptions all occur on lead water pipes (Wright and Richmond 1955, 48–9; Wright and Hassall 1971, 273) (pl 4), and it is far from certain at what stage in the life of the fortress it was provided with running water (Strickland 1980, 8). The pipe most recently discovered, for example, had clearly been laid after the foundations of a large stone elliptical building were almost complete. On the other hand even if the installation of running water was a secondary phase in the construction of the fortress, the water pipes all date to early in AD 79, almost two years after Agricola's operations in North Wales. All the more important, therefore, is the growing evidence that the early military occupations of Chester was far more complex than has previously been assumed. The probability of an earlier fort somewhere beneath the fortress has long been postulated because of the discovery of Roman cremations in the Deanery Field (Jarrett 1969, 39). Burial within a Roman settlement was forbidden by law, so that a pre- or post-Roman fortress context must be indicated. Since cremation largely went out of fashion by the mid-third century AD, the former is the more likely. Recent excavation on the northern defences of the fortress at Abbey Green nearby has revealed several phases of rampart and associated military timber buildings (McPeake et al. 1980, 15–18). A box rampart, an uncommon and generally pre-Flavian style of construction (Jones 1975, 82–3), had undergone repairs suggestive of a lengthy occupation. This was then replaced by a much larger rampart on a slightly different alignment. Associated timber buildings had been reconstructed at least once before the end of the first century when they were replaced in stone, though the precise date of the phases has not yet been fully determined. Examination of the samian pottery from the early phases at Chester led Hartley to suggest that an auxiliary fort of Neronian–Flavian date, too late therefore to belong to Suetonius Paullinus, was replaced by a legionary fortress well before the governorship of Agricola (1981, 243–4). Indeed, there is independent confirmation of Roman control and exploitation of the area at least by the time of Frontinus, for lead pigs from the territory of the Deceangli, precisely dated to AD 74, have been recovered from the vicinity of the fortress (*C.I.L.* VII, 1204–5) (pl 5).

At only two auxiliary forts in Wales can a reasonable case be made for an Agricolan foundation. Excavation and recording in advance of gravel extraction at Pen Llystyn provided the nearest thing we yet have to the complete plan of a timber-built auxiliary fort in Britain (fig 3). On historical grounds it was firmly identified with Agricola, the date supported by the parallel between the earliest decorated samian from the site and that from deposits at Pompeii which were sealed, and thus closely dated, by the historically attested eruption of Vesuvius in AD 79 (Hogg 1968, 145 and 161). Recent large-scale

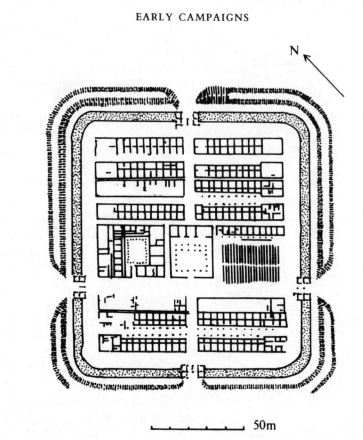

N

50m

3 Timber-built auxiliary fort at Pen Llystyn (after Hogg)

work at Caernarvon indicated that the earliest fort was Agricolan on the basis of the discovery of coins of the emperor Domitian (AD 81–96) in apparently primary levels (*A.W.* 1979, 27), though this has yet to be confirmed in the full publication.★ Both forts, however, are situated in the extreme north-west corner of Wales so that the archaeological evidence need not be seen to conflict with Agricola's own view of his first military action, that it was no more than a minor policing exercise, or at most the completion of the process of consolidation after the main conquest had been achieved by his immediate predecessors. To imply that this brief episode in North Wales was a brilliant campaign of conquest by Agricola is typical Tacitean hyperbole.

THE BRIGANTES AND BEYOND?

What Tacitus says about the operations of Agricola's second summer is extremely vague. The descriptions of his activities – his presence everywhere on the march, his personal selection of camp sites and reconnoitring of terrain – are no more than the stock literary characteristics of a good general, readily paralleled in the writings of Sallust and Livy (Ogilvie and Richmond 1967, 217–8). Accordingly it is not entirely safe to rely on these asides to give clues to the precise whereabouts of Agricola's activities (*contra* Salway 1981, 141). Traditionally this campaign is seen as resulting in the occupation of Brigantian territory (Ogilvie and Richmond 1967, 55–7; Todd 1981, 103–4), though Tacitus does not mention the tribe by name (*Ag.* 20). Such an oversight may simply reflect Tacitus' typical geographical vagueness; alternatively it might be explained as a device to ensure the maximum credit accruing to Agricola. To have specified that the campaign was directed against the Brigantes when their conquest had already been attributed to Petillius Cerialis three chapters earlier would inevitably have detracted from Agricola's perceived achievements.

There can be little doubt, however, that Agricola was operating somewhere in northern England or Lowland Scotland, for the end of the following season sees him penetrating as far north as the Tay estuary (*Ag.* 22). Yet this provides only a very general frame of reference. Tacitus does give some other clues, though his lack of precision and obscurity of expression leave considerable grounds for speculation. Firstly, he indicates that many states or tribes (*multae civitates*) succumbed to Agricola. This seems straightforward enough and has usually been taken to refer to the Brigantes, whose political structure is thought to have been a loose confederacy (Salway 1981, 45; Frere 1978, 72 and 77). Yet in an earlier chapter the Brigantes are specifically referred to as a *civitas* in the singular (*Ag.* 17). This may be no more than inconsistency on Tacitus' part, but if the text is taken literally other tribes ought also to have been involved (Birley 1973, 189). Since Brigantian territory seems to have covered virtually all of northern England (see below) apart from eastern Yorkshire, this in turn perhaps implicates at least one of the Lowland Scottish tribes. Tacitus goes on to state that these tribes had previously operated on equal terms *against* Rome, though the translation of this sentence is disputed (Birley 1973, 190 *contra* Mattingly 1948, 71 and Ogilvie and Richmond 1967, 219). This could mean that some of the Scottish tribes had actually come into contact with Roman forces before Agricola's second campaign. In addition, the fact that Agricola is not credited with encountering new tribes until his third season of campaigning, during which he penetrated as far north as the Tay, or previously unknown tribes until his fifth, would seem to support the view that previous governors may have been active in Scotland (*Ag.* 22 and 24; Birley 1953, 15–16 and 40–1).

This may seem rather too elaborate an interpretation to base on the finer nuances of one or two phrases in Tacitus' account, particularly in respect of the Brigantes, for elsewhere in the *Agricola* he confuses them with the Iceni (*Ag.* 31) and may well have been further confused over the chronology of the dispute between Cartimandua of the Brigantes and her husband Venutius (Hanson and Campbell 1986). On the other hand there is some independent corroboration for the extent of the northward penetration of Roman forces by the early 70s AD. While discussing the geography of Britain, Pliny the Elder states that:

> In nearly thirty years now, Roman arms have extended knowledge of it (*sc.* Britain) not beyond the neighbourhood of the Caledonian Forest. (*Nat. Hist.* 4, 102)

The Caledonian Forest is located by Ptolemy in the north of Scotland, somewhere in the vicinity of the Great Glen (*Geog.* 2, 3, 8), though in general classical usage the name seems to mean simply 'the wilds of Caledonia', an area usually located north of the Forth–Clyde isthmus (Rivet and Smith 1979, 289–91). But even if the geographical reference was being used in a very general way to mean north Britain, it still ought to imply some contact with the far north. Indeed, Clarke has suggested that it was initial progress through the forest of the upper Forth which brought this classical literary stereotype of dense undeterminably large forest into being (1969, 193). The translation of the first phrase (*triginta iam prope annis*) has been rendered as 'nearly thirty years ago' (Rackham 1942, 197–8). While possible linguistically, this would require special pleading in historical terms, for we would then have to postulate the presence of Roman troops in Scotland not long after the invasion of Britain in AD 43. *Exactly* thirty years from that event would place us at the interface between the governorships of Petillius Cerialis and Julius Frontinus. Even if allowance is made for the approximation inherent in such chronological expressions, it could not stretch to include Agricola's activities, for Pliny's *Natural History* was dedicated to Titus in AD 77, the very year that Agricola took up office. It seems unlikely that Cerialis was operating quite as far north as the Forth–Clyde isthmus, but perhaps not improbable that he would have obtained intelligence of the area if active slightly further south.

The name Brigantes may mean 'the high or mighty ones' and

occurs relatively widely in the Celtic world. Whether it is simply a flattering self-description, or has more specific connotations, is uncertain, but the senses of 'overlords' or 'upland people' are both potentially applicable to the British tribe (Rivet and Smith 1979, 279). Their territory was widespread. Tacitus refers to them as the most populous tribe in the island (*Ag.* 17), while Ptolemy remarks that they were situated below the Votadini and Selgovae, and extended from sea to sea (*Geog.* 2, 3, 10). He goes on to confirm the large size of their territory by reference to some nine 'cities' within it, in contrast to only one for the Parisi who were located on the coast to the south. The northern and southern limits of Brigantian territory are more difficult to define. The most southerly places attributed to the tribe by Ptolemy are Rigodunum and Camulodunum, identified tentatively as Castleshaw and Slack, the names having been transferred to the Roman forts at those locations from nearby native sites (Rivet and Smith 1979, 142) (fig 8). On the other hand, the distribution of the coins of the Coritani, or the Corieltauvi as they may now be more correctly known, to the south suggests that their lands did not extend far to the north and west of the river Trent (Allen 1963, 13–19). That the southern limit of Brigantian territory skirted the edge of the Pennines would fit well with the distribution of the most northerly pre-Flavian forts in that area which may have served as a watch on the border (Hanson and Campbell 1986) (fig 4). In the north the Tyne–Solway isthmus is usually taken as a convenient geographical demarcation which might define their domains, but if the distribution of later dedications to the goddess Brigantia may be taken as a guide, their territory extended into southern Scotland, for one such inscription is recorded from Birrens in Dumfriesshire (*R.I.B.* 2091; Birley 1953, 33).

Given the vast size of this territory and its climatic and topographical variety, it is perhaps not surprising that the Brigantes have been considered to be a loose confederation of smaller groups rather than one large tribe. This is borne out by other literary and epigraphic evidence. In describing the British coastline, Ptolemy refers to a bay and a harbour in the north by ethnic names (*Geog.* 2, 3, 2 and 4) (fig 1). Since neither of the peoples referred to, the Setantii and Gabrantovices, occurs in his full list of tribes, they may well have been smaller groups within the Brigantian confederacy (Rivet and Smith 1979, 364 and 457). Similar arguments apply to otherwise unknown groups recorded on inscriptions in the area – the Textoverdi near Chesterholm in Northumberland (*R.I.B.* 1965) and perhaps the Corionototae, though the latter may have dwelt further

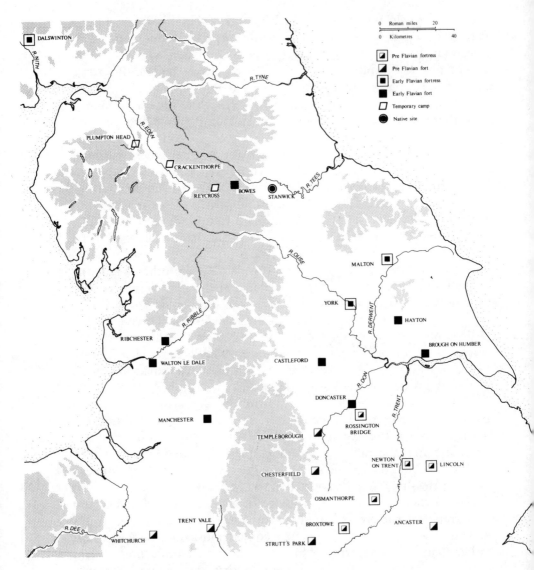

4 Pre-Agricolan penetration into north Britain

north, for it is a successful military action against them that is commemorated by a Roman officer from Corbridge in Northumberland (*R.I.B.* 1142). Finally, there are the Carvetii, recorded on only two inscriptions in Cumberland, a milestone and a tombstone, both of which refer to the *civitas Carvetiorum*, a later tribal administrative unit based on Carlisle (*R.I.B.* 933; Wright 1965, 224).

At present the archaeological evidence does not appear to demonstrate sufficient distinction to aid closer identification of such regional units, with the possible exception of the territory of the Parisi in eastern Yorkshire (Stead 1979). What is notable, however, is the general lack of any settlement hierarchy. Hillforts are surprisingly rare, even in terrain which would seem admirably suited to their construction, and none is of any great size. This has led to the suggestion that the tribal structure was unstable and lacked either a well-developed political superstructure or a large elite group whose position was based on absolute distinctions of wealth and rank (Haselgrove 1984, 20–2).

The obvious exception to this picture of the Brigantes is the massive fortified complex at Stanwick in north Yorkshire which covers some 730 acres (295 ha) at its fullest extent, and is a clear manifestation of an authority with sufficient power to mobilise considerable resources of labour (fig 5). The long-accepted interpretation of the site places it in the context of the disaffection between the pro-Roman queen of the Brigantes, Cartimandua, and her husband Venutius, the various phases of its defences being

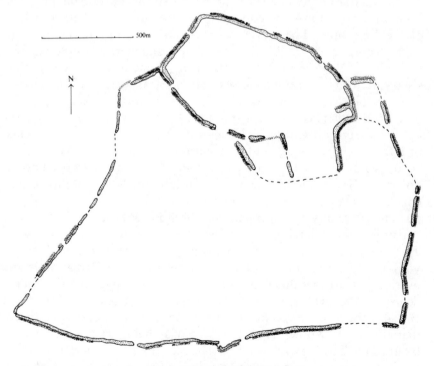

5 Cartimandua's capital at Stanwick (after Wheeler and Haselgrove)

constructed by him against Roman troops after he had deposed his wife (Wheeler 1954). Recent work at the site has prompted a reassessment which makes this interpretation no longer tenable (Haselgrove 1984, 21: Hanson and Campbell 1986). The site has produced large quantities of pre-Flavian samian and Roman building materials which indicate wealthy occupants with direct Roman contacts; not what one would expect at the capital of a rebel king. It is hard to avoid the conclusion, therefore, that Stanwick represents the power centre of Queen Cartimandua and thus provides archaeological support for the existence of the centralised authority which Roman dealings with the Brigantes imply. However, since the massive defences do not seem to have been built until towards the middle of the first century AD, a treaty with Rome may have been the catalyst to ensure the superior position of one faction within the shifting alliances which may have characterised Brigantian politics (Haselgrove 1984, 21). On the other hand, Cartimandua's party must already have been sufficiently dominant to offer guarantees of peace to Rome: perhaps they were the 'overlords' implied by the name Brigantes.

The alternative meaning of the tribal name, 'upland people', has been one of the dominant concepts in some modern characterisations of the Brigantes. They have been seen as nomadic hillmen (Frere 1978, 71–2), even 'Celtic cowboys and shepherds, footloose and unpredictable' (Piggott 1958, 25). More recent studies have emphasised variable topographic factors within the area and indicated that a more sophisticated mixed farming economy is likely to have predominated (Haselgrove 1984, 18–19). Nor should the Brigantes be seen as culturally impoverished or backward, for there is evidence of a fine metalworking tradition within their territory (MacGregor 1976, 184), though it is perhaps no coincidence that the only known hoard of Brigantian bronzework, largely made up of horse and chariot fittings apparently deposited by a craftsman, was found just outside the Stanwick complex (MacGregor 1962) (pl 6).

Despite the relatively poor reputation assigned to Cerialis by Tacitus, it is likely that he was responsible for the defeat of Venutius who had led the main Brigantian opposition to Rome after the ousting of Cartimandua in AD 69. If Agricola had had any hand in the defeat of the man described elsewhere by Tacitus as the greatest British general since Caratacus (*Annals* 12, 40), there can be no doubt that the story would have constituted a major part of Agricola's biography. There is no need to assume, however, that any major battle took place at Stanwick as Wheeler suggested (1954, 23–6), if only because it would have been military madness to attempt to defend a perimeter 3.5 miles (5.6 km) long against the Roman army (Hanson and Campbell 1986). Moreover, Tacitus describes Cerialis' campaign as a series of battles over a wide area, not a decisive victory at a single power centre. We may even have some archaeological indication of his line of march, for across the Stainmore pass to the north-west of Stanwick a distinctive group of three temporary camps of legionary size has long been known (Richmond and McIntyre 1934), further examples of which have come to light more recently (Goodburn 1979, 283; Wilson 1975, 232–3) (fig 4). Approximately one day's march apart, they mark the overnight encampment of a Roman force on campaign in hostile territory. Though not dated by excavation, which in any case is less likely to produce datable artefacts from such sites than from those occupied over a longer term, various factors suggest an early date. Their trapezoidal shape and the provision of multiple gateways are features without parallel among the many camps recorded in Scotland of Agricolan and later date. Moreover, the first of the group at Rey Cross seems to be earlier in date than the Roman road which diverges from a straight line as it passes through one of the camp's eastern gates (fig 6). The size of the camps, c. 20 acres (8.1 ha), indicates that the force involved was not very large and might suggest that Cerialis' army had been split up to deal with localised resistance.

Continuation of this line of march leads down the Eden valley to Carlisle where an early Flavian occupation has long been postulated on the basis of the samian pottery known from the site (Bushe-Fox 1913, 299–301). However, despite quite extensive excavation within the city in recent years, no certain structural evidence has yet come to light which could be so early (below, p 85). Either the pottery evidence has been misinterpreted, though apparently confirmed by analysis of the coin evidence (Shotter 1980, 6), or the earliest Roman presence was of a more ephemeral nature than has previously been assumed.* Further north still, at Dalswinton in Dumfriesshire, we have the opposite problem. Aerial reconnaissance has revealed a two-period double-ditched enclosure at Bankfoot which looks like a large Roman fort (fig 7). Its topographical position on low-lying ground by the river is inferior to that of the smaller two-period Flavian fort at Bankhead nearby (pl 11) which suggests an earlier date, but at present no artefactual material has been recovered to confirm this (St Joseph 1977, 131–3). Its size, as indicated by more recent aerial work, is similar to that of the so-called vexillation

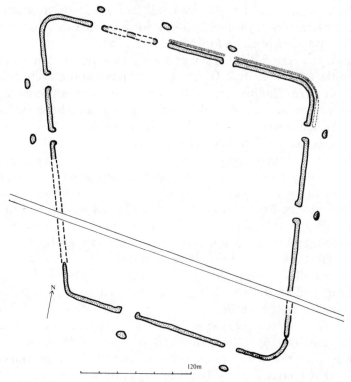

6 Rey Cross temporary camp (after Richmond and McIntyre)

fortresses. These are now being recognised in greater numbers and seem to have been used as short-lived bases during the campaigning phase rather than for permanent occupation (Frere and St Joseph 1974, 5–7).

It is not impossible that Cerialis' successor, Julius Frontinus, was also active in the north, for he is said by Tacitus to have 'shouldered the heavy burden' (*subiit sustinuitque molem*) left by Cerialis, which may have been meant to convey the fact that he continued the war against the Brigantes (*Ag.* 17; Birley 1981, 71). Although Tacitus summarises his governorship in a single sentence, it must not be forgotten that Frontinus was a distinguished author, particularly in the field of military science, an accomplished strategist and one of the major figures of his day. It would surely have been out of character if such a man had not taken the opportunity to build upon successes already achieved in the north even though the main thrust of his own achievement was against the Silures in Wales. On the other hand, the very fact that Frontinus was able to concentrate his attention against

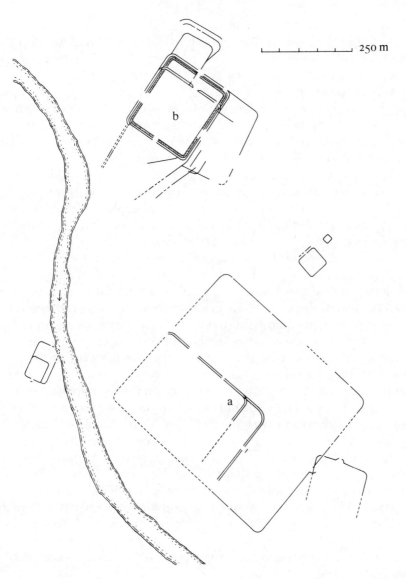

250 m

7 Roman forts at Dalswinton: (a) Bankfoot, (b) Bankhead (after St Joseph with additions) (by permission of Edinburgh University Press)

the Welsh tribes may indicate the effectiveness of Cerialis' campaigning in Brigantia.

To what extent Cerialis or Frontinus was able to consolidate the conquest of Brigantia by the construction of forts is uncertain. Because of Tacitus' narrative, modern commentators have assigned Flavian forts in northern England to Agricola unless there is very positive evidence to the contrary. Simple arithmetic makes this assumption difficult to sustain. Even disregarding the limited number of Agricolan foundations in North Wales, there are some thirty to thirty-five auxiliary forts in northern England conventionally dated to this period of his governorship. A further twenty to twenty-five between the Tyne–Solway and the Forth–Clyde lines gives a total of between fifty and sixty forts supposedly founded over a period of three or four seasons. The fluctuations in the size of the garrison of Britain are not fully charted. Many troops were undoubtedly withdrawn for service elsewhere at various times in the later first and early second centuries AD (below, pp 135, 152), but this need not imply that none were returned or replaced (Holder 1982, 16–17). Thus it seems unreasonable to assume that the army in Britain in the later first century AD was very much larger than in the first half of the second century when the total number of auxiliary units attested epigraphically is sixty-five (Frere 1978, 182–4). Clearly the surviving data are unlikely to furnish us with the total number of units present in the second century, but the archaeological record for the first century is equally fragmentary: there are notable gaps in fort distribution in south-western Scotland, for example. Thus, Agricola is reckoned to have placed up to seventy-five per cent of the total auxiliary force at his disposal in new forts in a three or four year period, yet few of the forts previously established appear to have been abandoned. This will not work. Either many of the forts in northern England are later in date, not being established until the withdrawal from Scotland in the late 80s AD or they must be presumed to have been founded earlier than previously thought to allow time for occupation before abandonment, either temporarily or permanently, to facilitate the expansion into Scotland (below, pp 113–14). More detailed work at a number of sites has begun to confirm that in fact both explanations may be correct, though it is important to stress once more the difficulty of assigning forts to a particular governorship on the basis of archaeological dating evidence.

It has long been accepted that Cerialis was responsible for the establishment of the legionary fortress at York when *legio IX Hispana* was moved there from Lincoln. Early activity of some kind is indicated beyond doubt by the pottery finds, though the structural evidence might better be interpreted as indicating the construction of a vexillation fortress subsequently replaced by a full legionary garrison under Agricola (Hartley 1966, 10–11). The remainder of the legion may originally have been stationed at Malton, where widespread distribution of early Flavian finds suggests quite extensive occupation at this time (Jones 1975, 164–5). Several auxiliary forts of early Flavian date are now attested as a result of recent work in eastern and southern Yorkshire (fig 8) at Doncaster (Buckland 1978, 247), Castleford (Sumpter 1984, 84), Brough on Humber (Wacher 1969, 19–20) and Hayton (Johnson 1978, 78), though most of these probably lie in Parisian rather than Brigantian territory. There are also hints of activity in the west: pottery of early Flavian date has been found in the fort at Manchester, startegically located at an important road junction (Jones and Grealey 1974, 83), while Ribchester, the next fort to the north, may also have been established at this time. Recent excavations revealed a line of defences cut by ditches of the known fort on its north side, while there are a number of pre-Flavian bronze coins from the site which ought to indicate occupation slightly earlier than the governorship of Agricola (Edwards and Webster 1985, 47 and 88). Further support for the early occupation of this area is provided by recent work at Walton-le-Dale only a few miles to the west. Here, on a site which subsequently developed into an industrial complex, occupation may even have begun as early as the pre-Flavian period, though the site has not previously been assigned to a military context (Frere 1984, 284–5 and information from Mr A.C.H. Olivier). The only other fort for which an early Flavian foundation date has been suggested is at Bowes, not far to the north-west of Stanwick (Hartley 1971, 58 and 66). While not impossible, it seems rather too far to the north of any other postulated early sites to be a likely candidate.

At the other extreme none of the forts in the Cumbrian massif seems to have been established earlier than _c._ AD 90, and some are of second-century date (below, pp 161–2). Nor is it certain that all the other forts in the north may be attributed to Agricola. On present evidence a number in the Pennines and across the Tyne–Solway isthmus may not have been built until the later Flavian period, though for most the dating evidence is not sufficiently precise (Breeze and Dobson 1985).

In conclusion, the northern part of Brigantian territory, though perhaps extending some little way beyond the Tyne–Solway isthmus, seems the most likely area for Agricola's second season of operations, but there is no reason to suggest that this was other than the process of occupying terrain already overrun by Cerialis or even Frontinus. The continuation of their work, establishing forts at fairly regular intervals along major lines of penetration, would reasonably comply with Tacitus' assertion that 'a ring of garrisoned posts was

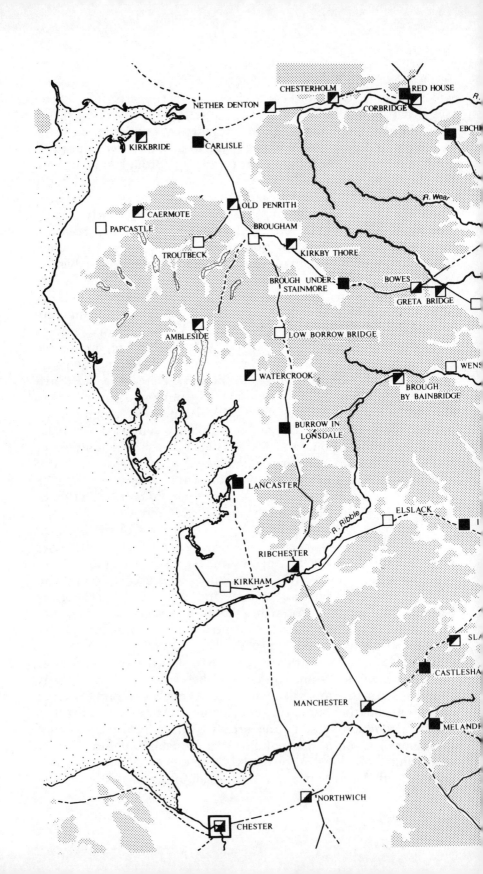

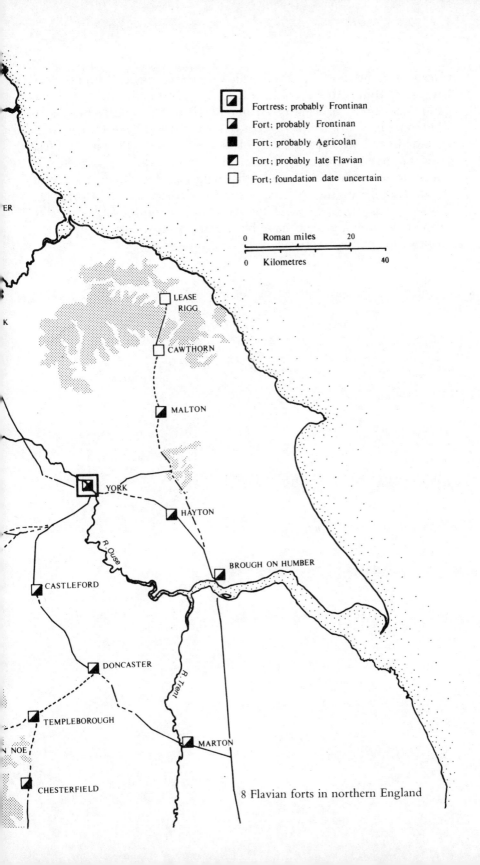

0   Roman miles   20

0   Kilometres   40

LEASE RIGG

CAWTHORN

MALTON

YORK

HAYTON

R. Ouse

BROUGH ON HUMBER

CASTLEFORD

DONCASTER

R. Trent

TEMPLEBOROUGH

NOE

MARTON

CHESTERFIELD

8 Flavian forts in northern England

placed around them' (*Ag.* 20) (fig 8). This should include sites such as Lancaster, Binchester and Ebchester, though at only the first is the dating evidence sufficiently strong to assert this with confidence (Potter 1979, 356). We have already seen that the Lake District was excluded, and perhaps also the less crucial trans-Pennine routes. How far northwards this fort-building programme progressed is uncertain, but what is arguably the main base for the next stage of the advance lies on the crossing of the Tyne at Red House, Corbridge (Hanson *et al.* 1979, 84–5). Thus Agricola's second 'campaign', like his first, would appear to have been based almost entirely upon the work of his predecessors.

· 4 ·

CIVIL RESPONSIBILITIES

THE conquest of new territory or the defence of the frontier against invasion were major news items and, accordingly, they figure strongly in contemporary literary sources. It is in such contexts that we hear most about actions by provincial governors, and so it is on his role in the expansion of the province of Britain that Agricola's fame largely depends. But even governors of provinces with a large standing army, such as Britain, had other duties and responsibilities. The governor's dealings with native states on the borders of his province were not confined solely to military action. The role of diplomacy in the often delicate relationships with leaders of tribes beyond the frontier should not be underestimated (Braund 1983), particularly in the first century AD. The importance of maintaining relations with client kings, more accurately described as friendly kings, is indicated in Britain by the problems which arose on the breakdown of such relations with the Iceni and the Brigantes; the first resulting in a major revolt, the second in the undermining of the security of the northern frontier. Agricola's involvement in diplomatic negotiations during his governorship is not directly attested, but a case can be made for some such dealings with at least one tribe in Scotland (below, pp 91–2, 120), while the welcome he accorded to a fugitive Irish prince indicates his awareness of the potential value of contacts of this kind (*Ag.* 24).

The next most important non-military role of the governor was the administration of justice. He was the Chief Justice of the province with authority extending over both civil and criminal cases. This is not to say he tried all cases, but rather that he acted as a court of appeal in provincial law suits: problems might occur, for example, in reconciling local law codes with Roman Law or disagreements between two communities might require arbitration. When not campaigning it was the governor's duty to go round the province holding judicial sessions (*conventus*) at specified towns (Millar 1967, 64–6), though he also held court in the provincial capital. The governor tried all serious criminal cases where condemnation to the

69

mines or the death penalty was involved, and all those concerning Roman citizens. In serious cases the latter could appeal to the emperor, though the precise nature of this right in the first century is disputed (Millar 1967, 68).

The legal aspect of the governor's duties could be quite onerous. It was in recognition of this that a specifically legal post was created, the *legatus iuridicus* (law officer), whose rank was equivalent to that of a legionary commander, though given the very limited number of known office holders, such appointments were probably only made when the governor was particularly preoccupied with military matters (Birley 1981, 404–5). The first known holder of this office in Britain, C. Salvius Liberalis Nonius Bassus, was appointed during Agricola's governorship. The precise date is uncertain, but Salvius Liberalis may even have been the very first *iuridicus* in the Empire (Birley 1981, 213 and 404). He had a reputation as an outstanding advocate and was looked upon favourably by the emperor Vespasian (Pliny *Ep.* 2, 11, 17; Suetonius *Vespasian* 13). His successor, with the striking name C. Octavius Tidius Tossianus L. Javolenus Priscus, who served under the next governor, became a famous jurist and followed a very distinguished career in the imperial service (Birley 1953, 51). One case, involving the disputed inheritance of the chief helmsman of the British fleet, which he must have heard whilst serving in Britain, found its way into the *Digest*, the famous codification of legal opinion compiled under Justinian (*Digesta* 36, 1, 48). The eminence of these early holders of the post of *iuridicus* gives some indication of the importance of judicial matters in the government of the provinces, though Tacitus makes no mention of this aspect of Agricola's responsibilities.

The governor also had numerous other general administrative duties. He was responsible for the supervision of the *civitates* (states or communities), the largely self-governing administrative divisions of the province; for the construction of roads and the efficient functioning of the *cursus publicus* (imperial posting service); and, of course, for recruitment into the army. In addition to whatever personal friends the governor might bring with him to assist or advise him, he had a permanent staff attached to his headquarters made up mainly of soldiers seconded from the legions (Jones 1960, 161–3). It is presumably to this group that Tacitus is referring when describing Agricola's first actions after his brief foray into North Wales. It is uncertain to what extent we should take literally Tacitus' claims that Agricola enforced discipline in his staff and made subsequent selection on the basis of merit rather than recommendation (*Ag.*19), for it was a common rhetorical claim that a good commander began by setting his own house in order (Ogilvie and Richmond 1967, 213). It is interesting to note, however, the specific exclusion of slaves and freedmen from his staff. This perhaps reflects the disdain felt by the senatorial class for the power of freedmen and slaves in the imperial service and is likely to have been well received by Tacitus' audience (Millar 1977, 69–86). More specifically it emphasises the contrast with the staff of the imperial procurator which would have been dominated by precisely this group.

In one very important area, however, the governor had no direct authority. All financial matters were dealt with by the procurator, appointed by and directly responsible to the emperor (Stevenson 1939, 47–8). This division of responsibility for the running of imperial provinces was quite deliberate, so that too much power was not concentrated in the hands of any individual. The possibility of collusion between the two strands of government was further reduced by the background of the relevant officeholders, for the procurator was drawn not from the senatorial class, like the governor, but from the lower ranking equestrian order. Indeed, friction between governor and procurator was not uncommon. One of the most famous cases concerned Britain in the aftermath of the Boudican revolt when the new procurator, Julius Classicianus, was instrumental in the recall of the governor, Suetonius Paullinus (Tacitus, *Annals* 14, 38–9). Since he was serving in Britain at the time, Agricola will have been familiar with this incident and may well have taken it to heart in his own dealings, for Tacitus points out that he was careful to avoid conflict with the procurator during his first governorship in Aquitania (*Ag.* 9).

Nevertheless, in the face of corrupt practices in the requisition of grain, Agricola does seem to have interfered, assuming Tacitus' account is not merely a stock description of the action of a good governor, as has recently been suggested (Mann 1985, 22). Provincial *civitates* were obliged to provide grain for the army which was purchased at a fixed price, a system known as *frumentum emptum* (Millar 1967, 96; Rickman 1971, 271–2). Two methods of extortion, both well known from a famous case during the Republic (Cicero *Verres* 2, 3, 170–80 and 188–200), seem to have been employed in Britain. If the communities could not supply grain they were obliged to purchase it from the imperial granaries in order to sell it back again at a reduced price, thus making a loss on the transaction; if they could provide grain, they might be instructed to deliver it not to the local fort but to one some considerable distance away. Since transport, especially overland, was expensive, they would often be willing to make cash payments to be excused this additional burden. The illicit profits from these transactions would have been pocketed by corrupt officials. Exactly who was responsible for organising this grain supply is uncertain, for the evidence is very limited and some of it difficult to interpret (Rickman 1971, 272–8). It has been suggested, on the basis of the account in the *Agricola*, that it fell to the governor (Ogilvie and Richmond 1967, 195 and 215; Jones 1970, 183–4), but this was entirely contrary to the general principle of division of responsibility between governor and procurator which Tacitus himself emphasises:

> We used to have one king at a time; now two are set over us – the governor to wreck his fury on our life-blood; the procurator on our property. (*Ag.* 15)

The governor may have led the army, but the procurator paid the soldiers. It seems to be the case that the procurator's responsibilities may also have covered the requisitioning of military supplies (Jones 1960, 123).

We do not know the identity of the procurator serving in Britain at this time, but the severe criticism of corrupt practices (*Ag.* 19–20) is surely directed at him and his immediate predecessors, for Tacitus consistently presents these equestrian officials in a hostile light (*Annals* 14, 32 and 38). If this had been the understanding of Tacitus' audience in Rome, it would have conveniently detracted from the implied criticism of Agricola's immediate predecessor as governor, Julius Frontinus. By the time of the publication of the *Agricola*, he had become a leading statesman, soon to be exceptionally honoured with a third consulship. Frontinus' integrity, eye for detail and commitment to exposing fraud and correcting abuses are amply attested in one of his own published works (*de Aquis*). Provincial officials were sometimes tried for corruption, but we have no way of knowing whether the culprit was in this instance. It seems to have been the case, however, that honesty was less common amongst Roman officials than we might naturally assume from our twentieth-century standpoint, and central government was, in the main, unable to do much about it (Brunt 1960, 222–3).

The success of Rome in establishing a large and long-lived empire across much of the known world was not entirely dependent upon the success of its army. It is obvious that the maintenance of direct military control over such a large area with the resources available to a single city state would have been logistically impossible, even if we grant that the reputation of Roman arms increased her perceived power far beyond the scope of her finite forces (Luttwak 1976, 195–200). Unless the conquered peoples had come to accept the Roman presence as beneficial and, moreover, had eventually identified themselves with Rome, the empire could not have continued to expand.

The process of romanisation was, then, as crucial to Rome's success as the strength and morale of her army. We have ample evidence that it was taking place, but the question remains whether it was a conscious policy or simply a spontaneous side effect of Roman administrative organisation. Here Tacitus' account of Agricola's activities in the winter of his second year of office assumes considerable importance, for it is a clear statement of a policy of romanisation:

> He encouraged individuals and helped communities to build temples, public squares and good houses. He praised the energetic and scolded the slack; and competition for honour took the place of compulsion. Furthermore, he educated the sons of the chiefs in the liberal arts, and expressed a preference for British abilities over the trained skills of the Gauls. The result was that instead of loathing the Latin language they became eager to speak it effectively. In the same way our national dress came into favour and the toga was everywhere to be seen. (*Ag.* 21).

If this was not an expression of *imperial* policy, we have an example of a major initiative by Agricola which demonstrates understanding and foresight of statesmanlike quality. It has been asserted that there is no other direct statement of a general policy of romanisation by the imperial government, for this passage is unique in classical literature (Jones 1970, 184). But such a view is hard to sustain in the face of consistent evidence from the western empire of the deliberate foundation of towns and cities by Roman authorities and the extension of Roman citizenship in the provinces, particularly during the Flavian period (Sherwin-White 1973, 251–3 and 258). Indeed, an earlier remark by Tacitus with reference to the governor Trebellius Maximus, which alludes to the attractive weaknesses of the Roman lifestyle, would seem to imply that Agricola was not the first to pursue this policy in Britain (*Ag.* 16; Ogilvie and Richmond 1967, 202), while one reason for the establishment of a colony of veterans at Colchester in AD 49 was to provide an example of the rule of Roman law for the natives to follow (*Annals* 12, 32). This was not a question of altruism. As already indicated, the policy had its roots in pure pragmatism, which Tacitus himself makes perfectly clear:

> Agricola had to deal with people living in isolation and ignorance, and therefore prone to fight; and his object was to accustom them to a life of peace and quiet by the provision of amenities. (*Ag.* 21).

This approach is particularly evident in the encouragement of urban development. Once an area was deemed to be sufficiently pacified it was handled over to local administration. In general the Romans preferred to adapt an already existing system rather than create something entirely new, so that the administrative areas (*civitates*) in Britain, or in Gaul, were loosely based on pre-Roman tribal territories. Naturally each *civitas* required an administrative centre and, accordingly, Mediterranean-style towns were deliberately founded, now referred to as the *civitas* capitals, on sites of pre-existing native centres or newly formed settlements outside Roman forts (Wacher 1975, 21). Since self-government was the intention, local leaders, probably the old tribal aristocracy, were given positions of authority within these new towns, whose constitution and administrative organisation seems to have been based upon that of Roman colonies. How these settlements subsequently developed was left largely to their inhabitants. It was in the interests of Roman central authority, however, that they should develop successfully, and support was frequently provided.

There is ample archaeological and epigraphic evidence for this aspect of romanisation in Britain. The hallmarks of these new towns were a planned street layout and the provision of a central administrative block, the forum, both of which are quite readily identifiable archaeologically. Though *civitas* capitals were being established as early as the 50s AD, as at Canterbury and Verulamium (St Albans), the latter already elevated to the rank of *municipium* by AD 60 (Tacitus, *Annals* 14, 33), the Flavian period saw a major surge of building activity. Because of Tacitus' remarks about his father-in-law, much of this latter work tends to be attributed to Agricola, but the archaeological evidence suggests that it began before his arrival and continued after he left.

The only town in Roman Britain furnishing direct evidence of Agricola's personal involvement is Verulamium. His name appears on a monumental inscription in the forum there (pl 7), which was dedicated probably in AD 79, though an alternative restoration of the second line could indicate a date in AD 81 (Frere 1983b, 69). At first glance this would seem to provide excellent epigraphic confirmation of Tacitus' account, but the construction of a magnificent stone-built forum (fig 9) was not something which was achieved overnight. A timescale of at least two years for its construction would be a conservative estimate, so that, accepting the earlier date for the dedication, if any credit is due for official encouragement, it should perhaps go to Frontinus rather than to Agricola (Frere 1983b, 9). Moreover, by AD 79 the town was already a thriving self-governing community of some thirty years standing, so in the dedication we may be seeing only the improvement of public facilities, perhaps in recognition of new status (Wacher 1975, 18–19), and not the manifestation of a new policy initiative; it must be borne in mind, however, that there is as yet no archaeological evidence of an earlier forum.

After the death of the client king, Tiberius Claudius Cogidubnus, the extensive domains which he controlled in south-west England would undoubtedly have been annexed by the Romans. The same system of administrative organisation as already existed elsewhere in the pacified province would then have been instituted, probably

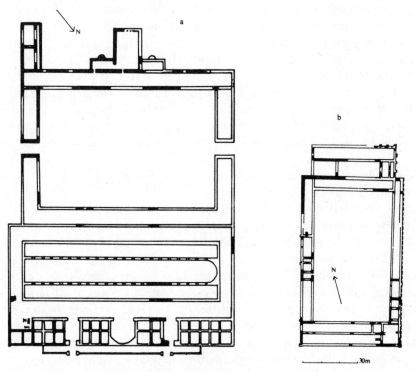

9 Early Flavian fora at (a) Verulamium and (b) London (after Frere and Marsden)

giving rise to the official creation of three new *civitates*, the Regni, the Atrebates and the Belgae, administered from Chichester, Silchester and Winchester respectively (Barrett 1979, 230–4). It is generally accepted that Cogidubnus died at some time in the Flavian period, and Agricola is frequently assumed to have borne the responsibility for making the necessary arrangements and setting up the new towns (Wacher 1975, 27). Indeed, some scholars even suggest that it was for this onerous legal and administrative task that the first *iuridici* were appointed (*P.I.R.*[2], 4, 1, 14; Boon 1969, 38). Unfortunately, close examination of the evidence will not allow this superficially attractive interpretation.

To begin with, we do not know when Cogidubnus died. Tacitus tells us only that he had 'remained most loyal down to our own times' (*Ag.* 14), an extremely vague chronological expression. It seems barely credible, however, that had the famous king died during Agricola's governorship, Tacitus would not have mentioned the fact. Since the *Agricola* was written in AD 98, Cogidubnus' demise might well have occurred within the previous decade, in which case it would have been one of Agricola's unknown successors who was responsible for the development of the urban centres of each of three south-western *civitates*. This interpretation would certainly fit the archaeological evidence for the date of construction of the massive 'palace' complex at Fishbourne near Chichester in the mid-70s AD; but the building seems then to have been occupied until the end of the century, with very little change in form and presumably, therefore, function, for a further fifty years or so thereafter (Cunliffe 1971, 77–159). If this was the residence of the client king, such sustained use of the building would seem to imply excessive longevity on his part. In fact, it should be emphasised that Cogidubnus' association with the site at Fishbourne has not been established beyond doubt, so that the date of the main occupation there need have no bearing on the present debate. Moreover, it is becoming more and more difficult to put back urban development at Winchester, Chichester and Silchester even as late as Agricola's term of office. At Chichester major changes occur in the later Neronian-early Flavian period with the demolition of structures followed by the erection of timber buildings on stone sills and the construction of a new public bath suite (Cunliffe 1978, 180). At Winchester the settlement was provided with defensive earthworks at around the same time, a mint coin of Nero perhaps deliberately deposited in one post-hole of the military-style timber gateway (Biddle 1975, 111), and timber buildings of early Flavian date are aligned with the street grid (Biddle 1975, 297–8). At Silchester a defensive earthwork, the so-called Inner Earthwork, seems to be even earlier in date and a number of the stone internal buildings – one of them a bath building from which a tile of Nero was recorded – appear to be aligned on a line between its east and west gates (Boon 1969, 14–15 and 40–41). Furthermore, recent excavation of the amphitheatre suggests that it originated in the Neronian period (Fulford 1985, 68). A case could thus be made for planned urban development at these sites possibly as early as the end of Nero's reign, which would coincide nicely with the most recent suggestion for the date of Cogidubnus' death in the mid-60s AD (Barrett 1979, 241–2).

It would be reasonable to respond, however, that within the territory of a pro-Roman monarch urban development and roma- nisation in general is likely to have proceeded in already established settlements even before formal annexation of the area. Clearly this was the case, for there is epigraphic evidence of a formal Roman- style dedication at Chichester as early as the late 50s AD, while the famous inscription which mentions Cogidubnus by name records a guild of artisans erecting a temple to the classical gods Neptune and Minerva (R.I.B. 91 and 92). The provision of administrative buildings, the forum and basilica, however, must relate to the formal creation of a self-governing *civitas*. By far the best evidence for this comes from Silchester where the large stone forum, which appears to precede the known street pattern, has generally been seen as a late Flavian construction (Boon 1969, 48; Wacher 1975, 260). Current excavations on the basilica, however, have demonstrated that beneath it lie several timber phases (Fulford 1985). The immediate precursor, of massive construction, is clearly identified as an earlier basilica of Flavian date. Beneath that, however, lie two earlier phases of uncertain identification, the second of which is on the later Roman alignment, its construction dated by pottery to the Claudio– Neronian period. There is little doubt that this is an earlier official building, though the excavator remains cautious about its precise identification. Three possible interpretations have been proposed: that it represents the residence of the local client ruler, presumably Cogidubnus; that it was in fact a forum; or that it was part of a military establishment (Fulford 1985, 56–7). The first possibility seems least likely, for given Nero's attitude towards the Iceni following the death of their king, Prasutagus, it seems unlikely that imperial support would have been provided to another client king for building work at this time. Similarly it is difficult to understand the circumstances under which a military post would have been required. It would have been grossly insensitive to have placed a fort in the centre of an already thriving pro-Roman settlement, particularly so soon after the Boudican revolt had demonstrated the importance of tact and diplomacy during the changeover from client kingdom to Roman authority. Though the plan is too fragmentary to be certain, the location and alignment of the building does, indeed, suggest that it was an early forum, so that we may postulate that Silchester, and with it probably Winchester and Chichester, became *civitas* capitals very early in the Flavian period. Nonetheless, improvement of the amenities, though still in timber, may have taken place during Agricola's governorship.

London is something of a special case. It was never a *civitas* capital, but became capital of the province and formal centre of its administration. Exactly when this occurred is uncertain, but the procurator was probably already in residence from the early 60s AD, since Classicianus, who was in office immediately after the Boudican revolt, was buried there (*R.I.B.* 12). London, too, seemed to have undergone some major development in the Flavian period, for the earliest forum and basilica are of that date. This in turn would indicate that the town had achieved self-government, presumably with the grant of formal municipal status, a process entirely in keeping with general Flavian policy in the provinces (see below). Whether Agricola was responsible for establishing London as a self-governing community and instituting an appropriate public building programme is uncertain, for the precise date of the forum is much disputed. After recent work on the site the excavator concluded that the building was erected in the decade AD 60–70 (Philip 1977, 18–19), but his interpretation has been challenged for a coin of Vespasian dated to AD 71 provides a *terminus post quem* for the construction. A mid-Flavian or Agricolan date has been proposed (Marsden 1978, 100–102), but an early Flavian date is perhaps to be preferred, for in size and grandeur the building bears no comparison with that completed in AD 79 at Verulamium (fig 9). This would be more understandable if the London forum was the earlier of the two, for both towns were probably of equal municipal rank and London was certainly not inferior in wealth (Merrifield 1983, 64–9). That the first London forum may have been quickly judged too modest is confirmed by its replacement perhaps in the last decade of the first century by a very large and architecturally imposing structure on the same site (Philip 1977, 24–6). But even this is credited by some to Agricola (Merrifield 1983, 71), such is the influence of one sentence in Tacitus' biography.

The expansion of Roman territory during Agricola's long governorship must have placed considerable stress on the supply of
troops, and numbers would have had to be released from garrison
duties in the south for more northerly locations. Inevitably this will
have prompted the creation of new *civitas* capitals to fill the
administrative vacuum, but it remains difficult to attribute specific
examples to Agricola. At Exeter the legionary fortress was finally
evacuated by AD 75, or slightly earlier, when *legio II Augusta* was
moved to Caerleon in South Wales. There seems then to have been
an interregnum. It has been suggested that the administration may
have been under the control of a *praefectus civitatis* until local
self-government could be formalised, as is attested in some of the
Danube provinces (Mocsy 1974, 69), for the forum and basilica were
not constructed till approximtely AD 80 (Bidwell 1979, 87–8). There
is, however, no direct evidence for such officials operating in Britain.
Nonetheless, some such explanation may also serve to explain the
situation at Leicester. When its garrison was withdrawn around AD
80 the street system was laid out but the forum plot apparently left
empty for some considerable time. On the other hand the limited
investigations in the area could easily have missed the often very
tenuous remains which might mark an earlier timber version of the
forum (Hebditch and Mellor 1973, 36–7). That Agricola was
responsible for the creation of the *civitas* capital at Cirencester has
also been suggested (Wacher 1975, 32), but if, as is now argued, the
fort there was abandoned somewhat earlier than was previously
thought (Wacher and McWhirr 1982, 58–9), this may carry with it
the date of the town's foundation. Other towns, such as Wroxeter,
seem to have been established in the late Flavian period.

Clearly the Flavian period saw a great programme of urban
development in Britain, but it would be misleading to attribute it all,
or even the major part of it, to Agricola. He would certainly have
been involved, but was only carrying out a policy already established. Various factors may be seen as responsible for the stimulus
that the policy received during this period. We have already seen the
importance that Rome placed upon urbanisation as part of the
administrative organisation of the province. After thirty years of
Roman occupation it is perhaps not surprising that a number of areas
should have been judged ripe for conversion to self-government.
The Boudican rebellion, which undoubtedly set back the progress of
romanisation in the province, was then a decade or more away and a
new dynasty ruled the empire. Indeed Vespasian pursued a general
policy of expanding the citizen body and founding cities in the

provinces, which was duly followed by his sons (Garzetti 1974, 249–50). The advances into Wales, northern England and subsequently Scotland by successive Flavian governors would have stretched military resources and prompted the rapid release to civilian administration of areas in the south still under military control. Finally, the death of one important client king, even if it occurred as early as the mid-60s AD, considerably extended the territory under direct Roman control and resulted in the creation of perhaps three new *civitates* whose establishment would probably still have been in hand in the early Flavian period.

The extent to which direct assistance in town building was provided by the Roman authorities is a matter of debate. The *ordo*, the town council elected from among the wealthiest citizens, was responsible for both the maintenance and development of its town. Public buildings were paid for either by subscription or by donations. Indeed, public munificence was a common feature of the Roman empire and civic pride played a large part in urban development (Duncan-Jones 1985). Provincial authorities may occasionally have overstretched their resources but although showing concern, government assistance seems to have been restricted to the provision of advice (Pliny *Ep.* 10, 37–40). It has been argued that British towns were given more direct help, both financial and practical. The calling in of loans, perhaps made to facilitate such urban expenditure by local officials, was one of the factors which prompted the Boudican revolt, though some at least of these loans seem to have been part of a private investment by Seneca, one of Nero's advisors, rather than emanating from official sources (Dio Cassius 62, 2). The form and construction methods of some early civil buildings may hint at construction by the army. The plans of most fora in Britain are unlike those in Gaul and closely resemble military headquarters buildings. This has led to the suggestion that military architects were employed in their design (Frere 1978, 276), though this conclusion is disputed (Blagg 1984). Military assistance in the erection of more humble buildings is implied by the early use of sophisticated construction techniques not attested in the pre-Roman Iron Age. At Verulamium, as early as the reign of Claudius, sleeper-beam construction, a distinctive method employed on early military sites (Hanson 1982, 177), was found in one block of shops whose plan is distinctly reminiscent of a barrack block (Frere 1972, 10–11). Even if such direct assistance had been provided, the date range of the archaeological evidence involved serves to weaken any specific link with Agricola.

Agricola's encouragement of temple and house building (*Ag.* 21) may seem less likely to have had any immediate practical motivation, but in fact makes sense in the context of administrative efficiency and political loyalty. There was a close link between religious adherence and the state, most obviously illustrated by the cult of the emperor. This was not simply confined to Colchester, where the temple dedicated to the deified emperor Claudius had been established to provide a focus for provincial loyalty, but widespread throughout the province (Henig 1984, 68–76). Priests of the imperial cult, the Seviri Augustales, are attested epigraphically at York and Lincoln, though these examples are of third-century date. The building of classical temples may then be seen as a manifestation of loyalty to Rome and her emperor. Similarly, the provision of appropriate places of residence within the towns was essential if the wealthier members of native society, who were expected to take on a local administrative role, were to be involved. Indeed, their interest might be greater and their participation more enthusiastic if physically part of that community. In fact, under normal circumstances members of the town council were obliged by law to live within the town (Salway 1981, 55–6). Tacitus states that competition for honour made any such compulsion unnecessary (*Ag.* 21), but by implication, therefore, it could have been applied. Here the archaeological evidence provides an interesting counterpoint. Though private buildings of Flavian date are attested in towns, they largely take the form of shops and relatively humble dwellings. The widespread occurrence of town houses of the size and form which might reasonably be taken to reflect the presence of wealthy councillors does not become evident until the mid-second century (Walthew 1975). In the first century, at least, despite what Tacitus implies, the rich local aristocracy seem to have preferred to live on their country estates where the Roman-style villa was quite rapidly adopted.

In addition to the provision of amenities, Agricola is praised for his encouragement of less tangible aspects of Roman culture, including the adoption of the Latin language and Roman national dress, the toga. Such a policy, however, had a long pedigree, for the desire to make Britain into a toga-wearing nation is ascribed by Seneca to Claudius (*Apocolocyntosis* 2, 3). It is strange that in this context Tacitus does not mention any grants of Roman citizenship, particularly in view of the general propensity of the Flavian dynasty to increase its award in the provinces. Though undoubtedly class conscious, the Romans were not nationally elitist. Accordingly, they were quite willing to see expansion of the citizen body and, indeed, subsequent movement up the social scale. We have already noted how Agricola's own family may have made the transition from native provincial aristocracy to membership of the Roman senatorial class over some three generations (above, pp 33–4). Few provincials might anticipate such success: we have no certainly attested British senator, for example. In fact not many could even expect to acquire Roman citizenship. It was only those who had previously held power, the local aristocracy, who could aspire to such favour and in whom Roman authority would subsequently be vested as members of the town councils. The attractions of romanisation and education were mutual: by maintaining the political *status quo* Rome could achieve quite rapid assimilation of conquered areas and ensure their continued peaceful development while the native aristocracy were able to maintain their position in society and had before them the prospect of further advancement. Moreover, it was a general Flavian policy to advance scholastic education in the provinces by indirectly subsidising municipal schools and granting personal privileges to members of the teaching guilds (Sherwin-White 1966, 287). It is into this context that we should place Agricola's cultural initiative, noting in particular that it was specifically the sons of chiefs who were to be the beneficiaries. It may not be coincidence that we have an independent record of the presence in Britain at this time of a Greek schoolmaster, Demetrius of Tarsus, who may reasonably be identified with the man who dedicated two plaques while at the governor's winter-quarters in York (Plutarch *de defectu oraculorum* 2; *R.I.B.* 662–3). Some individuals may even have been educated abroad, for the process of sending the sons of conquered kings or chiefs to Rome to be brought up in the Roman way was a common principle intended not only to provide hostages for good conduct but to insure the future pro-Roman stance of the provincial native leadership (Braund 1983, 12–17). The principle is not dissimilar to that followed during the flourishing years of the British empire when the sons of the native aristocracy were educated in England. Thus, there is no need to postulate any particular altruistic motive involved, akin to Kipling's concept of the white man's burden, either on the part of Agricola or the Flavian dynasty (Garnsey 1978, 252–3). It was simply a matter of effective government, as Tacitus himself recognised:

> The unsuspecting Britons spoke of such novelties as 'civilisation' when in fact they were only a feature of their enslavement. (*Ag.* 21)

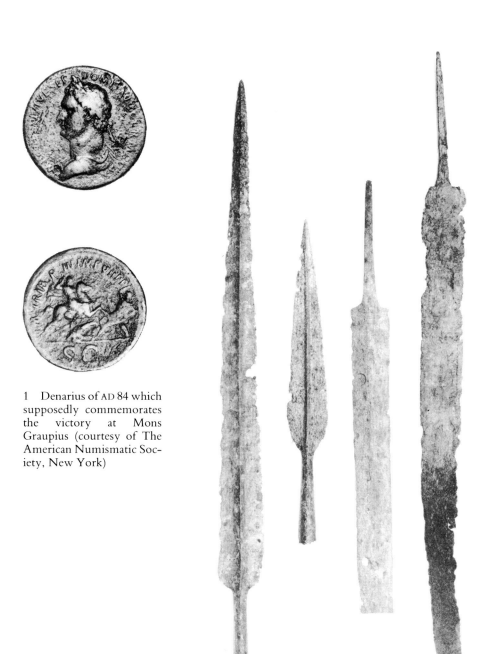

1 Denarius of AD 84 which supposedly commemorates the victory at Mons Graupius (courtesy of The American Numismatic Society, New York)

2 Weaponry from Llyn Cerrig Bach, Anglesey (by permission of The National Museum of Wales)

3 Chariot and horse gear from Llyn Cerrig Bach, Anglesey (by permission of The National Museum of Wales)

4   Lead waterpipe from the legionary fortress at Chester inscribed
IMP. VESP. VIIII T. IMP. VII COS. CN. IULIO AGRICOLA LEG. AUG. PR. PR.
(by permission of the Grosvenor Museum, Chester)

5   Lead pig from Chester inscribed (top) IMP. VESP. AUG. V T. IMP.
III (side) DECEANGL. (by permission of the Grosvenor Museum,
Chester)

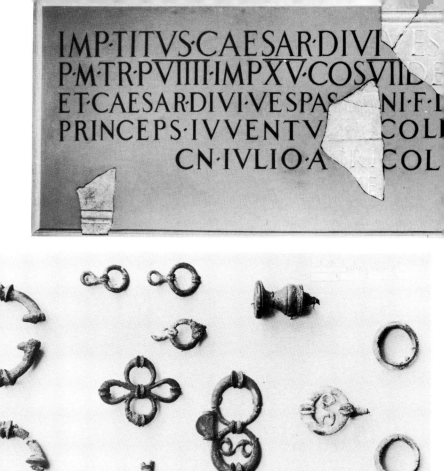

IMP·TITVS·CAESAR·DIVI·VES
P·M·TR·P·VIIII·IMP·XV·COS·VII·DE
ET·CAESAR·DIVI·VESPAS·NI·F·I
PRINCEPS·IVVENTV·COL
CN·IVLIO·A·COL

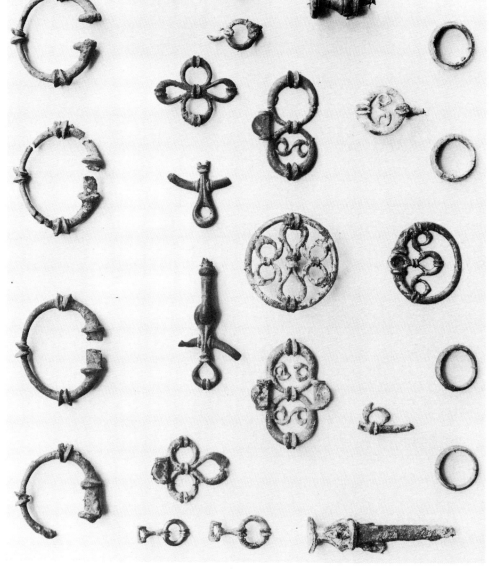

SIANIE   SPASIANVS·AVG
·VIII·CENSOR·PATER·PATRIAE
MITIANVS·COS·VI·DESIG·VII
IORVM·OMNIVM·SACERDOS
EG·AVG·PRO

left 6 Horse and chariot fittings from the Melsonby hoard, Stanwick (by permission of the British Museum)

top 7 One possible restoration of the Agricolan dedicatory inscription from the forum at Verulamium (by permission of the Verulamium Museum)

8   Walls Hill native fort from the air

9 Roman fort at Birrens from the air showing as crop marks the additional complexity of its defences (Cambridge University Collection: copyright reserved)

top right 10 Roman fort and annexe at Easter Happrew from the air (Royal Commission on Ancient Monuments, Scotland)

right 11 The two-period Roman fort with annexes at Dalswinton (Bankhead) from the air (Royal Commission on Ancient Monuments, Scotland)

12 Stracathro-type camp and adjacent Roman fort at Dalginross from the air (Royal Commission on Ancient Monuments, Scotland)

top right 13 The hill of Bennachie from above the site of the camp at Durno (Cambridge University Collection: copyright reserved)

right 14 Iron Age carnyx (war trumpet) from Deskford, Banffshire (by permission of the Royal Museum of Scotland)

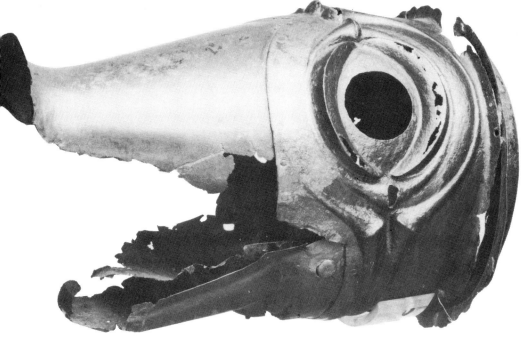

15   Roman fort and Stracathro-type camps at Malling from the air (Royal Commission on Ancient Monuments, Scotland)

top right 16   The Sma' glen from the watchtower by Fendoch Roman fort

right 17   The Roman fort and Stracathro-type camp at Inverquharity (Royal Commission on Ancient Monuments, Scotland)

18 *Asses* of AD 86 from Inchtuthil (a and b) above better preserved
copies of similar types (c and d) (Hunterian Museum, Glasgow)

19 The line of the Gask ridge from the west with the watchtower at
Muir o' Fauld in the foreground (G.D.B. Jones)

Top left 20 The wall trenches of two timber-built barracks at Elginhaugh showing only one period of construction (by permission of Historic Buildings and Monuments, Scottish Development Department: Crown copyright)

left 21 Part of the timber gateway of the Roman fort at Carlisle burnt after partial demolition

above 22 Severed heads on display outside a Roman camp on Trajan's Column

23 Part of the Flavian temporary camp at Dun and adjacent native
settlement revealed as crop marks from the air (Royal Commission on
Ancient Monuments, Scotland)

But what of the bulk of the population? For the most part they seem to have been relatively little affected by the Roman presence (see also below, pp 166–73). Even in the civil province, only gradually did they acquire some of the material manifestations of Roman civilisation. The evidence of graffiti suggests that a know-ledge of Latin at least spread to urban artisans (Boon 1973, 62–3), though it is doubtful whether this reflects a policy of widespread formal education, rather than the process by which those in regular contact with officialdom picked up Latin gradually. Regular use of Latin is unlikely to have spread far down the social scale in the countryside, except among those who had been recruited into the Roman army (Dobson and Mann 1973, 198–205).

There is a suggestion that one tribe, the Ordovices, suffered rather badly at Agricola's hands, apparently in contrast to his otherwise sympathetic dealings with provincials. In describing their defeat Tacitus states that 'almost the whole tribe were killed' (*Ag.* 17). Combined with the paucity of Roman finds on native sites in central and north-west Wales, at least until the third century AD, this has led to the suggestion that Agricola was responsible for tribal genocide as a punishment for resistance to Rome, the area being recolonised in the third century by new settlers (Hogg 1966, 30 and 35). This interpretation of the evidence may be quickly dismissed. Tacitus' expression is simply intended to emphasise the completeness of the victory, which the absence of early Roman finds from local native sites may confirm, reflecting a retarded pace of assimilation in the area. More recent work makes clear, moreover, that the stone-built setlements of third-century date have earlier enclosures beneath them, suggesting continuous occupation from the pre-Roman Iron Age (Lloyd Jones 1984, 47; Davies 1980b, 109–112 and 133–8). There is, thus, no cause to challenge Agricola's reputation on the basis of his treatment of the Ordovices.

In fulfilling the civil responsibilities of government, Agricola may be seen to have followed the general provincial policy of the Flavian dynasty, just like his predecessors and, indeed, his successors. There is absolutely no need to see his actions as in any way unusual or remarkable just because we are fortunate enough to have more detailed literary information about him than about any other governor of the province; but neither is there any reason to doubt Agricola's honesty and efficiency in the performance of these duties.

· 5 ·

FROM TYNE TO FORTH

CONQUEST

Traditionally Agricola is credited with the conquest of Scotland. His third campaign penetrated as far as the estuary of the Taum or Tanaum (*Ag.* 22). It has recently been proposed that this should be equated with the name Tameia, one of the places attributed by Ptolemy to the Vacomagi (*Geog.* 2, 3, 8), which itself is then identified with the newly discovered fort at Doune on the river Teith (Maxwell 1984, 222–3). However, palaeographers seem to be agreed in preferring the reading Taum, while philologists suggest its derivation from Tavum and its equation with the Tava (*Ταουα*) of Ptolemy (Rivet and Smith 1979, 470). Moreover, the estuary of the Tay is a far more striking topographical feature and as such more likely to have featured in the account of the campaign as recalled by Agricola himself, particularly if the fleet had been employed to scout ahead. In any case, the Teith is a tributary of the Forth so that even had it been the limit of Agricola's penetration, reference would surely have been to the more obvious feature, the Firth of Forth.

Agricola's line of march is usually assumed to have followed the two main routes north, through Annandale to Clydesdale in the west and through Redesdale to Lauderdale in the east, both subsequently formalised as permanent roads. One way to determine his campaign route archaeologically is to identify the temporary camps built by his army when they stopped overnight. Although these are quite numerous in the Lowlands, they are notoriously difficult to date. The distribution of the examples identified by Maxwell as probably Flavian would seem to confirm that in general the traditional routes were followed (fig 10), but dating of the camps is not sufficiently refined to allow the distinction between their use in one campaign as opposed to another (1980b, 28–40). It is noticeable, however, that the camps are all quite small, the largest, at Castledykes, being less than 50 acres (20 ha), so that Agricola's forces were probably split in order to follow separate routes northwards. But if the two 115-acre (46.5 ha) camps at Dunning and Abernethy in Perthshire are correctly assigned to this campaign (fig 11) – and they are confidently

84

dated to the Flavian period as a result of the fortuitous discovery of a fragment of South Gaulish samian in the ditch of the latter (St Joseph 1973, 219–21) – then Agricola's army must have been reunited beyond the isthmus for the final march to the Tay.

An alternative approach is to seek evidence of the base or bases for Agricola's advance as an indication of his starting point. One such base has been identified recently at Red House, Corbridge, at a crossing of the Tyne. Here a large section through what seems to have been one of the category of 25–30-acre (10–12-ha) sites, known as vexillation fortresses, was excavated ahead of modern road construction. The presence of numerous open-ended sheds or store-buildings and the provision of a workshop point to the function of the site as a supply base, while the dating evidence indicates occupation for a relatively short time in the mid-Flavian period (Hanson *et al.* 1979) (fig 12). There can be little doubt that this served as the base for the advance north along the line of what subsequently became Dere Street. It is usually assumed that Carlisle served a similar purpose in the west. That Agricola initiated building work there may be asserted with almost as much confidence as if there was an inscription recording his presence, for dendrochronological analysis of one timber used in an early Roman structure there, which had survived in the prevailing waterlogged conditions, indicates that the tree from which it derived was felled *c*. AD 79 (McCarthy 1984, 65). The timber concerned came not from the fort, but from a strip building of uncertain function situated a quarter of a mile away. The fort itself is securely dated by pottery and coins to Agricola's governorship, and although its size can only be guessed, considerations of local topography suggest that it cannot be larger than some 8 acres (3.2 ha) at most (Charlesworth 1980, 210). This seems too small to have served as a supply base. The separation of the fort and the strip building referred to above implies that other structures filled the gap in between. One, a massive timber platform of uncertain function, has long been known (Ferguson 1893). This might support the location of a base here if its identification as a granary was accepted (Hanson 1978b, 4), but it is not yet securely dated. It could just as easily relate to the postulated early Flavian presence as to Agricola, though recent excavation in Castle Street nearby hints at a slightly later context (McCarthy 1984, 68). Thus the presence at Carlisle of a base for Agricola's third campaign remains unconfirmed, and so a two-pronged advance concentrating on the eastern side of the country would be commensurate with all the evidence currently available.

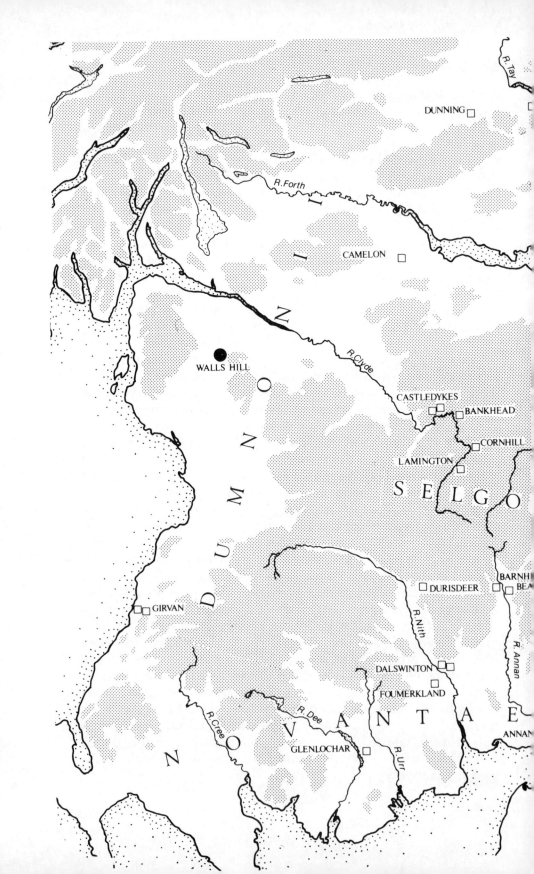

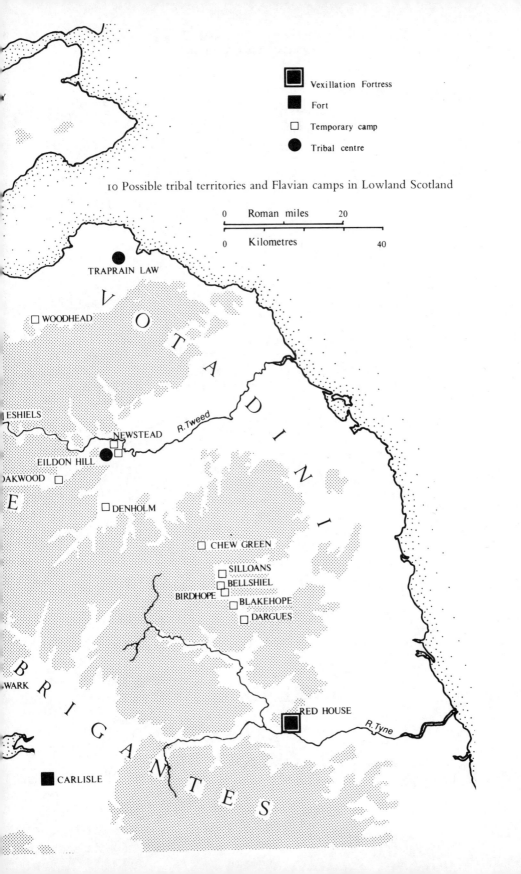

■ (filled square, bold)	Vexillation Fortress
■	Fort
□	Temporary camp
●	Tribal centre

10 Possible tribal territories and Flavian camps in Lowland Scotland

Roman miles 0 — 20

Kilometres 0 — 40

● TRAPRAIN LAW

□ WOODHEAD

V O T A D I N I

ESHIELS

R. Tweed

NEWSTEAD

● EILDON HILL

OAKWOOD □

□ DENHOLM

E

□ CHEW GREEN

□ SILLOANS
□ BELLSHIEL
BIRDHOPE □
□ BLAKEHOPE
□ DARGUES

WARK

B R I G A N T E S

■ RED HOUSE

R. Tyne

■ CARLISLE

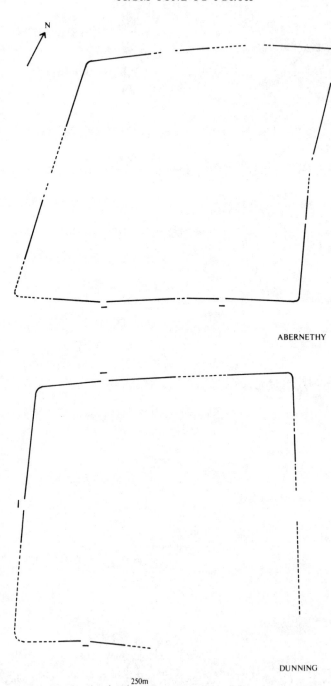

ABERNETHY

DUNNING

250m

11 Large Flavian temporary camps at Dunning and Abernethy

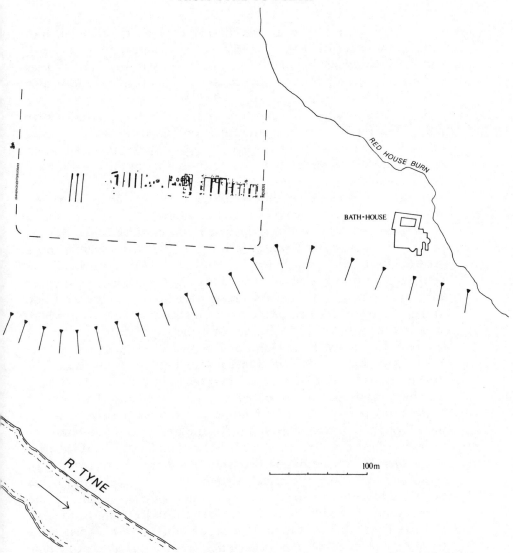

12 Agricolan supply-base at Red House, Corbridge

Tacitus makes clear that Agricola's third campaign met with little resistance despite the depth of penetration into new territory. Indeed, there was even time to spare for the building of forts in the area before the end of the season. If we take this narrative at face value, it would appear that the conquest of Lowland Scotland was virtually over, for the following season was spent in consolidating all the territory to the south of the isthmus, while in the fifth campaign Agricola appears to have been advancing once more beyond the

Clyde (*Ag.* 23–4). However, the contrast between the time taken to subdue the tribes of Wales (at least thirteen campaigning seasons), and that to conquer Lowland Scotland (only two seasons), requires some explanation. Why was it that Lowland Scotland succumbed so readily to Roman arms?

Some have suggested that the tribes of the Lowlands were politically divided or decentralised and consequently could be picked off easily tribe by tribe or in small groups (Clarke 1958, 48; Frere 1978, 127). Such a suggestion is not without its problems. Political decentralisation can be a positive advantage in warfare, for it can be even more difficult, especially in rough terrain, to break resistance which is widely scattered. Nor need the failure of tribes to organise a concerted opposition to Rome be disadvantageous for, if the Roman army had a weakness, it was in facing guerrilla tactics such as those used so effectively by the Silures in South Wales (Tacitus, *Annals* 12, 39). According to Ptolemy Lowland Scotland was occupied by four tribes (*Geog.* 2, 3, 5–7). The Novantae were located on the west side of the country to the east of the peninsula bearing their name which is clearly identifiable as the Rhinns of Galloway. Further to the east lay the Selgovae, with the Dumnonii to their north and west and the Votadini yet further east, allowance having been made in all cases for the notorious turning of Scotland evident in Ptolemy's map (fig 1). Of the various places attributed to each tribe only Trimontium (Newstead) and Bremenium (High Rochester) are positively identified, though Rerigonium and Vindogara are presumably linked to the gulfs of the same name which may be confidently identified with Loch Ryan and Irvine Bay respectively (Rivet and Smith 1979, 133). Assuming that Ptolemy's tribal attributions are correct, this further ties the Novantae to the south-west, the Selgovae to the upland massif centred on the upper Tweed basin, the Votadini to the east and the Dumnonii to the north-west. In the broadest sense these tribal regions do seem to be reflected in archaeological terms. There are, for example, notable differences in settlement forms between the eastern and western Lowlands. Hillforts are far more common in the east, while the heavy stone-walled settlements or duns and distinctive lake dwellings or crannogs are largely restricted to the west, though small enclosed settlements abound on suitable soils throughout the Lowlands. If the recently proposed identifications of the other places named by Ptolemy are also correct, such as Alauna/Ardoch (Rivet and Smith 1979, 245), the Dumnonii may have extended beyond the Forth–Clyde isthmus into southern Perthshire. This may explain the restricted distribution pattern of brochs, duns and palisaded enclosures in Stirlingshire apparently demarcating an area with a different settlement tradition from that seen only slightly further north (Maxwell 1983b, 246). As yet, however, the detailed comparative surveys of settlement patterns which might enable more precise definition of regional groupings on archaeological grounds are very few (e.g. Macinnes 1983).

Despite the predominance of small hillforts and other small native settlements in Lowland Scotland, there are a few examples of much larger sites, the so-called minor oppida, which seem to indicate a relatively highly stratified native society whose upper echelons had considerable coercive powers (Feachem 1966, 77–80). In the south-west, though perhaps still in the territory of the Brigantes, the hillfort of Burnswark covers an area of 17 acres (7.1 ha), while in Renfrewshire, in the territory of the Dumnonii, the fort of Walls Hill is slightly larger (pl 8). By far the largest and best known hillforts, however, are those in the east at Eildon Hill North and Traprain Law, in the territory of the Selgovae and Votadini respectively. Both enclose areas of approximately 40 acres (16.7 ha) at their most extensive, the large size of their population being confirmed at the former where some 300 house platforms are still visible on the ground (fig 13). Possible confirmation of a social structure based on wealth and rank is provided by occasional finds of rich metalwork, often relating to horses. Most famous are the pony-cap from Torrs in Kirkudbrightshire and the Middlebie hoard of harness gear from Dumfriesshire, though such material is often difficult to date and its place of manufacture hard to identify (MacGregor 1976).

If some of the tribes were more politically centralised than has previously been credited, their differing attitudes towards Rome may also be of some relevance. The Votadini seem to have been favourably inclined towards Rome and may even have had some formal treaty or client relationship in the manner of the Brigantes somewhat earlier. The large hillfort at Traprain Law, generally accepted as the capital of the tribe, seems to have continued in importance throughout the Roman occupation and may even have maintained its defences, something which seems unlikely to have been allowed by the Roman authorities if the site had been considered a probable centre of resistance (Jobey 1976). Moreover, despite extensive aerial reconnaissance in the Lothian plain, an area highly susceptible to cropmark production, no Roman military installations are known to the east of Dere Street. This special relationship with Rome may have applied only to Votadinian territory north of the Tweed, which recent work on native

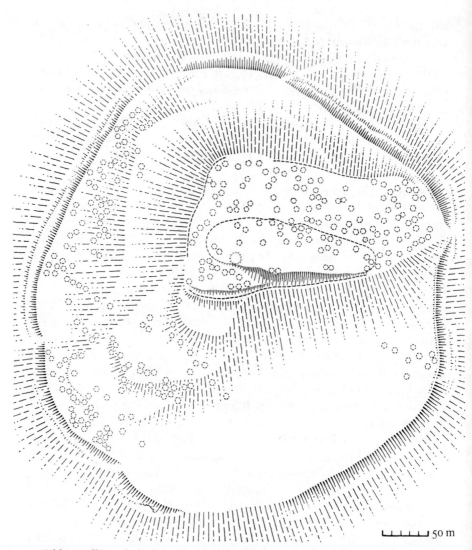

13 Eildon Hill North: hillfort capital of the Selgovae and site of Roman watchtower (after R.C.A.H.M.S.) (by permission of Edinburgh University Press)

settlement patterns suggests may have been a boundary between different tribal groups (Macinnes 1983, 393), for to the south of that river Flavian forts are known or assumed from the configuration of the road system. On the other hand there is no reason to suggest that the other tribes of the Lowlands, the Selgovae, Novantae and Dumnonii, were necessarily inclined towards such ready acceptance of Roman suzerainty. The treatment of Eildon Hill North, probable capital of the Selgovae, contrasts sharply with that of Traprain Law: in the very centre of the settlement the Romans placed a watchtower to serve the large fort at Newstead nearby (Steer and Feachem 1952a). This implies that the inhabitants of the hillfort had fled or been forcibly expelled, assuming, of course, that it was still occupied at the time of the Roman arrival (below, p 167). If the subsequent location of Roman forts is any guide, eastern central Scotland required quite close supervision, while the later history of the Annan and Nith valleys, in particular, suggests the presence of an unsettled and consistently hostile population at least until the mid-second century (Hanson and Maxwell 1983, 63). There is, however, no direct evidence to suggest that these anti-Roman tribes were so busy fighting amongst themselves that the Roman army was able to deal with them in piecemeal fashion. As we shall see later, in the face of a threat of the magnitude of Rome, inter-tribal differences could be shelved (below, p 120).

Perhaps the solution to our problem is that the conquest of the Lowlands in fact took rather longer than the single season implied by Tacitus. Indeed, the process of conquest can be expanded at both ends. As already noted, there are some indications that Roman penetration into Scotland may have occurred before Agricola's third campaign (above, pp 55–6), so that at least the Selgovae may already have been softened up. But earlier penetration beyond the Tyne–Solway line, either by Agricola or one of his predecessors, is unlikely to have been either deep or sustained: the latter would already have been operating well beyond any permanent bases, while Agricola's troops would probably have been much occupied in the construction of forts in northern England.

At the other end of the scale, operations may have continued rather longer than Tacitus allows. In Agricola's fourth season the building of forts is once again unlikely to have allowed much time for serious campaigning. However, Agricola's fifth year in the field involved the subjugation of 'hitherto unknown tribes' (*ignotas ad id tempus gentes*) (*Ag.* 24). The location of this campaign has always been problematical, argument concentrating on the precise stretch of water which Agricola crossed (*nave prima transgressus*) at the beginning of the operation. Both the grammatical construction of the passage, which ought to refer back to the stretch of water referred to at the end of the previous chapter, and the sense of the narrative would seem to imply that a crossing of the Forth–Clyde isthmus was involved (Mann 1968, 307; Reed 1971, 143–7). More specifically, since the following sentence refers to troops being drawn up on the coast which faces Ireland, the campaign must have been confined to the west side of the country. There is, however, an immediate problem: there is as yet no archaeological trace of any Roman activity to the north and west of the Clyde. One need not anticipate any permanent installations, but the construction of temporary camps would surely have been essential in hostile territory. Even if the action had been confined to naval reconnaissance with minor skirmishes, coastal camps would have been constructed when it was necessary to replenish provisions or reconnoitre on land. Indeed, the rugged terrain and difficulties of movement by land are still the dominant characteristics of Argyll so that a seaborne operation would make sound military sense. But what of the troops subsequently drawn up on the coast facing Ireland? While it would fit the geographical description, the idea of concentrating a major force on the Mull of Kintyre, whether intended as a springboard into Ireland or not, seems improbable. A more likely point from which to contemplate such an invasion would have been the coast of Ayrshire or Galloway. Moreover, if Ptolemy's map of Britain is an accurate reflection of what had become the accepted shape of the island as seen from Rome, then the Kintyre peninsula (*Epidium promontorium*) would not have complied with Tacitus' conception of the local geography, for it was thought to face northwards well away from Ireland (fig 1). Reed accepts these points and is thus forced to see the two elements of Tacitus' account – the crossing of a stretch of water and the drawing up of troops opposite Ireland – as entirely separate events (1971, 146). Even if this was the case, it would still have resulted in a concentration of forces in the western Lowlands. Tacitus explains this in terms of preparation for an invasion of Ireland (*Ag.* 24). Agricola may have put this forward as an alternative to advance beyond the isthmus (Dobson 1980, 8), but no such invasion took place and it would have been the height of folly to have seriously contemplated it when so much of the mainland remained unexplored.

Thus, it seems far more reasonable to explain the presence of Agricola's army in the west in terms of the completion of the conquest of the Lowlands, even though this flies in the face of Tacitus' assertion that everything south of the Forth–Clyde isthmus was held by the end of the fourth season. To accuse Tacitus of slight rhetorical exaggeration is not too serious a criticism. Reed objects to the suggestion that the south-west was by-passed during the third campaign because this would have resulted in dangerously long supply lines and an unprotected western flank (1971, 145). Such criticism has been weakened by recent discoveries. It is now quite clear that Agricola ignored the Lake District, which is similarly located in relation to the rest of northern England, during the consolidation following his second campaign (below, pp 161–2). Presumably a similar policy of divide first and conquer later could have been applied in Lowland Scotland.

Several scholars have felt it necessary to emend the text of Tacitus specifically in support of a south-western location for Agricola's fifth campaign suggesting a crossing either of the Solway Firth (Itunam) or the river Annan (Anavam) in place of the Latin phrase *nave prima* (Postgate 1930, 8; Wellesley 1969b, 267). While both these emendations are possible in palaeographic terms, there is no reason to suggest that the surviving text of Tacitus is corrupt at this point. Moreover, it seems highly unlikely that Tacitus would have mentioned the Annan, a very minor river, for geographical precision is not one of his strengths; while a crossing from one side of the Solway to the other is unacceptable on archaeological grounds (see below). In fact, the Latin makes sense as it stands, meaning that Agricola was in the leading ship (Lacey 1957, 121). Alternatively, as Hind has recently suggested (1985, 7–8), the phrase may have been intended to combine two meanings somewhat elliptically – the first use of the fleet at the beginning of a new season.

Although it has been argued that no sensible commander would invade south-west Scotland by sea when he could move on dry land (Wellesley 1969, 267), a landing on the northern shore of the Solway Firth would have facilitated easy advance up the valleys of the rivers Annan, Nith, Urr, Dee and Cree which run predominantly from north to south. The recently discovered 8–9-acre (3.2–3.6-ha) site at Annan Waterfoot, though on the small side, may represent such a beachhead camp despite its preliminary interpretation as a fort (*D.E.S.* 1979, 4 *contra* Goodburn 1978, 418). Further west at Ward Law the long-known but undated military work appears to be attached to an adjacent native hillfort by a ditch (Goodburn 1978, 419). The reuse of native forts as Roman bases during the early stages of consolidation of an area is becoming more frequently attested (Frere 1986), so there is a strong possibility that Ward Law relates to the period of the conquest of the south-west. Moreover, the recent identification of certain eccentricities at one entrance, with the provision of multiple stretches of *titulum* ditch, cast some doubt on the interpretation of the site as a permanent fort (information from Mr G.S. Maxwell). The two newly discovered camps at Girvan in Ayrshire, the southernmost point on the west coast from which uninterrupted penetration to the north and east is feasible, may provide further support for the concept of a seaborne invasion of south-west Scotland, though St Joseph prefers to see them associated with the drawing up of troops on the coast at the end of the fifth campaign (1978a, 399). One of the camps is 36.7 acres (14.9 ha) in area, which is large enough for a reasonable campaigning force, while discovery of a second camp nearby, probably covering less than 15 acres (6 ha), has led to the suggestion that there was possibly a permanent site in the vicinity (Rankov 1982, 339). A Flavian date for the smaller camp is implied by the discovery of first-century glass form its ditch bottom (Frere 1984, 276). Thus a reasonable case can be made for a seaborne invasion of south-west Scotland in Agricola's fifth campaign presumably against the Novantae and subsequently the Dumnonii.

The starting point for this move cannot have been the Cumbrian coast since that was not occupied until the 90s AD (below, pp 161–2). The normal operating procedure during a series of campaigns was for the army to withdraw to winter quarters at the end of each summer. Thus the forts constructed in Lowland Scotland during the fourth campaign (see below) would have housed over winter many of the auxiliary troops which made up Agricola's army, but the legions would have withdrawn either to their permanent bases (York, Chester and Caerleon) or possibly to vexillation fortresses not quite so far in the rear such as is postulated at Red House, Corbridge. The governor will have accompanied his legions southwards, for he had other duties to attend to in the conquered province, as we have seen already (above, chapter 4). The fifth campaign could well have set out, therefore, from much further south than is normally suggested, perhaps from Chester which subsequently became the base of Agricola's own legion, *XX Valeria Victrix*. The legionary fortress is accessible by sea and has possible naval connections (*R.I.B.* 544; Jarrett 1969, 34; Furneaux and Anderson 1922, lvii). The only alternative, which does not have the advantage of fitting the sense of Tacitus' account, is to postulate that the fleet first crossed the Clyde, but then backtracked southwards towards the Rhinns of Galloway (Hind 1985, 8–9).

CONSOLIDATION

It is essential that the distinction is made between campaigning and consolidation. It was possible for a Roman army to campaign in an area and yet leave behind no garrisons whatsoever. If one takes only the example of Britain, the first appearance of a Roman army upon these shores under Julius Caesar did not result in the construction of any permanent garrison posts; nor did Cerialis' campaign in northern England, nor, indeed, Agricola's own campaigns in northern Scotland.★ The establishment of permanent garrisons was the natural concomitant of a campaign of conquest, but they usually followed its completion (Breeze 1980; Hanson 1986a). The very fact that Agricola had time to build forts during his third campaign is used by Tacitus to emphasise the speed and ease of the conquest precisely because it was unusual. To have been building forts while campaigning was still going on could have been hazardous, for it would have necessitated a considerable reduction in the fighting manpower. What is less clear, however, is the extent to which forts were constructed at the end of a single campaign rather than the end of a series which resulted in the conquest of the area. The apparently gradual way in which the consolidation of Wales and northern England progressed suggests that consolidation could follow upon single campaigns but that the area covered need not be as extensive as that in which the army had been operating (Davies 1980a; Hanson and Campbell 1986).

In the absence of precisely dated inscriptions, archaeological dating can never hope to distinguish between forts established in succeeding years. Thus we have little chance of isolating those forts constructed during Agricola's third campaign, although the strategically important site at Newstead must be a prime candidate. Unfortunately, we know very little about it other than its large size (10.5 acres; 4.2 ha) and its unusual outline (Richmond 1950, 2–7). The design is a very clever one, allowing additional defensive firepower to be mustered at the gateways, which are potential weakspots in any defensive circuit (fig 14). However, the complication of the design with its additional angles in the turf rampart, always the most difficult element to construct, probably militated against its general adoption. Only the fort at Milton in Nithsdale is in any way comparable, though there the design seems to have been simplified so that only two of the

*It has recently been claimed in public lectures and in the local press that two enclosures discovered from the air, one at Easter Gallcantray in Nairn and the other at Thomshill in Moray, may be the sites of Roman forts of first century date. While the detailed evidence upon which these assertions are based has not yet been presented in any academic publication, neither site has the distinctive morphological characteristics of a Roman military work and, despite trial excavation, neither has produced indisputably Roman pottery. Since the presence of permanent garrisons so far north would dramatically alter our understanding of the occupation of northern Scotland, it seems best to regard these works as of native character until there is more definite proof to the contrary. It would not be the first time that supposedly Roman military establishments discovered from the air subsequently proved to be settlements of local origin (below, p 102).

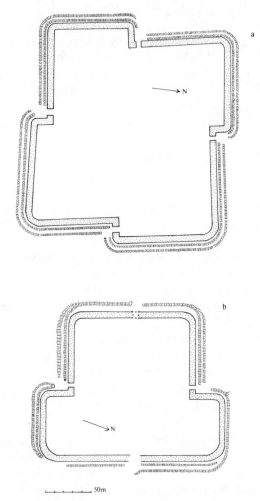

14 Agricolan forts at (a) Newstead and (b) Milton (after Richmond and Clarke)

gateways received additional protection. Whether this indicates that Milton also falls into this earliest phase of construction is uncertain. Despite several seasons of excavations between 1947 and 1950, dating of the sequence of forts there remains imprecise (Clarke 1947, 20–3).

The method of controlling a recently conquered area of rugged terrain was already well established: it had been employed by Frontinus in Wales (Davies 1980a, 261) and subsequently by Agricola himself in northern England (above, chapter 3). Thus we see the creation of a network of forts and fortlets linked by a system of roads. The spacing between posts is normally quoted as the equivalent of one day's march, which is a suitably vague phrase since the actual distances vary considerably. Even this generalisation can only really be applied to the major north–south routes, for elsewhere our knowledge is too scant with large areas totally devoid of military sites or roads. The problem is always one of determining whether the blanks on the map reflect the situation in the Roman period or merely modern lack of information.

If the interpretation of the campaigns presented above is correct, Agricola's fourth season would have been spent building forts and roads in the central and eastern Lowlands along the main north–south routes as well as across the isthmus itself, leaving the west unoccupied until the end of the following year (fig 15). Some 23 miles (37 km) north of Red House, Corbridge, along Dere Street a Flavian foundation date is postulated for High Rochester on the basis of the samian ware from the site. Very little structural evidence was noted in the limited investigation below the later fort, although two phases of construction were apparent in the early turf rampart (Richmond 1936, 179; Hartley 1972, 9). The situation at the small fort at Cappuck, just over 11 miles (17.7 km) south of Newstead, is very similar, though it has produced coarse ware as well as samian of Flavian date (Richmond 1951, 139; Hartley 1972, 9). However, the suggested early date for the small ditched enclosure beneath the Antonine fortlet at Chew Green, only seven miles (11.3 km) north of High Rochester, is supported by only one sherd of coarse ware (Richmond and Keeney 1937, 46). Approximately 13.5 miles (21.7 km) north of Newstead is a small fort at Oxton for which a Flavian date has been assumed (Frere 1978, 136), although the only pottery recovered from the site is Antonine (*D.E.S.* 1967, 17). A further 13 miles (21 km) on, however, a fort of some three acres (1.2 ha) in internal area has recently been discovered from the air at Elginhaugh. Trial excavation indicated a Flavian date (Maxwell 1983a, 172–77), which has since been confirmed by large scale work. This discovery makes contemporary occupation at Inveresk, only three miles (4.8 km) to the north-east, highly unlikely and confirms the recent re-assessment of the artefactual evidence from that site which cast doubt on the Flavian date of the material (Richmond 1980, 298 and fns. 18–21). It also raises the question of whether there were any forts on the southern shore of the Firth of Forth at this time. Maxwell has suggested that Dere Street originally pursued a more inland route (1983a, 175) and, like Inveresk, the fort at Cramond provides no clear evidence of Flavian occupation (Rae and Rae 1974, 163). The importance which may be attached to the line of the road serves to

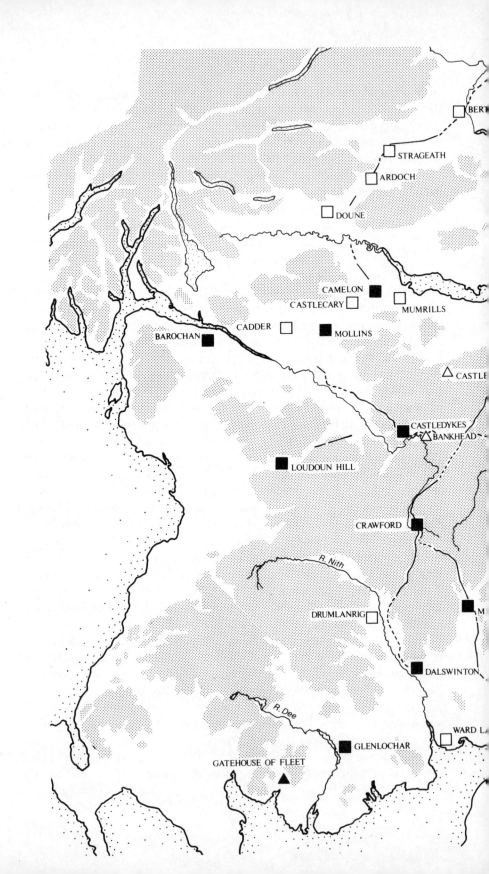

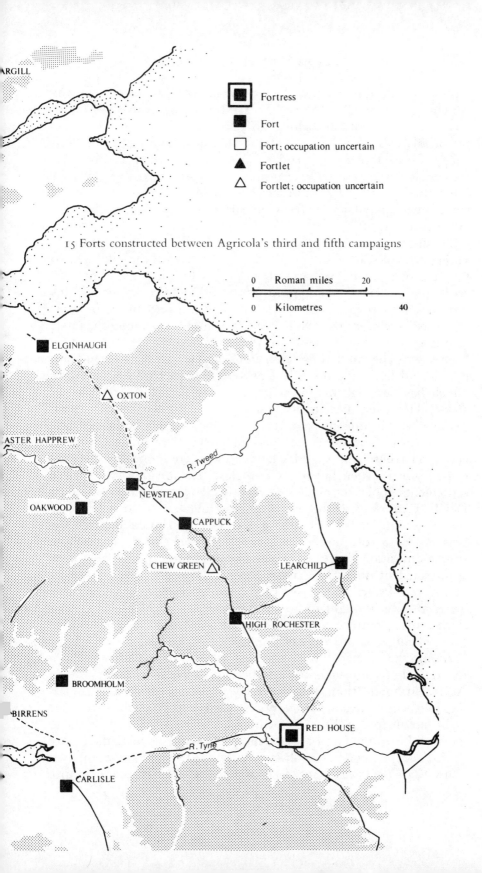

ARGILL

Fortress

Fort

Fort; occupation uncertain

Fortlet

Fortlet; occupation uncertain

15 Forts constructed between Agricola's third and fifth campaigns

0   Roman miles   20

0   Kilometres   40

ELGINHAUGH

△ OXTON

ASTER HAPPREW

R. Tweed

NEWSTEAD

OAKWOOD

CAPPUCK

CHEW GREEN △   LEARCHILD

HIGH ROCHESTER

BROOMHOLM

BIRRENS

RED HOUSE

R. Tyne

CARLISLE

remind us of the general deficiency in our knowledge of the contemporary road network. Even those fragments which are recorded need not all belong to the Flavian period. It seems reasonably clear that the known road alignment in the upper Tweed valley, for example, is not laid out in relation to the Flavian fort at Easter Happrew, but to its Antonine successor across the river at Lyne. Indeed, the lack of association with a known road line is sometimes quoted as evidence in support of a Flavian date for unexcavated sites.

To the east of Dere Street only one Flavian permanent site is known. Small-scale excavation many years ago at Learchild defined the area of a small fort, at least 0.6 acres (0.3 ha) in extent, and recovered pottery of the appropriate date (Taylor 1957, 206). This post has two road connections with Dere Street and numerous attempts have been made to locate some installation along the more southerly, the continuation of the road known as the Devil's Causeway. The latest contender, Longshaws, was discovered from the air and lies some distance from the known road line, a factor which has been taken to support an early date (St Joseph 1969, 105–6). However, the dangers of attributing a Roman military origin to small enclosures in that area simply on the basis of their rectangular plan have been emphasised in recent years by excavations at both Hartburn and Apperley Dene. Both were at one time thought to be Roman fortlets but proved on closer examination to be native settlements (Jobey 1973, 51–3; Greene 1978). The continuation of the Devil's Causeway to the north of Learchild, traced to within one mile (1.6 km) of the mouth of the Tweed, should indicate the presence of a fort in the vicinity of Berwick on Tweed whose strategic position and fine harbour facilities must surely have been appreciated at an early date. The site, however, remains to be discovered. Professor St Joseph has recorded a site from the air near Tweedmouth, thought to be a military post, but it produced only third-century pottery during trial excavation (1951, 56) and it seems more likely to be of native origin.

Along the western route the fort at Milton has already been mentioned. Its unusual shape is perhaps a point in favour of an Agricolan foundation, but the relevant dating evidence remains unpublished in detail. Midway between it and Carlisle lies the well-known fort at Birrens. Although a Flavian presence there is indisputable in the face of abundant artefactual evidence, the nature of that occupation remains obscure despite extensive excavation over many years (Robertson 1975a, 42 and 73–75). Aerial reconnaissance suggests that the fort was of even greater complexity than has generally been appreciated (pl 9). Some 16 miles (26 km) to the north of Milton lies the small fort at Crawford. Small-scale excavation in the 1960s confirmed its Flavian origin and, on the basis of its layout, suggested the presence of a cavalry vexillation (Maxwell 1972, 169). There is, however, some dispute over the nature of the earliest Flavian occupation of the important site at Castledykes. A proposed direct road link with Crawford, some 17 miles (27 km) to the south, has been examined and rejected, but the strategic value of the position, which lies astride a major land-route and commands wide prospects along the various natural corridors which meet at this point, is attested by the concentration of temporary camps in the vicinity of the fort (fig 16). According to the excavator the earliest permanent establishment on the site, a large fort of some 6.5 acres (2.6 ha), was late Flavian in origin, its Agricolan predecessor being only a semi-permanent enclosure (Robertson 1964, 259–62). However, it seems unlikely that this nodal point would not have been provided with a permanent fort at an early stage. A brief

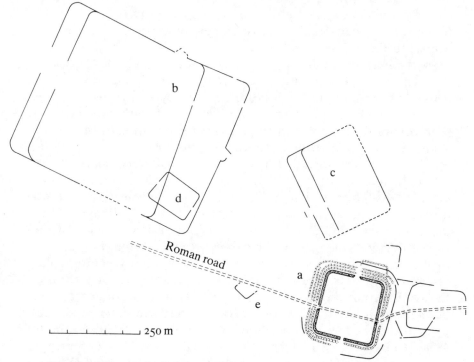

16 Fort and camps at Castledykes (after R.C.A.H.M.S.) (by permission of Edinburgh University Press)

reassessment of the samian ware has emphasised the absence of definitely late Flavian material and suggested a rather earlier occupation of the permanent fort than that envisaged by the excavator (Frere 1966, 270; Hartley 1972, 10). Moreover, the so-called Agricolan semi-permanent enclosure is questionable as an independent structure. It may have served as a construction camp, but since it follows closely the outline of the fort's defences, contemporary use seems likely. An enclosure for baggage or animals is a possible explanation (Frere 1966, 270; Jones 1975, 139), for similar outworks are coming to light as a result of aerial reconnaissance at other sites (Wilson 1984, 57–61). But even if an early date is accepted for the first permanent installation at Castledykes, we know virtually nothing of its internal arrangements or garrison. No other sites are known on this western route south of the isthmus, though one might be expected further down the Clyde valley, perhaps in the vicinity of the Antonine fort at Bothwellhaugh.

Between the two major north–south routes a few other permanent establishments are known. The fortlet at Castle Greg, Midlothian, lies well away from any known road line and is thus assumed to be an early foundation, though no modern excavation has taken place (R.C.A.H.M.S. 1929, 140). The recent discovery from the air of a similar fortlet at Bankhead some 4.5 km east of Castledykes may mark the junction of the missing road south from Castle Greg with the east–west trunk route (Frere 1985, 265). Along this route, between Bankhead and Newstead, lies the 3.5-acre (1.4-ha) fort at Easter Happrew. Limited excavation demonstrated that the fort had been occupied only once in the Flavian period, though the dating evidence was insufficient to determine whether it was early or late within that timespan (Steer 1957, 101). Aerial reconnaissance, by which the fort was originally discovered, has further augmented our knowledge of the site by revealing the outline of some of the internal timber buildings, an annexe to the west and further buildings outside the fort to the east (pl 10). Still further south in the valley of the Ettrick Water, which almost links Newstead and Milton though no road line is recorded in the valley, is another aerial photographic discovery, the 3.5-acre (1.4-ha) fort at Oakwood, Selkirkshire. Excavation confirmed a Flavian date, with two phases of occupation, but nothing of the interior was revealed (Steer and Feachem 1952b, 97). Finally, the fort at Broomholm, Dumfriesshire, located some 10 miles (16 km) east of Birrens, also appears to have been occupied in the Flavian period, but remains unpublished in any detail (Wilson 1965, 202).

Thus, apart from the central massif of the Southern Uplands, much of which is relatively sparsely inhabited even today, the only major gap in the distribution of forts in the central and eastern Lowlands is to the north-east; the possible significance of this in relation to differing tribal allegiances has already been suggested (above, p 91). The forts seem to have been fairly regularly distributed along the major routes, presumably as much to facilitate control of movement as to keep an eye on the recently subjugated inhabitants of the area, but rather less attention seems to have been paid to the interior.

When we turn our attention to the far west, the area overrun probably in Agricola's fifth campaign, the Roman military presence is poorly attested. Most of the sites are concentrated in the south, the best known being Dalswinton in the Nith valley. This 7.9-acre (3.2-ha) fort, later expanded to almost 10 acres (4 ha), is one of the most impressive aerial photographic discoveries in Scotland (pl 11). Both phases of the site were shown on excavation to be Flavian, though the limited nature of the investigation precludes much further comment, except to note the presence of a large garrison (Richmond and St Joseph 1956). The significance of the discovery, also from the air, of a further two phase work nearby, probably of permanent or semi-permanent nature, has already been discussed (above, pp 61–3). To the south, at the mouth of the Nith, lies the 7.5-acre (3-ha) site at Ward Law. Little excavation has taken place and no dating evidence has been recovered, though the site is usually thought to be Hadrianic (St Joseph 1952, 117–120). However, its location away from the established road line may indicate an earlier date, and reasons have already been adduced for regarding it as a possible campaign base rather than a permanent fort (above, p 95). Further west on the Dee lies the fort at Glenlochar. A well known aerial photograph shows the superimposed late Flavian and Antonine forts, but beneath these were found traces of earlier occupation which the excavators thought were civilian rather than military in character, believing the associated fort to lie elsewhere (Richmond and St Joseph 1952, 12). Given the limited area that was sampled it is difficult to characterise the nature of the occupation in such terms, but two Flavian phases seem to be attested. Around the fort are a series of temporary camps at least one of which is also likely to be Flavian. The most westerly permanent outpost known at present is located at Gatehouse-of-Fleet, Kirkcudbrightshire, where a fortlet only 0.5 acres (0.2 ha) in internal area contains sufficient accommodation for perhaps a single century (St Joseph 1983). Finally, though not published in detail, Flavian occupation is well attested at Loudoun Hill, a small fort covering some 2.8 acres (1.1 ha), in a seemingly isolated position further north in central Ayrshire (Taylor 1949, 98). Four phases of Flavian occupation are recorded here though the first two are of a somewhat ephemeral nature.

This is the limit of the certain Flavian forts in the western Lowlands. The area may have been pro-Roman and thus left largely ungarrisoned, but the absence of further permanent military installations may be explained in other ways. Because of relatively high rainfall and a high percentage of permanent pasture land, cropmark formation in the west is considerably inhibited and thus the chances of finding new sites from the air, the most common method of discovery, are much reduced. In fact there are a number of direct hints that further forts remain to be discovered. It seems unlikely that such a small post as Gatehouse-of-Fleet would have represented the most westerly Roman presence in Galloway and recent trial excavation by Professor St Joseph has confirmed the presence of a well built Roman road leading to a crossing of the Water of Fleet to the south of the fortlet (Frere 1985, 267). Indeed the advantages of Loch Ryan as a harbour are so manifest that a Roman fort there, probably in the vicinity of Stranraer, is to be expected. This finds some support from Ptolemy. As already noted above he attributes the 'city' of Rerigonium, located in the vicinity of Rerigonius Sinus (Loch Ryan), to the Novantae. Since Ptolemy is probably mapping Roman places this is likely to be the site of a Roman fort to which the native name has been transferred (Rivet and Smith 1979, 447). A similar argument may be applied to Vindogara in relation to Vindogara Sinus (Irvine Bay) (Rivet and Smith 1979, 501–2), where a Roman fort on the coast at Irvine to the west of Loudoun Hill might reasonably be predicted to take advantage of the good harbour. The only archaeological evidence, however, are occasional finds of first century Roman coins in the vicinity of Stranraer and Ayr (Robertson, 1975c, 394–6), though an earthwork of possible Roman date is mentioned at Irvine in one early antiquarian account (Pococke 1887). Finally and most interestingly, aerial reconnaissance in the very dry summer of 1984 recorded a previously unsuspected 3.7-acre (1.5-ha) Roman fort at Drumlanrig in the upper Nith Valley some 12 miles (19.3 km) north of Dalswinton (Frere 1985, 267). This fort, though as yet undated, lies away from the well known loop road which links Dalswinton and Crawford (fig 15) and strongly suggests a line of Roman penetration and subsequent consolidation westwards along the Nith valley in the direction of Irvine Bay. It is perhaps unwise, therefore, to speculate on the attitude of the tribes in the south-west towards Rome on the basis of the distribution of forts in their territory as known at present.

The Forth–Clyde isthmus was already garrisoned at this time, Agricola having recognised the value of this natural frontier line. Indeed, Tacitus makes it clear that for a time it was considered as the point at which to terminate the advance in Scotland:

> If the valour of our army and the glory of Rome had pemitted such a thing, a good place for halting the advance was found in Britain itself. The Forth and Clyde, carried inland for a great distance on the tides of opposite seas, are separated by only a narrow neck of land. This isthmus was now firmly held by garrisons (*praesidia*). (*Ag.* 23)

Such a decision lay not with the governor, but with the emperor. It has been suggested that this halt coincided with the death of the emperor Titus, for it seems to have been standard practice for a general to cease campaigning under such circumstances and await new orders (Breeze and Dobson 1976, 125), as did Vespasian whilst operating against the Jews when he heard of the death of the emperor Galba (Josephus *Bell. Jud.* 4, 498). But the halting of a campaign of conquest is not quite the same as ceasing the deliberate consolidation of an area previously overrun, which is what Agricola's task seems to have been for the whole of his fourth season (AD 80). Moreover, even if the later date for Agricola's governorship were accepted, the death of Titus on 13 September AD 81 would still have been too late in the season for news to have reached Britain in time to have had any effect on activities in the field that summer. Thus the decision to halt on the isthmus must have been a deliberate one on the part of Titus (Frere 1978, 126).

The fact that it proved to be only a short-lived frontier does not mean that it was not originally intended as a permanent one. By the time that he had reached the Forth–Clyde isthmus, Agricola had already completed three seasons of operations in Britain and as a result Roman occupied territory had been advanced all the way from north Wales. The consequent strain on resources and manpower must have been considerable with, on present estimates, the construction of between fifty and sixty new auxiliary forts or fortlets in the areas overrun. Titus had already received his fifteenth imperial acclamation (Dio Cassius 66, 20), probably as a result of Agricola's third campaign, and may simply have considered it time to call a halt. There are some indications that Agricola favoured this decision amd may even have proposed it in dispatches. Tacitus' reference to the halt on the isthmus is strangely ambivalent. He is clearly sympathetic to the idea, yet the renunciation of further conquest runs contrary to both Roman tradition in general and Tacitus' own criteria of success for a provincial governor. Morever, the subsequent change of tactics is ascribed to 'the valour of Roman arms and the glory of Rome', not to belated acceptance of Agricola's good counsel (Dobson 1980, 7–8). Already in the fourth year of his governorship, Agricola might well have anticipated imminent recall. To fix a permanent frontier at this point would still have allowed him to claim the glory of completing the conquest of Britain.

Paradoxically, given the unusual geographical accuracy of Tacitus' narrative at this point (*Ag.* 23), the identification of Agricola's *praesidia* across the Forth–Clyde isthmus has proved difficult. Too many archaeologists have let the later line of fortifications across this narrow neck of land colour their thinking, almost as if Agricola's eye for suitable fort sites (*opportunitates locorum*) (*Ag.* 22) was such as to influence the builders of the Antonine Wall some sixty years later. Undoubtedly many Flavian forts throughout Scotland were reoccupied in the Antonine period, but a number, such as Easter Happrew, Elginhaugh and Oakwood, were not. More importantly, the tactical and topographical criteria which determined the siting of individual forts were not necessarily the same as those which influenced the line chosen for a linear barrier, as the position of Hadrian's Wall in relation to the earlier Stanegate forts should serve to emphasise. Hadrian's Wall did not join together the pre-existing forts on the Stanegate road but was positioned some distance to the north to take advantage of the best topographical line. If the siting of forts still under occupation did not determine the line of Hadrian's Wall, there seems no logical reason why the line chosen by the builders of the Antonine Wall need have been in any way influenced by the location of forts abandoned some half a century earlier.

Nonetheless, at least nine of the sixteen forts on the Antonine Wall have been put forward at one time or another as candidates for the sites of Agricolan *praesidia*. However, most may be readily dismissed (Hanson 1980a). Some of the structural evidence supposedly indicative of Flavian occupation is very tenuous: for example, there is nothing to support Macdonald's suggestion that either the *lilia* at Rough Castle or the awkwardness of the ditches around the fort at Westerwood relate to earlier fortifications at those sites (1934, 234 and 257–8). The small enclosures beneath the forts at Croy Hill and Bar Hill have long been accepted as part of the Agricolan frontier.

Fortunately, both sites have been re-examined in the last decade and both may now be shown to be of Antonine date. The ditch of the Croy Hill enclosure was still open at the time of the construction of the Military Way bypass route around the Antonine fort since, for part of its length, the ditch served to drain that road. Moreover, quantities of Antonine pottery have been recovered from the ditch (Hanson 1979, 19). Similarly, the ditches of the Bar Hill enclosure had been carefully and deliberately packed with turf and branches before the construction of the Antonine fort. The lack of silting in these ditches indicates that they had been in use up to that point and are, therefore, unlikely to relate to any Flavian activity on the site. Unfortunately, no dating evidence was recovered during the excavation to confirm this (Keppie 1982, 104–5). The postulated presence of Agricolan *praesidia* at the remaining five Wall forts depends upon the identification of a few Flavian artefacts amongst a large quantity of Antonine material. But great care must be taken in assessing the significance of such discoveries (Hanson 1980a, 60–2). Coins, even low-value bronze denominations whose life might generally be thought to be quite short, could continue in circulation for a long time. To use a modern analogy, prior to decimalisation it was not unusual to receive in change pennies which were fifty or more years old. Thus the identification of Flavian sites beneath Antonine forts on the basis of nothing more than one or possibly two such coins, as at Balmuildy and Kirkintilloch, is dubious in the extreme. Slightly different arguments may be applied to coarse pottery. Although it has a relatively short life-span, since once broken it is merely rubbish to be disposed of, its dating is based upon changes in morphological characteristics which often occur quite slowly. Thus we must allow for the possibility that certain pottery forms could occasionally have been in use for longer than we would normally expect. At both Bearsden and Croy Hill, for example, a few ostensibly Flavian sherds were found in indubitably Antonine contexts. It could be argued that this pottery derived from an earlier occupation, but in neither case was there any indication of occupation other than of the Antonine period. Thus when the suggestion of Flavian occupation at an Antonine site rests solely upon the identification of a few sherds of coarse pottery, as at Old Kilpatrick, it must also be viewed with suspicion. At only three Wall forts has artefactual evidence been found of sufficient variety and quantity to warrant serious consideration of the existence of a Flavian site nearby: four first-century bronze coins and some sherds of coarse pottery have been recovered from excavations at Mumrills, while fragments of coarse pottery, samian and glass are known from both Cadder and Castlecary, the latter also producing one bronze coin of Nero. Without the testimony of Tacitus, however, it is unlikely that even these sites would have been considered as potentially Flavian foundations.

The only certain Agricolan sites across the isthmus in fact lie off the line of the Antonine Wall (fig 17). At Camelon, just over half-a-mile (1 km) north of the Wall on the line of the road to Strathmore, the existence of a Flavian fort beneath the annexe of the later Antonine fort has long been suspected (Macdonald 1919, 129–31), though the complexity of the remains has only recently become apparent (Maxfield 1980). Only one other fort is known on the isthmus proper, the recent aerial photographic discovery at Mollins just two-and-a-half miles (4 km) south of Bar Hill. Sample excavations within the small fort (0.9 acres; 0.4 ha) produced little structural evidence, but the only dateable pottery was Flavian (Hanson and Maxwell 1980). A second aerial photographic discovery may also be included here even though, strictly speaking, it is not located on the isthmus. Immediately to the south of the Clyde estuary the 3.2-acre (1.3-ha) fort at Barochan Hill has produced traces of timber buildings and quantities of Flavian pottery (*D.E.S.* 1972, 35–6: Newall 1975, 84–9).

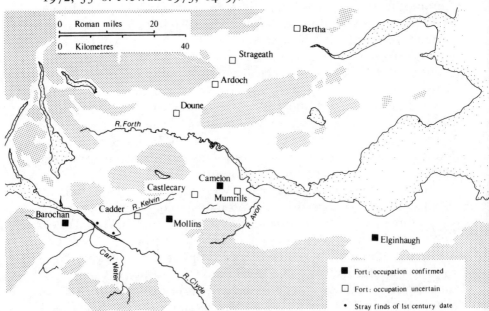

17 Agricolan *praesidia* across the Forth–Clyde isthmus

It has been noted that fortifications along a frontier line tend to be positioned rather closer together than those placed along strategic routes, the intervening distance usually being referred to as half a day's march (Gillam 1975, 52). A spacing of between six and eight miles (9.7–12.9 km) is consistently recorded between the forts on Hadrian's Wall, those on the Antonine Wall, as originally planned, and those along the Stanegate frontier, if the smallest forts are excluded. If we accept the implication of Tacitus' description of the isthmus as a *terminus*, a frontier, we might expect a similar disposition of forts across it too. If we add to the two certain examples those on the flank and three sites on the Antonine Wall with the relatively strong artefactual evidence of first century occupation, the spacing of installations across the isthmus would be as follows:

Site		Distance		
	Miles			Km
Barochan Hill				
	12.8			20.7
Cadder				
	6			9.7
Mollins				
	6.1			9.9
Castlecary				
	4.8			7.6
		8	12.9	
Camelon				
	3.6			5.8
Mumrills				
	25.9			41.6
Elginhaugh				

It is not difficult to see a possible 6–8-mile (9.7–12.9 km) mean distance between these sites and thus provide some tentative archaeological support for the existence of a frontier line (fig 17). The further implication would be the existence of a fort between Barochan and Cadder, perhaps in the vicinity of the confluence of the Clyde and the Cart Water or the Clyde and the Kelvin, from both of which stray finds of Roman material have been recorded (Macdonald 1918, 237; Buchanan 1877, 256–7). The large gap between Mumrills and Elginhaugh might be filled by a fort at the crossing of the river

Avon near Linlithgow, where first-century Roman pottery is recorded (Curle 1932, 353; Hanson 1980b, 66 *contra* Laing 1969, 137), and perhaps another at the crossing of the Almond or slightly further east near Gogar, where two temporary camps have recently come to light (Rankov 1982, 340).

The spacing of the forts to the east of Castlecary is even closer than the suggested mean. Although this is not without parallel, as for example along the Stanegate if the small forts at Haltwhistle Burn and Throp are included, it might indicate that Camelon relates to the occupation of the lands between Forth and Tay rather than to the frontier on the isthmus. This was certainly its strategic function at a later date when the fort lay immediately to the *north* of the Antonine Wall. The number and complexity of the temporary camps around the fort continue to grow and suggest that the area was an important jumping off point for further advance. That at least some elements of the complex were of first century date is implied by the provision of clavicular gateways at two of the camps, though a mint *as* of Vespasian was found too high in the fill of one excavated ditch to allow its use an indication of a more precise date (Frere 1984, 275). It has even been suggested that Camelon may have served as a harbour and supply depot for Agricola and subsequently for the Antonine Wall (Tatton-Brown 1980, 342). The relationship of the fort at Corbridge to the military presence in Scotland rather than to the occupation of Hadrian's Wall, which lies less than 2.4 miles (4 km) to its north, provides a possible analogy. The corollary of this might be to postulate occupation beyond the Forth–Clyde isthmus, at least along the known road line as far as Bertha, by AD 80 (see below pp 120–1), for the Flavian pottery from Camelon is as early as any recorded in Scotland. Indeed, it includes small quantities of what would normally be interpreted as pre-Flavian material, which has led the excavator to argue for a date as early as the historical context will allow (Maxfield 1980, 77).

The importance of the provisions made by Agricola across the Forth–Clyde isthmus to the military occupation of Britain and to the development of Roman frontiers in general requires emphasis. The decision to halt the advance into Scotland as recorded by Tacitus marks the earliest recognition that a policy other than complete conquest was being seriously considered for Britain. Perhaps more significantly, this line represents the first example in Britain, if not the whole Empire, of a frontier demarcated solely by a series of military installations rather than some natural feature, such as one of the major European rivers. However, before we can be completely confident of this assertion, the existence of further forts requires confirmation and a system of watch-towers must be located, for it is these smaller posts which are the hallmark of such frontier lines.

Indeed, it has recently been proposed that Agricola's *praesidia* were in fact located rather further to the north along a line skirting the southern fringe of the Highlands from Dumbarton to Stirling (Maxwell 1984, 218–21). This suggestion stems from the discovery of a new fort at Doune on the river Teith. This has been linked with two other recent aerial photographic discoveries at Malling and Drumquhassle and one long known site at Bochastle to define an arc of forts which might comply with one possible translation of the term *sinus*, as a salient, used by Tacitus when describing the effect of the fort building campaign. But it requires special pleading to apply Tacitus' very specific description of the Forth–Clyde isthmus to such a disposition of garrisons: all the more so when the two important terminal forts at Stirling and Dumbarton are both hypothetical. As we shall see, the strategic context of the forts skirting the highlands is perhaps better explained in relation to the pattern of occupation further north at a slightly later date (below, pp 146–9).

The problem presented by Agricola's major programme of fort building between his second and fifth seasons has already been discussed (above, p 64). Even allowing for a number of much later constructions in northern England the process would still have necessitated the abandonment of forts further south, for the number of garrison troops available was not infinite. The likely effect of Flavian military advances on urban development in the south and west has also been noted (above, p 79), but the number of troops still stationed in these long-conquered areas cannot have been great. Unless Agricola's army was considerably reinforced, for which there is no evidence, his campaigns must also have put pressure on troop dispositions in more recently subjugated areas.

If recognition of the date at which a fort was founded is difficult to establish on archaeological grounds, the time at which such occupation ceased is no less of a problem to define, particularly if reoccupation took place subsequently. There are, however, a number of sites where such evidence is beginning to accrue. In Wales temporary abandonment at the time of Agricola's Scottish campaigns has been suggested at Caernarvon, Caersws, Jay Lane, Erglodd and perhaps Brithdir (Davies 1980a, 263–4), though the evidence is very tenuous. In the north of England, on the other hand, forts established under Cerialis may have been evacuated by Agricola. At Brough on Humber the samian pottery suggests a date not later than AD 85 for the departure of Roman troops, and perhaps slightly earlier (Wacher 1969, 19–20), while at Hayton, the next fort to the north, the pottery gave the impression of abandonment by the early 80s AD (Johnson 1978, 78). Slightly further west the similarly early fort at Doncaster apparently had a more complicated history. The first fort was deliberately demolished, its timbers collected together and burned. A *terminus post quem* for its rapid replacement is provided by numerous finds of bronze *asses* of AD 86–7, but the excavator suggests that this probably occurred after a period of neglect, perhaps while the troops were in Scotland (Buckland 1978, 247).

· 6 ·

TOTAL CONQUEST

THERE can be no doubt that by Agricola's sixth campaign the northward advance had been resumed, for Tacitus is quite specific that the tribes involved, though unnamed, lay north of the Forth (*Ag.* 25). He goes on to imply that the stimulus for this forward movement was the fear of a general rising of these northern tribes who were making threatening moves. But there is no particular need to see this as other than the justification for a policy decision made in Rome, for the expansion of the empire was emphatically the emperor's business (Dobson 1980, 7).

On the revised dating for Agricola's governorship, the sixth campaign would have been the first under the new emperor Domitian who came to power in September AD 81 after the death of his brother Titus. Perhaps because he lacked the military background of his father and brother, Domitian seems to have favoured a more expansionist policy in general: in Germany, for example, we see a resumption of Roman activity beyond the Rhine involving the emperor personally (Schönberger 1969, 158–9). A desire for military glory was a common trait amongst Roman emperors, particularly those whose previous military experience was limited, both as a reflection of the consistent Roman militaristic ideology and a recognition of the importance of the army for the maintenance of imperial power. That it was Domitian who had decided to abandon the isthmus frontier would further serve to explain Tacitus' strange phraseology when describing its construction (*Ag.* 23): the vagueness of his expression effectively avoiding a direct reference to the initiative taken by the emperor, since this would not have fitted the derogatory picture of him being presented.

The general course of the sixth campaign is relatively clear from the brief Tacitean account (*Ag.* 25–7). Agricola made use of his fleet to reconnoitre and strike ahead, as well as to supply his main column. Reference to frequent contact between soldiers and marines confirms the impression of a combined operation and, of course, implies that the land forces maintained fairly close touch with the coast. The inhabitants of Caledonia seem to have reacted violently and proceeded to attack one or more Roman forts. Learning that a major attack was imminent and fearful that he might be surrounded, Agricola split his forces into three divisions and advanced. The Caledonians then singled out the ninth legion as the weak link and attacked by night. It was only by virtue of good intelligence and speedy reaction that Agricola was able to bring the rest of his forces to the rescue. The enemy were routed but the campaigning season seems to have been drawn to a close shortly thereafter.

When we try to identify the location of these events more precisely, however, we run into difficulties. That the hostile natives are named as the inhabitants of Caledonia is important given the paucity of geographical references in Tacitus' narrative, but the identification of that territory is disputed. According to Ptolemy, the Caledonii stretched from the Varar estuary (Beauly Firth) to Lemannonius gulf (Loch Long) (2, 3, 8). This has been taken by most scholars to indicate occupation of the central highlands: Rivet and Smith (1979, 141) suggest that Ptolemy may really have meant Loch Linnhe, thus placing the tribe neatly in the Great Glen (fig 18). Recently, however, this location has been challenged primarily because of doubts about the area's ability to sustain a population of sufficient size and power to head the opposition to Rome. Moreover, the Romans appear to have skirted the Highlands (see below) so that they are less likely to have made contact with the occupants of that area (Hind 1983). While not disputing that the mountains themselves are unlikely to have proffered any major attractions to settlement, the straths and glens which divide them have much to offer. In particular recent detailed underwater investigations of Loch Awe and Loch Tay suggest that our estimate of population density in the Highlands in prehistory needs to be drastically revised to take into account the number of crannogs or man made islands (Dixon 1982; Morrison 1985). Moreover, contrary to Hind's assertion, the place name evidence that he quotes for the location of the Caledonii – the mountains of Schiehallion and Rohallion – would place them within the Highland massif not to the east of it. Finally, it is important to note that, in contrast to some other tribes located to the north of the isthmus, no places in Caledonian territory are named by Ptolemy. Since he seems to have been describing Roman places, and for the north, therefore, predominantly Roman forts, we must conclude that no significant forts were located in Caledonian lands. Thus, these can hardly be located to the east of the Highlands where many forts and a legionary fortress are known.

Ptolemy names a dozen tribes in Scotland north of the Forth–Clyde isthmus, but the majority are recorded nowhere else. They were probably small groups who had relatively little contact with Rome, several located along the west coast where the broken terrain tended to discourage the formation of large tribal groups (fig 1). Allowing for the misplacing of Scotland in relation to the rest of the British Isles, to the east of the Caledonii were the Vacomagi to the south-east of whom were the Venicones and to the north of these the Taexali. The location of the latter in northern Aberdeenshire may reasonably be fixed by their association with the promontory of the same name, probably Kinnaird's Head, the most north-easterly point in the county. Also included within their territory is a place called Devona, the name probably derived from its location on the river Don or Dee (Rivet and Smith 1979, 141), though no Roman fort is known that far north. The only other named place attributed to any of the tribes which can be tied down with any confidence is Tuesis somewhere on the river of the same name, the Spey, whose estuary Ptolemy identifies on the north coast (*Geog.* 2, 3, 4) (fig 1). Ironically, this immediately causes problems, for the location is not entirely consistent with the position of the Vacomagi, to whom it is credited, in relation to the other tribes nor with the coordinates for the other places in their territory, unless the tribe is seen to have followed the eastern highland fringe all the way from the upper reaches of the Forth to the Moray Firth (Maxwell 1980a, 7). At present the combination of the turning of northern Scotland by Ptolemy, the difficulties of identifying the places named and the omission of at least one tribe, the Boresti (below, p 140), makes it impossible to fix the location of the northern tribes with any certainty.

However, one or two relevant points may be made from the archaeological evidence of native settlement patterns. There is sufficient distinction between Fife and Angus to suggest that the areas were inhabited by groups with different cultural affiliations (Macinnes 1982, 70–2 *contra* Ordnance Survey 1978), differences which are also reflected in the disposition of Roman garrisons (see below). Similarly, the distribution of souterrains, underground stone-lined passages for storage or refuge, show separate concentrations in Perthshire and Angus, and in Aberdeenshire, and sufficient differences in form between these two areas to hint at a further possible tribal distinction, though the more northerly group have not been fully studied (Wainwright 1963, 7–8). This Aberdeenshire group lie within the area attributed to the Taexali, while it is

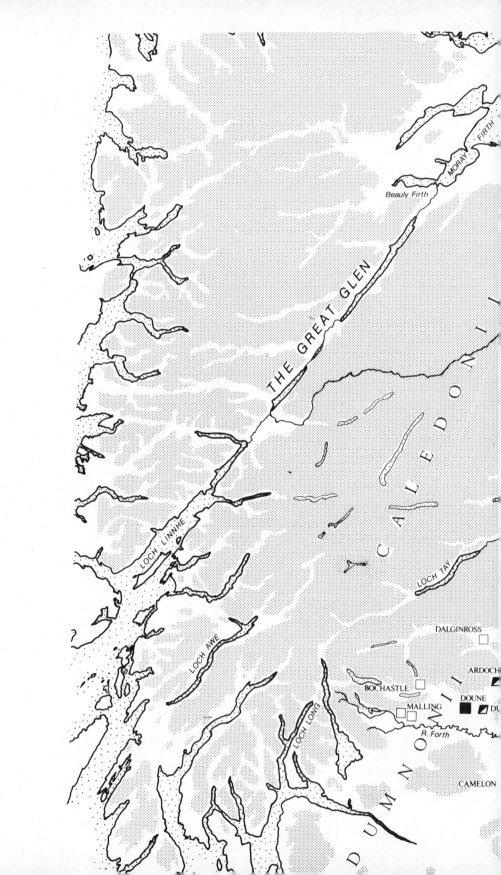

THE GREAT GLEN

Beauly Firth

MORAY FIRTH

C
A
L
E
D
O
N
I
I

LOCH LINNHE

LOCH AWE

LOCH TAY

LOCH LONG

DALGINROSS

ARDOCH

BOCHASTLE

DOUNE

MALLING

R. Forth

DU

CAMELON

D
U
M
N
O
N
I
I

Tribal territories and possible Agricolan temporary camps in north-east Scotland

BELLIE
DESKFORD
MUIRYFOLD
AUCHINHOVE
TAEXALI
YTHAN WELLS
DURNO
R. Don
KINTORE
NORMANDYKES
R. Dee
RAEDYKES
THE MOUNTH
STRACATHRO
FINAVON
DUN
INVERQUHARITY
R. South Esk
VACOMAGI or BORESTI
CARDEAN
R. Tay
HA
DUNNING
ABERNETHY
BONNYTOWN
E N I C O N E S
Kinnaird's Head

■ Fort
□ Camps of 100 acres or more
□ Stracathro-type camps
◩ 30 acre camps
◩ Small camps
● Deskford

0   Roman miles   20

0   Kilometres   40

generally accepted that Fife was occupied by the Venicones. The question remains, however, who occupied the area in between? At present the most likely candidates are the Vacomagi or the Boresti (fig 18).

We may reasonably suggest, therefore, that the tribes faced in Agricola's sixth campaign were the Venicones, the Vacomagi or Boresti and perhaps the Taexali. Why is it then that Tacitus apparently refers only to the Caledonii in opposition to Rome? The simplest explanation is that Tacitus has reverted to his usual imprecision in matters geographical. In particular it should be stressed that nowhere does he actually refer to the Caledonii as such, but rather to the inhabitants of Caledonia (*Ag.* 11, 25 and 31), this area being generally equated with Scotland north of the Forth–Clyde isthmus (Rivet and Smith 1979, 289–91). Thus the expression could be simply a catchall phrase for the tribes of the far north. The general implication of Tacitus' various remarks and of the subsequent development of the area is that it was bound by some form of loose confederacy. The men finally gathered to meet Agricola's army at Mons Graupius, for example, had been assembled from many tribes by sending envoys and invoking treaties (*Ag.* 29), and by the third century AD the Caledonii are one of only two tribal groups referred to in Scotland (Dio Cassius 75, 5; 76, 12 and 15) subsequently to be encapsulated within the Picts (Ammianus Marcellinus 27, 8, 5). Indeed, this alliance between different groups in the north may even have been stimulated by the Roman threat.

But the whole of northern Scotland may not have been united in their opposition to Rome. Like the Lothians, much of the peninsula of Fife east of the Ochils, comprising the old counties of Fife, Kinross and Clackmannan, is highly susceptible to cropmark production, yet traces of Roman military presence are extremely limited. Only two or possibly three temporary camps of Flavian date are known and no permanent forts (fig 18), in sharp contrast to the heavily garrisoned road immediately to the west which at some stage served as a frontier line (below, pp 152–3). It is difficult to avoid the conclusion that the Venicones, like the Votadini, had Roman sympathies and may even have had their territory protected by treaty (Hanson 1980b, 24). The forts along the road from Camelon to Bertha may have been established already, perhaps as early as Agricola's fourth campaign to serve as outposts to the *terminus* on the Forth–Clyde isthmus (fig 17) (Frere 1980a, 91), a role they subsequently were to play for the Antonine Wall, for Roman arms had penetrated as far as the Tay the previous year.

That the establishment of the fort at Camelon should be placed as early in the Flavian period as possible has already been noted. Though the picture is far from clear, recent excavations at the fort confirmed that its development was much more complicated than previously assumed, with at least two phases of Flavian occupation (Maxfield 1980, 77). Since on historical and archaeological grounds (below, p 157) we know that the Flavian permanent presence in the area was very short-lived, no more than a decade, sites which show more than one phase of occupation are likely to have been early foundations. The fort at Ardoch offers a similar picture, for there a semi-permanent work has been identified (information from Professor St Joseph) to the north-east of the well-known fort (fig 19), which itself has produced evidence of Flavian occupation both structural (Breeze 1983) and artefactual (Hartley 1972, 5). Current excavations at Strageath have provided hints of two phases of Flavian occupation, with dating evidence indicative of an early foundation (Frere 1980a, 95), though the nature and extent of the first phase is very limited. Finally at Cargill a Flavian fort of perhaps two or even three phases has been found only 300m. away from a fortlet of the same date (information from Mr G.S. Maxwell). Thus the archaeological evidence would tend to indicate an early construction date for the forts along the only known road north of the isthmus. Whether the well-known watchtowers along the middle section of this road were also constructed at this time is uncertain, but the establishment of a frontier along the Gask Ridge contemporary with the formal halt on the Forth–Clyde isthmus seems unlikely, and a later context would seem more appropriate (below, p 153).*

There is also a hint in Tacitus' narrative that forts had indeed already been constructed to the north of the isthmus (*contra* Breeze and Dobson 1976, 128; Breeze 1982, 53). The reaction to the Roman dual advance by land and sea was a Caledonian attack on a Roman fort, or perhaps forts, for the manuscript tradition is ambiguous on this point. Although Tacitus does not state specifically that these sites were north of the isthmus, this is surely the implication of the consequent advice offered to Agricola:

> There were cowards in the council who pleaded for a strategic retreat behind the Forth, maintaining that evacuation was preferable to expulsion. (*Ag.* 25)

Various attempts have been made to work out the route and scope of Agricola's campaigns beyond the isthmus in more detail than is provided by Tacitus. These rely solely upon the analysis of Roman

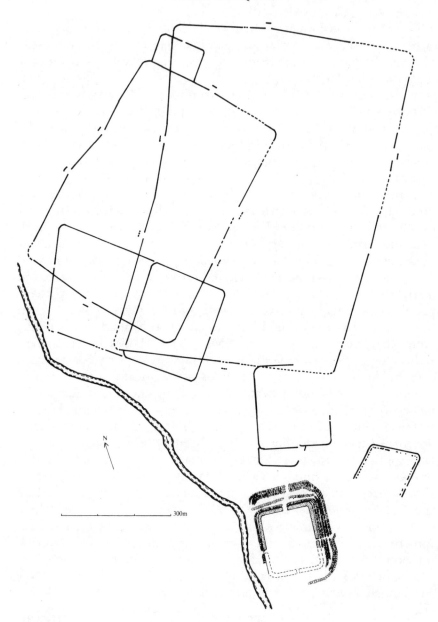

19 Forts and camps at Ardoch (after St Joseph)

temporary camps which mark the halting places of an army on campaign (St Joseph 1969, 113–119; 1973, 228–33; 1977, 143–5). Indeed, the study of this area is a classic example of the methodology whereby camps are divided into groups on the basis of their size, shape and gateway design and the groups, in turn, assigned to specific campaigns because of their date, where it can be established, and distribution in relation to the historical account. The whole process is possible only because the number of different occasions when the Romans were campaigning in the area is limited, although perhaps not as limited as has generally been assumed (Hanson 1978a, 140–1). Two particular groups of medium-sized camps are usually assigned to Agricola's sixth campaign when the army was divided into three parts (*Ag.* 25): one distinguished by its unusual gateway design, the so-called Stracathro-type named after the site of the best known example (fig 20); the second categorised in terms of its size, nominally 30 acres (12.1 ha) (St Joseph 1973, 229). Unfortunately this neat picture does not stand up to detailed critical examination.

The Stracathro camps do not make up a coherent grouping which can be related to any single campaign. They are scattered throughout Scotland (figs 10 and 18) and vary in size from as little as 3.7 acres (1.5 ha) to as much as 60.5 acres (24.5 ha) (Maxwell 1980b, 34–6) (table 1). Moreover, when studied more closely the gateway form itself shows some variety (Maxwell 1980b, 31–4). Even if consideration is restricted only to the examples north of the Forth–Clyde isthmus, there is still considerable diversity in their size (fig 20). We can, however, be quite confident of their general attribution to the Flavian period, though none have been dated on the basis of associated artefacts. The clavicular style of gateway, of which the Stracathro type is a variant, is not usually found in camps later in date than the reign of Trajan (Lenoir 1977, 716). Thus the examples in Scotland north of the isthmus should be Flavian since the next period when Roman activity might be expected in that area falls at the beginning of the reign of Antonius Pius at the earliest. More specifically, several of the camps are directly associated with forts of known or presumed Flavian date. Stracathro-type camps are found adjacent to the forts at Bochastle, Dalginross (pl 12), Inverquharity and Malling (Menteith), the first two of which have been established as Flavian by excavation. Finally at the type-site, Stracathro, the north-east side of the camp intersects the annexe of the Flavian fort which it may, therefore, be presumed to predate, although this point has not actually been tested by excavation.

This group of Stracathro camps may have housed the troops engaged in the construction of the adjacent forts although they would appear to be rather too large for that purpose. Simple proximity need not imply such a relationship, as is clear, for example, at Ardoch (fig 19), Camelon, Glenlochar and Castledykes

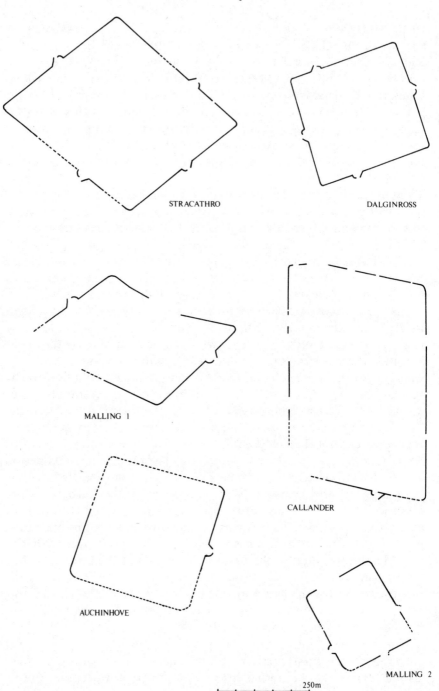

20 Comparative plans of Stracathro-type camps north of the Forth–Clyde isthmus

Table 1   Temporary camps in Scotland with Stracathro-type gateways

Site	Area		Approximate dimensions in metres
	acres	ha	
Castledykes	60.4	24.5	550 × 445
Callander	48.2	19.5	530 × 365
Beattock	c.40	c.16.3	c.440 × 370
Stracathro	38.8	15.7	425 × 370
Ythan Wells	33.9	13.7	435 × 315
Auchinhove	c.32	c.13	c.350 × 310
Dalginross	22	8.9	305 × 295
Lochlands	c.23.7	c.10	c.350 × 275*
Malling I	26	10.5	370 × 285
Malling II	13.4	5.4	250 × 215
Inverquharity	c.5	c.2.1	c.150 × 140
Dalswinton I	61.3	24.8	535 × 465
Dalswinton II	c.4.9	c.2	c.150 × 140
Woodhead	3.7	1.5	140 × 110

*Information from Professor J.K. St Joseph and Mr. G.S. Maxwell.

(fig 16) where each fort is almost surrounded by camps. Indeed, a second Stracathro camp at Malling may better fit into the category of construction camps by virtue of its smaller size. Of the Stracathro camps north of the isthmus only two, Auchinhove and Ythan Wells, may be confidently identified as demarcating successive stages of a single campaign. They are of similar size in so far as we know the dimensions of the former, and are 14.8 miles (9.2 km) apart, approximately one day's march. To these might be added the eponymous site, since it is presumed to predate the fort at Stracathro and is also of broadly similar size.

We are then left with a group of three Stracathro-type camps of varying size which, though not members of a series demarcating a line of march, may nevertheless relate to campaigning up the glens. The rows of pits, presumably for the disposal of rubbish, recorded at Dalginross (pl 12) suggest occupation for rather longer than just an overnight stop (St Joseph 1973, 224), which in turn implies that the camp may have been used as the base for the exploration and pacification of the surrounding area (Maxwell 1980b, 35). In which case the large camp at Dalginross, and perhaps those at Callander (Bochastle) and Malling also, might relate to activities in Agricola's sixth campaign, though since they lie too far inland to allow any link with the fleet they may rather belong to the activities of his successor.

The second group of camps which supposedly relate to Agricola's sixth campaign, the so-called 30-acre (12-ha) group, are even less helpful. Their attribution to this period depends very largely upon circumstantial evidence. Because in size and distribution they are broadly complementary to the Stracathro group (fig 18), the 30-acre (12-ha) group have been seen to provide ideal accommodation for another part of Agricola's army while it was divided into three, given that at some stage in the campaigns his full forces were brigaded together in camps of *c*.115 acres (46.5 ha). Moreover, the example at Ardoch appears to be early in the sequence of camps attested there (fig 19). The serious doubts already cast on the Stracathro group partly undermine one part of this argument, while the evidence from Ardoch indicates no more than that the camp there, which in any case had been extended from a smaller one, is probably earlier than the third century AD (St Joseph 1970, 169; Hanson 1978a, 144–5). More fundamentally, since the group is supposedly characterised by a common size, it is disturbing to find variation akin to that already noted between the Stracathro-type camps north of the isthmus (table 2). On present evidence, the identity of the group cannot be maintained nor their Flavian date confirmed, let alone any association with a particular campaign. Indeed, at least three examples may be rather later in date. A propensity for Flavian camps to be square in plan has been noted in a recent analysis (Maxwell 1980b, 29), yet the camps at Bonnytown, Ardoch and Strageath are distinctly elongated, the latter also occupying rather awkward terrain as if it were a later addition to the various Roman structures in the immediate area.

Given Tacitus' emphasis on Agricola's use of combined operations during his sixth campaign, we might reasonably expect to see this reflected in the archaeological evidence. At present only one camp, at Dun on the north shore of the Montrose basin (pl 23), can reasonably be associated with the link between Agricola's naval and land forces. An ideal spot for the sheltered beaching of ships, its Flavian date has been confirmed by pottery finds (St Joseph 1973, 225–6). Yet even this site presents problems for at only eight acres (3.2 ha) in area it is too small to have held more than a couple of thousand men at most and might better be identified as a stores compound, or simply

Table 2   So-called 30-acre (12-ha) camps

Site	Area		Approximate dimensions	Spacing	
	acres	*ha*	*in metres*	*miles*	*km*
Dunblane	34.3	13.9	375 × 370		
				7.3	11.7
Ardoch	29.5	12	460 × 260		
				5.8	9.3
Strageath	33	13.5	– –		
				1	1.6
Dornock	23.1	9.4	360 × 260		
				31	50
Cardean	33+	13.4+	*c.*435 × 310		
				14	22.5
Finavon	37	15	425 × 355		
				–	–
Bonnytown	*c.*35	*c.*14.2	*c.*490 × 290		
				–	–
Bellie	25+	10.1+	*c.*400 × 300		

temporary accommodation for elements of the fleet alone.

Thus, at present, archaeological support for Tacitus' account of Agricola's campaign is extremely limited. Tacitus' narrative (*Ag.* 25) suggests that the dividing of Agricola's army into three occurred relatively late in the season after the war had been pushed forward by land and sea, so that, assuming a starting point somewhere on or about the Forth–Clyde isthmus, we might expect a group of large camps following a coastal route and then a series of smaller camps further north. The Flavian camps at Dunning and Abernethy could fit into this context, but given the postulated pro-Roman stance of the Venicones they are perhaps better seen in relation to the much earlier penetration to the Tay (above, pp 84–5). The two or three most northerly Stracathro-type camps, on the other hand, are likely to have been constructed well on in the summer and their size (34.6 acres; 14 ha) would suit a battle group formed from the tripartite division of an army earlier housed in camps of *c.*115 acres (46.5 ha). Most importantly they serve to confirm the depth of penetration into northern Scotland implied by Tacitus.

Agricola's seventh and final campaign follows almost as though the winter had not intervened. Employing his fleet to plunder and spread terror ahead, and with his army marching light, Agricola reached Mons Graupius where the enemy awaited (*Ag.* 29). Why they chose to meet him in a set-piece battle, rather than to employ guerrilla tactics as in the previous season (*Ag.* 26), is unclear. It is perhaps unfair to castigate the Caledonians for their military ineptitude, for it is only with hindsight that we can predict the inevitability of their defeat in the face of a better equipped, better trained and better organised foe. Nor were they the first to succumb to the Roman principle of deliberate and persistent frightfulness as a means of drawing an enemy into battle. They may have had little choice, for Agricola had struck at their economic heartland: the coastal strip of Angus is one of the few areas of first class agricultural land in Scotland, while the plains of Moray and Nairn and the plateau of Buchan represent the largest concentration of predominantly good land in the country (Coppock 1976, 13).

Despite limited investigation there is ample evidence of quern-stones from native sites in the north-east to provide archaeological confirmation of the arable potential of the area (Watkins 1980, 198). If souterrains are correctly identified as for the storage of foodstuffs, for their function has been much debated, their size indicates considerable production capacity and centralised storage (Macinnes 1983, 357–9 and 364–6). Unopposed, a Roman army could have done much damage to growing crops and stored grain. Despite Tacitus' narrative, which implies Agricola's speedy arrival at Mons Graupius, the battle clearly took place at the end of the campaigning season (*Ag.* 38). What had Agricola been doing in the previous months? Fort building has been tentatively suggested (Keppie 1980, 84), but this seems unlikely (below, pp 143–6). Recently it has been argued that the campaign simply got off to a late start because of Agricola's bereavement (Hind 1985, 11–12). We must be careful not to assume, however, that nothing was taking place just because Tacitus gives us no specific information. In fact he does provide a clue in Agricola's speech before the battle:

> Often on the march, when you were wearied with bogs, hills and rivers, I have heard the bravest of you ask: when will they come and fight us. (*Ag.* 33)

The process of march and countermarch, threatening native homes and crops *en route*, is exactly what is implied. Perhaps battle was finally deemed preferable to starvation.

This encounter was clearly seen by Tacitus as the climax of his narrative and Agricola's main claim to fame, for approximately 25 per cent of the book is devoted to it. Certainly it continues to capture the imagination, for of all the questions concerning the Roman conquest of Scotland, perhaps the most common is the location of Mons Graupius. Nor has concern been restricted to the layman: over the last 250 years considerable academic ink has been spilt postulating the whereabouts of the battle (Keppie 1980).

Various factors point to a location in the far north. Most importantly, the battle took place towards the end of the season and was followed by a slow march south, of sufficient duration to allow the fleet time to sail around the north of the island (*Ag.* 38). None of this is commensurate with the battle being fought anywhere much to the south of the Mearns. The pre-battle speeches attributed to the opposing generals, Calgacus and Agricola, point to the same conclusion. Both clearly indicate that Tacitus was of the belief that the farthest shores of the island had been reached before the battle took place. According to Calgacus:

> There are no more nations beyond us: nothing is there but waves and rocks. (*Ag.* 30)

while Agricola claims that:

> The farthest boundary of Britain, known previously only by report and rumour, we hold with arms and forts. (*Ag.* 33)

Though both speeches are almost certainly inventions of Tacitus, full of rhetorical expressions of dubious value, they are at least consistent in the general picture they present. On the other hand it is doubtful whether any weight should be placed on the detail they contain, such as the implication in Calgacus' speech that the sea was not far away (*Ag.* 32).

Nor is the topographical and etymological information in Tacitus' account of much assistance. The link between the Grampian mountains and Mons Graupius is the reverse of what one might expect: an error by an early editor of Tacitus produced Grampius, instead of Graupius, and it is from this that the mountains, formerly known as 'the Mounth', subsequently acquired their name (Ogilvie and Richmond 1967, 251). The etymology of the name Graupius has been much disputed, though the most likely derivative is Old Welsh 'crup' meaning a hump (Rivet and Smith 1979, 370). The Latin *mons* need not necessarily imply a mountain rather than a hill, and the name 'hill with a hump' is hardly likely to aid very specific identification. Nor is it entirely safe to extract topographical details from Tacitus' description of the battle, for in part at least it is modelled on other set pieces and, to quote one Tacitean scholar, 'such efforts are almost always so subjective as to be valueless, and are founded on the mistaken assumption that Tacitus was writing with a painterly concern for accuracy of detail' (Henderson 1984, 25). However, the presence of a temporary camp in the immediate vicinity is required by common sense as well as the narrative of Tacitus (*Ag.* 35).

Of the candidates for the battle site proposed in recent years, four deserve consideration in more detail. The etymological link between Duncrub, a hill in Perthshire, and the name Graupius combined with the identification of a nearby putative Stracathro-type temporary camp, were sufficient to convince Feachem that he had located the battle site (1970). Recently additional arguments have been marshalled and the case restated: the combination of a presumed late start for Agricola's final season and the speedy arrival at Mons Graupius implied in Tacitus' narrative has been taken to indicate a more southerly location for the final battle than is normally accepted (Hind 1985, 12–14). The supporting archaeological evidence is, indeed, now stronger, for the stretch of rampart in Kincladie Wood which Feachem thought was part of a Stracathro camp has since been demonstrated to belong to one of the 114-acre (46.1-ha) camps, now known as Dunning (fig 11), whose Flavian date seems assured (above, pp 84–5). In addition, the suggested allocation of the place name Victoria to Strageath, the nearest permanent fort to Duncrub, has been taken to provide further support for the location of a major victory in the vicinity (Hind 1985, 14–15). The place name evidence, however, is entirely circumstantial. The location of Victoria is disputed and need not in any case refer to a military victory, let alone to Mons Graupius (Rivet and Smith 1979, 499). Even though the two names Graupius and Duncrub have the same root, this does not mean that they refer to the same site: names for geographical features regularly recur and, as already noted, this particular description is hardly likely to be unique. Indeed, the hill of Duncrub itself is so insignificant as to be barely noticeable. Finally, and most importantly, the general arguments for a more northerly location for the battle still stand: Perthshire is much too far south. Moreover, Duncrub probably lay within the territory of the Venicones who seem to have been pro-Roman and, therefore, unlikely hosts for the battle.

The site which has been the favourite for the longest period of time is Raedykes, the eccentrically shaped Roman camp of some 93.5 acres (37.8 ha) near Stonehaven (fig 21). Since Caledonian forces were apparently drawn up in readiness for Agricola's arrival, they must have been able to anticipate his line of march. There are a number of possible routes north along Strathmore, but they all converge at the Mounth near Stonehaven where the Grampian foothills come closest to the sea. Precisely at this bottleneck lies Raedykes. Crawford bolstered this general argument by correlating the local topography with that described by Tacitus (though no specific eminence of the several in the vicinity was related to Mons Graupius) and drew attention to the ancient discoveries of chariot wheels at the site (1949, 131–2). The identification is superficially attractive, for the camp is of the right order of magnitude to house the forces known to have been at Agricola's disposal (see below), but the wheels recovered from the camp ditch are as likely to have come from Roman wagons as Caledonian war-chariots (Keppie 1980, 85), and the surrounding hills lack distinction.

Most crucial, however, is the date of the camp itself. For a number of years Raedykes has been grouped with camps of slightly larger size both to the north and south as part of a single line of march from Ardoch in Perthshire to Muiryfold in Banffshire, and dated to the Severan period (St Joseph 1969, 116–19). The third-century AD date for the camps to the south is still maintained, but the northern extension from Raedykes to Muiryfold has recently been reclassified to form a separate group attributed to Agricola (St Joseph 1973, 231–2: 1978b, 277–87) (fig 18). Admittedly the average size of the more northerly camps (109 acres; 44 ha) is sufficiently distinct from those to the south (by a factor of 10 per cent) to lend support to their separation, but the criteria for the redating are questionable. The more northerly camps do resemble the confirmed Flavian camps at Abernethy and Dunning in size, but not in shape (compare figs 11 and 21). The latter tend towards a square plan, while the former are distinctly elongated, a characteristic feature of third-century AD camps (Maxwell 1980b, 29 and 40) (table 3). The only direct dating evidence comes from Ythan Wells (Glenmailen) where the 111-acre (44.9-ha) camp overlies a smaller Stracathro-type camp. Excavation has demonstrated that the larger camp was clearly the later of the two and it was originally concluded that a considerable time had elapsed between their construction (St Joseph 1970, 177). That this observation was subsequently reconsidered and an alternative interpretation tendered to fit the hypothetically earlier dating of the camps (St Joseph 1973, 232) does little to encourage confidence in the other supporting data cited (see below). On present evidence, the so-called 109-acre (44-ha) camps could just as easily be related to the campaigns of Severus, who also penetrated to the far north (Dio

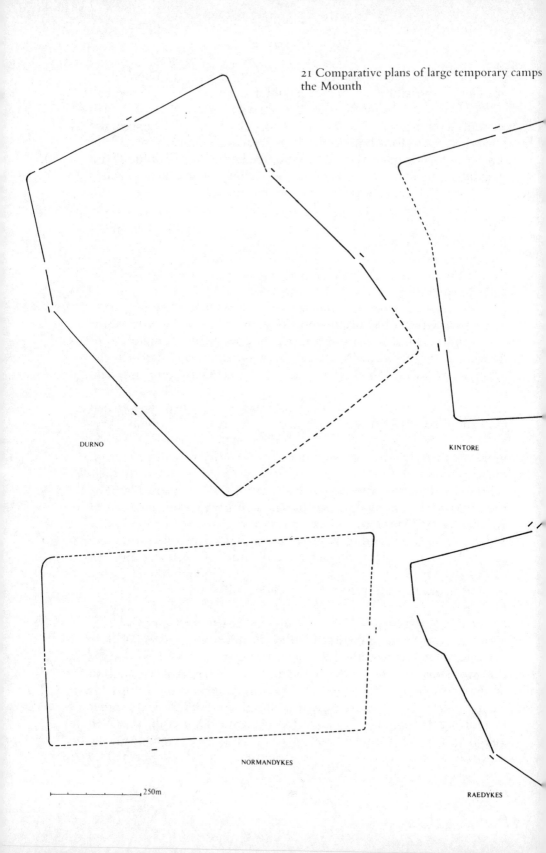

21 Comparative plans of large temporary camps the Mounth

DURNO

KINTORE

NORMANDYKES

RAEDYKES

250m

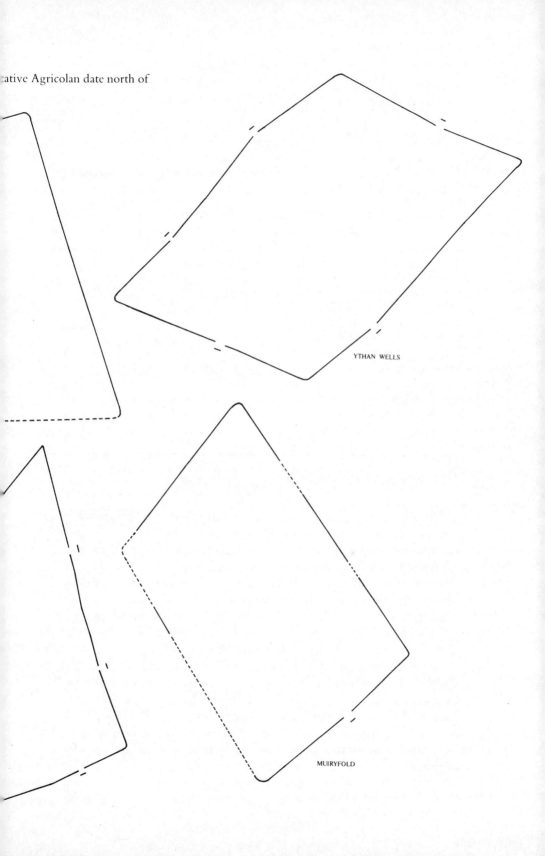

YTHAN WELLS

MUIRYFOLD

Cassius 76, 13, 3), as to those of Agricola. Having said all this, however, the aberrant size and morphology of the camp at Raedykes must always leave open the question of its inclusion within this group at all.

Table 3   Putative large Agricolan camps north of the Mounth

| Site | Area | | Approximate dimensions | Spacing | |
	acres	ha	in metres*	miles	km
Raedykes	93.5	37.8	c.670 × 560		
				5.8	9.2
Normandykes	106	42.8	860 × 495		
				10.8	17.3
Kintore	110	44.5	785 × 575		
				8.8	14.1
Durno	144	58.3	c.930 × 605		
				7.3	11.7
Ythan Wells	111	44.9	810 × 555		
				13.5	21.7
Muiryfold	109	44.1	790 × 555		

*Since the camps are not regular rectangles, the average dimensions provided will not necessarily agree exactly with the quoted area.

This redating of the large northern camps seemed to find further support in the discovery of an even larger example at Durno in Aberdeenshire (fig 21) which is the most recent contender for the site of Mons Graupius. The camp is situated approximately three miles (4.8 km) from the summit of the distinctive granite mountain of Bennachie, whose topography St Joseph carefully relates to Tacitus' account of the battle (1978b, 285). There is no denying the impressive nature of the mountain (pl 13), which is a conspicuous feature of the landscape for some many miles around, nor the apparent concentration of Iron Age hillforts in its vicinity (St Joseph 1978b, 282), though it is interesting to note that some doubt has recently been cast on the likely prehistoric origins of the fort on Bennachie itself (Ralston et al. 1983, 159–60). But the evidence presented to support the identification of Durno as the site of Mons Graupius is all circumstantial and fails to take into consideration a number of problems.

The first difficulty is the presence of a river, the Urie, between the camp and the hill which is not mentioned in Tacitus' account of the battle. Since caution in too close and literal a reading of the text on matters topographical has already been stressed, this objection should not be allowed to loom too large. On the other hand, the date of the camp is far from certain. St Joseph links it with the other large camps north of the Mounth (table 3), into which context it would plausibly fit; its extra large size he explains as the result of the amalgamation of two hitherto independent forces, one accommodated previously in camps of 109 acres, the other using adjacent Stracathro-type camps (Ythan Wells and Auchinhove) as their bivouac (1977, 144). The combination of a 109-acre (44.1-ha) camp with one of c. 33 acres (13.4 ha) adds up to an area extremely close to that of the camp at Durno (c. 144 acres; 58.3 ha). As we have already seen, however, the date of the 109-acre camps is far from clear and, even if they were to prove to be Flavian, they cannot be directly contemporary with the Stracathro-type because at Ythan Wells, only 7.3 miles (11.7 km) away to the north-west, examples of the two types overlap. Although it is clearly unsafe to place much weight on the chronological significance of rates of ditch silting, it is hardly feasible that the two camps could have been separated in time by only a matter of days or, at most, weeks, when some six or seven inches (15–18 cm) of silt had accumulated in the bottom of the earlier ditch prior to the superimposition of the larger camp (St Joseph 1970, 176). Moreover, a force of any size, particularly if accompanied by animals, is likely to have fouled both the ground and the water supply to such an extent that the immediate re-use of the same location would have been a distinctly unattractive proposition (Hanson 1978a, 142).

The very feature which drew particular attention to Durno as a 'unique concentration of military force' in northern Scotland and, therefore, the likely location of Agricola's final battle (St Joseph 1978b, 279) is the best reason for its rejection. Tacitus is surprisingly precise in his account of the size of the Roman forces assembled at Mons Graupius. Some 13,000 auxiliary troops are noted (*Ag.* 33–5), to which should be added a large legionary contingent. Since all four legions were already weakened by troop withdrawals to the German wars (*I.L.S.* 1025 and 9200), the total figure cannot have exceeded 30,000 and was probably rather less. St Joseph himself postulates only 20,000 Roman troops in attendance (1978b, 283), while Mann has recently suggested that there were no more than 17,000 (1986, 23). The density of troop dispositions within Roman temporary camps is disputed, with estimates varying from as few as 240 men per acre (*c.* 600 men per hectare) to twice that figure (Hanson 1978b, 142-3). Even with the most generous allowance of space, the maximum number of troops likely to have been present at Mons Graupius could have been housed in a camp no larger than 125 acres (50.6 ha). Coincidentally, a density of 300 men per acre (*c.* 750 men per hectare) and a force of 28,000 troops, both reasonable estimates, would give a required acreage almost exactly equal to the size of the camp at Raedykes. Clearly not too much emphasis can be placed on such precise equations, but the camp at Durno is too large for the forces known to be at Agricola's disposal. Nor can the additional space be explained away in terms of a larger than normal baggage train accompanying the troops, for Tacitus uses the word *expeditus* when referring to the army (*Ag.* 29), which is normally taken to mean that it was marching light (Ogilvie and Richmond 1967, 251). On the other hand, the one occasion when we do know that a force of sufficient size to fill the camp was operating in Scotland is during the campaigns of Severus (Reed 1976, 96), and the morphology of the camp at Durno, like the other large camps with which it has been linked, is most closely paralleled by the third-century AD camps south of the Mounth.

A more northerly location for the battle was favoured by Burn, and followed by other eminent scholars (Ogilvie and Richmond 1967, 65 and 252), influenced by the much earlier discovery of the Stracathro-type camp at Auchinhove in Banffshire (Burn 1953b). His suggested identification of Mons Graupius was the conspicuous cone of Knock Hill, overlooking the Pass of Grange, where the Grampians again come close to the sea between Buchan and the plains of Moray, although perversely he denied the relevance of any predictability in Agricola's line of march (1953b, 131). The topography of the battle was linked to nearby Sillyearn Hill, but Auchinhove was seen as the first step *after* the battle for it was some three miles (4.8 km) beyond it to the south-east. Though the Flavian date of the Stracathro-type camp there is assured, its estimated size (*c.* 32 acres; 13 ha) is too small to accommodate even all the auxiliary troops present at the battle. A further camp of more appropriate size (109 acres; 44.1 ha) was subsequently discovered slightly nearer at Muiryfold, but it still lies beyond, that is to the west of, the proposed battle site and is in any case of uncertain date (see above).

So far none of the various identifications put forward are conclusive, for the supporting evidence in each case is deficient in some respect. For the time being we can only fall back on the implication of Tacitus' narrative that a northern location is likely. Indeed, this argument has recently been pushed to its logical extreme and a case made for the most northerly tip of Scotland (Henderson 1984, 28). Not until the battlefield is located archaeologically will the debate be resolved. Mass burials of men and horses associated with broken arms and equipment may yet come to light as they have recently at Gellep in Germany, the site of the final battle of the Batavian revolt (Ruger 1980, 496–7). The only discoveries in the vicinity of any of the sites so far discussed are the wheels from Raedykes, though the well known carnyx or celtic war-trumpet from Deskford, Banffshire, should not be overlooked (pl 14): its identification, date and location all seem appropriate (Macgregor 1976, 87–9). Taking a broader historical perspective, however, the *precise* location of the battle is an irrelevance: only if it took place in the extreme north or the extreme south would its discovery have any effect on our interpretation of Agricola's campaigns.

What of the battle itself? On the Roman side perhaps 20,000–30,000 men were assembled, fairly equally divided between auxiliary and legionary troops. Tacitus is quite precise in his figures for the former: 8000 infantry in the centre were flanked by 3000 cavalry with a further four cavalry *alae*, some 2000 men, in reserve (*Ag.* 35 and 37). He subsequently names some of the infantry units present: four cohorts of Batavians, two cohorts of Tungrians and an unspecified number of Britons recruited from the tribes in the south long since conquered. The identification of these units is not certain. Two Batavian cohorts (*cohortes I* and *VIII Batavorum*) are attested epigraphically in Britain, one at the end of the first century AD the other early in the second (Holder 1982, 114), but others may have been transferred to the Danube where *cohors II Batavorum* was among the units whose dead were commemorated on the monument at Adamclisi, for the list also records a unit of uncertain identification which included two British recruits (Birley 1953, 21). On the other hand *cohortes I* and *II Tungrorum milliariae*, the latter part-mounted, still formed part of the garrison of Britain in the fourth century AD (Breeze and Dobson 1976, 251). The British troops may have been present in their own ethnic cohort, a *cohors Brittonum*, for such are attested serving overseas, but are perhaps more likely to have been recruited into already established units (Dobson and Mann 1972, 198–9).

Against them were allegedly ranged more than 30,000 Caledonians. Although the complement of Roman troops present was information which might have been fairly readily available to

Tacitus, the numbers of the enemy, if not entirely imaginary, will have been derived from Roman estimates. Given the difficulty of assessing the size of any large assembly with accuracy, the general tendency to exaggerate the size of the opposition and Tacitus' specific desire to show Agricola in the best possible light, it is more than probable that this figure is inflated. Indeed, Agricola seems to have judged that only 11,000 auxiliary troops would suffice for his front line, the legions, and a further 2000 auxiliary cavalry, being kept in reserve.

Fighting began with an exchange of missiles (*Ag.* 36). Then the auxiliary infantry in the centre advanced in close order pushing with their shields and stabbing with their swords as they were trained to do. Rapidly the Britons were pushed back. Meanwhile the cavalry had engaged the charioteers. Exactly how these war chariots operated is uncertain. Caesar, who had faced them in southern England more than a century earlier, is quite specific in describing them mainly as a means of transport to enable the warrior speedily to approach or retire from an engagement which was fought on foot (*de Bello Gallico* 4, 33). Yet his praise for their skill in manoeuvring the chariots at high speed, including the ability to walk along the yoke pole, and his reference to the hurling of missiles from chariots on the move, implies a method of operation not unlike that of the cavalry. But they are unlikely to have been numerous, since they will have represented the wealthy warrior elite, and were thus quickly routed. The Roman cavalry then began to wreak havoc on the British infantry until the terrain and the packed ranks brought them to a halt. The Britons on the hill tops, who had so far only watched the engagement, then descended to threaten the exposed rear, but were cut off and scattered by the four cavalry units which Agricola had kept in reserve (*Ag.* 37). The turning point came when these troops then attacked the remaining Britons in their rear. British resistance crumbled and the battle turned into a full-scale rout, with only a fleeting resurgence of resistance under cover of the nearby woods. The Romans were able to mop up till night fell.

According to Tacitus it was a Roman victory of some magnitude: 10,000 Britons dead for the loss of only 360 on the Roman side (*Ag.* 37). The former figure is likely to have been as exaggerated as the original estimate of the numbers present, while the latter may have been provided for dramatic effect to highlight the extent of Roman superiority, for Tacitus generally omits the numbers of Romans slain (Ogilvie and Richmond 1967, 280). It may, however, be claimed that the battle need not have been an exceptional victory, for even accepting Tacitus' figures for the number of Britons present, the two sides would have been fairly evenly balanced numerically, despite Tacitus' assertion to the contrary. Yet the natives were no match for the Romans in open battle. Tacitus mentions Roman superior weaponry, particularly their short thrusting swords, but this should not be taken to imply any great technological supremacy. Rather it reflects a difference in military tactics which came about as the result of the true Roman superiority: training, organisation and discipline. Tacitus himself stresses that 'the soldiers had been well drilled in this form of sword fighting, while the enemy were awkward at it' (*Ag.* 36). More importantly the Romans fought as a team, not simply as separate individuals. This is not to suggest that the Britons were a totally disorganised rabble, but they were facing professional and highly trained troops. In such circumstances the end result was rarely in doubt (Hanson and Maxwell 1983, 23–9). Thus, Agricola could afford to keep his legions in reserve, and the very fact that they were not employed simply serves to emphasise the ease with which the victory was achieved. Nor can the victory be put down to any outstanding or unusual tactics employed. He simply applied the well tried principles of a central infantry thrust, protected by cavalry on the wings, with reserve forces to combat any outflanking movement which might threaten the rear. Thus the battle was conducted, and won, with typical Roman efficiency; no more, no less.

What of reaction in Rome? The victory was well received and due honour paid to Agricola:

> Domitian therefore directed that the customary decorations of a triumph, the honour of a complimentary statue, and all the substitutes for a triumphal procession, should be voted to Agricola in the Senate, coupled with a highly flattering address. (*Ag.* 40)

Whether Domitian also took an imperial acclamation is uncertain, but probable. His third, the only one certainly attested on the coinage of AD 83, appears far too early in the year to relate to Mons Graupius (Buttrey 1980, 37). His fifth is first recorded at the very beginning of AD 84, so either it or his fourth acclamation could have been prompted by Agricola's victory. But the suggestion that it was further commemorated by a special coin issue has already been dismissed (above, p 42). Nor is there any need to herald the success as particularly outstanding: between March AD 82 and September AD 84 Domitian amassed six imperial acclamations (Buttrey 1980, 30).

Since the summer was already over and the enemy were not regrouping, Agricola began his return to winter quarters. According to Tacitus he led his army into the territory of the Boresti where he took hostages (*Ag.* 38). It is particularly ironic that one of the few ethnic names found in Tacitus' narrative is not attested elsewhere, so the location of this tribe remains a mystery. Various suggestions have been put forward. The name was at one time linked with modern Forres in Moray (Burn 1953b, 129), but the etymological basis for such a connection has been shown to be false (Ogilvie and Richmond 1967, 282). Recently attention has been drawn once more to a possible etymological link between the Boresti and the mythical dwellers at the top of the world, the Hyperboreans, implying a classical allusion to the northern tip of Britain (Henderson 1984, 28). Alternatively, it has been suggested that the problems presented by Ptolemy's listing of tribal attributions in northern Scotland, particularly in respect of the Vacomagi (above, p 117), might be resolved if the Boresti were actually located in Angus and had been omitted from his text in error (Breeze 1982, 29–31). At present no solution presents itself, though their location in Angus would suit the hint of differentiation in the native settlement pattern north and south of the Mounth, while the fact that hostages were taken confirms the formal conquest of the territory concerned and would tie in well with the extent of subsequent fort construction. Agricola then proceeded back to winter quarters, presumably to forts on the isthmus and in southern Scotland. Tacitus says he moved with deliberate slowness in order to impress and overawe the *new* tribes through whose territory he passed (*Ag.* 38). Taken literally this makes it difficult to accept a line of march skirting the Highlands, for the peoples there would already have been well familiar with the sight of Roman arms. Either Tacitus was being rather loose in his terminology, or we must postulate an alternative route south, perhaps down the Great Glen or following the valleys of the Spey and then the Tummel to reach Perthshire. Either of these would imply a more northerly location for the Boresti, perhaps in Moray, but at present we lack any archaeological confirmation of such a line of march.

Meanwhile the fleet, who had been assigned troops and ordered to circumnavigate the island, returned at about the same time as Agricola's land forces (*Ag.* 38). This particular passage has been much debated, for once more Tacitus' clipped style makes the exact meaning obscure. In particular the extent of the circumnavigation and the point to which the fleet returned is uncertain. The named port, Portus Trucculensis, does not help matters for it is otherwise unattested. Since place names are notoriously prone to error in the course of their transmission in the manuscript sources, various emendations have been put forward. One suggestion would equate the name with the Tunnocelum of the Notitia Dignitatum, known to be located on the southern shore of the Solway estuary (Hind 1974), but the likelihood of the suggested derivation is in doubt (Rivet and Smith 1979, 478–9). More fundamentally, however, the archaeological evidence indicates that Cumbria had not been occupied by Agricola's forces (below, pp 161–2), so that such a location for a fleet base at this time is highly improbable. Others have favoured a connection with Rutupiae (Richborough), which was certainly a naval base, Trucculensem in the text deriving from the emendation of the adjectival form Rutupensem (Ogilvie and Richmond 1967, 282). Though this change is relatively easy palaeographically, Rutupiae is one of the more widely known Romano-British place-names and as such perhaps less likely to have become corrupted to such an extent. Moreover, the adjectival form of the name plus *portus* is something of a circumlocution which, on analogy with other well-known port names, is unlikely to have been used for Richborough, while the more usual form, Rutupiae, could not easily have been corrupted to Trucculensem. The adjectival form of the latter better fits direct reference to a geographical feature, probably a river, in the absence of an established settlement name (Rivet and Smith 1979, 479). Nor does reference to a base on the south coast of England seem entirely relevant to Tacitus' narrative at this point. That Ugrulentum in the Ravenna Cosmography is a transformed version of Trucculensis is a further possibility (Reed 1971, 147–8), for that eighth-century AD list of place-names is notoriously corrupt. But other than suggesting a location north of the Forth–Clyde isthmus, this gets us no further since the Ravenna lacks sufficient logic in its organisation to allow the identification to be further refined (Rivet and Smith 1979, 212 and 478). The reference to a return *from* Portus Trucculensis has generally been taken to imply that the fleet reached only as far as a point, sailing from the east coast, which they had attained previously when operating in the west. By retracing their steps down the eastern coast the circumnavigation would have been achieved as the result of two separate operations (Burn 1969, 53). This seems an unnecessarily convoluted explanation and not really a true circumnavigation at all. More satisfactory would be to see Portus Trucculensis as a point in the extreme north which the fleet reached before returning along the other side of the island to its unnamed base. That a full circumnavigation was achieved is implied earlier in Tacitus' narrative when the Orkneys were subjugated and Thule, a name wrongly here applied to

Shetland, sighted, but further landings were prevented by the onset of winter (*Ag.* 10).

In the following spring or early summer (AD 84) Agricola finally returned to Rome after seven years in office in Britain. He had served more than twice the normal period (Birley 1981, 397–9) and had just reported a significant victory: his recall can have come as no surprise.

· 7 ·

THE ANATOMY OF
WITHDRAWAL

It has been widely assumed that all the Flavian forts north of the Forth–Clyde isthmus were established by Agricola (Frere 1978, 135–6). Indeed, in the past it has even been argued that the legionary fortress at Inchtuthil in Perthshire acted as Agricola's base for operations in the far north (Burn 1953b, 128–9). But once again Agricolan has become an overworked adjective. Simply because the forts are of Flavian date does not mean that they should be attributed to him. On the contrary, his involvement is becoming increasingly difficult to substantiate.

It has recently been argued that Agricola built no forts whatever north of the isthmus, mainly because Tacitus makes no mention of such activity (Breeze and Dobson 1976, 128; Breeze 1982, 53). We might well have expected that fort building, the physical confirmation that the area had been subjugated, would have deserved such mention. On the other hand it would have added little to the dramatic narrative and may even have been seen as a distinct anti-climax after the victory at Mons Graupius. It is thus rather unsafe to place too much stress on the negative evidence provided by Tacitus' account, and a reasonable case has already been made for the early establishment of forts probably as far north as Bertha (above, pp 120–1). However, this applies only to the forts which demonstrate two periods of occupation, all of which lie along the only road known beyond the isthmus. What of the rest? Debate centres on whether Agricola had time to indulge in fort construction during his last two years. It is highly improbable that he would have had much opportunity during the campaigning season, despite our ignorance of his actions in the early part of his last campaign, but this is not really a valid argument. Fort building usually occupied the winter months and did not normally impinge upon the period of active campaigning unless the whole season was devoted to it in order to consolidate an area previously overrun (Breeze 1980, 19–21; Hanson 1986a). If in theory there was time in the winter between Agricola's sixth and seventh seasons, was there the opportunity? As already

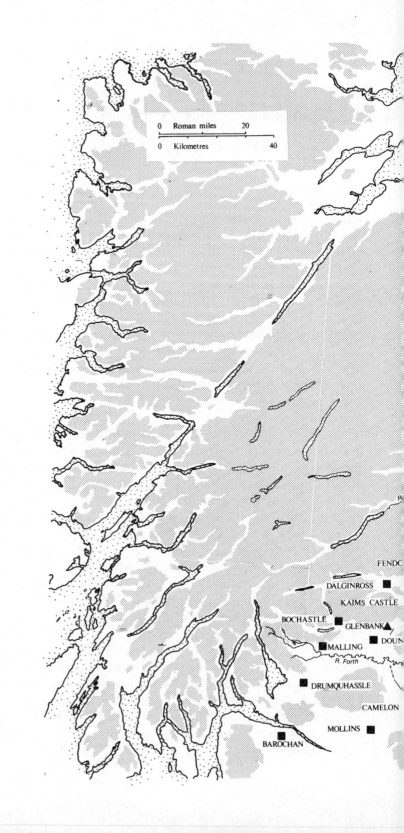

FEND[O]

DALGINROSS ■

KAIMS CASTLE

BOCHASTLE ■ GLENBANK▲

■MALLING   DOU[N]

R. Forth

■ DRUMQUHASSLE

CAMELON

MOLLINS ■

BAROCHAN

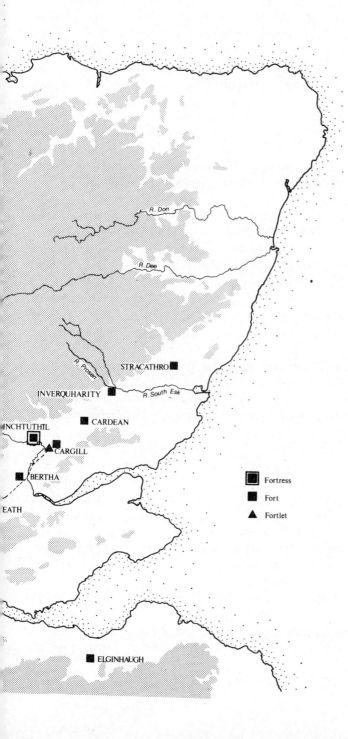

R. Don

R. Dee

R. Prosen

STRACATHRO ■

INVERQUHARITY ■

R. South Esk

■ CARDEAN

INCHTUTHIL ▣

▲ CARGILL

■ BERTHA

EATH

■ ELGINHAUGH

▣ Fortress

■ Fort

▲ Fortlet

noted, the process of Roman conquest and consolidation followed a fairly set pattern (above, pp 50–1). It was not a piecemeal affair. Forts were not constructed until the tribe occupying a particular area had been conquered. Manifestly Agricola did not achieve the conquest of any tribes north of the Tay before the battle of Mons Graupius. Fort building in northern Perthshire and Angus would have been premature before the winter following his seventh campaign, yet Agricola was recalled soon after his slow march back to winter quarters. At best he may have left orders for the work to begin in the spring, but can hardly have supervised its implementation. Fort building was probably left to his immediate successor. Nor should this be seen as at all out of the ordinary. As we have noted, Agricola himself was responsible for the construction of forts in northern England several years after the territory had been conquered by Cerialis (above, pp 65–8).

The conclusion that Agricola built few forts north of the Forth–Clyde isthmus is not without support in the archaeological evidence. The first point is obvious from the disposition of Flavian forts in the area. They are too densely distributed, too close together, for them all to have been contemporary (fig 22). Except along frontier lines, the normal spacing between forts established in conquered territory was some 10–20 miles (16–32 km). This is followed by forts along the road from Camelon to Bertha with the exception of the much closer distance between Ardoch and Strageath. But the outer line of forts, usually referred to as the Highland line or the glen-blocking forts, is too close by. Dalginross lies only eight miles (12.9 km) from both Ardoch and Strageath, and Fendoch seven miles (11.3 km) from the latter, though the nature of the terrain might add a mile to any journey between them. Even more striking, less than three miles (4.8 km) separates the legionary fortress at Inchtuthil from a Flavian fortlet at Cargill, immediately adjacent to which a further Flavian fort was recently discovered from the air (Rankov 1982, 335–6). One of the Cargill sites, perhaps the fortlet, could be contemporary with the legionary fortress intended to guard an important river crossing, but the additional fort, which itself shows signs of possibly two or even three phases of occupation, indicates that the consolidation of the area must have been a more complex process than is usually assumed.

If the argument that the inner line of road posts was an early development is correct (above, pp 120–1), then the outer line including Inchtuthil, if not contemporary, ought logically to be later. The evidence from excavations at Inchtuthil lends some support.

Although the date at which the fortress was founded has not been defined precisely, its abandonment may be placed no earlier than AD 86 or 87 because of the recovery of several unworn bronze coins (*asses*) of that date (Robertson 1968, 61–3) (pl 18). Yet building work was still incomplete (fig 23): the *praetorium*, the legate's private accommodation, had not been started; nor had several of his officers' houses, the internal bath-building or at least two of the granaries (Pitts and St Joseph 1985, 117, 136 and 187). The small external bath-house, though built, seems not to have been used, for the stoke holes of the hot rooms had never been fired (Pitts and St Joseph 1985,

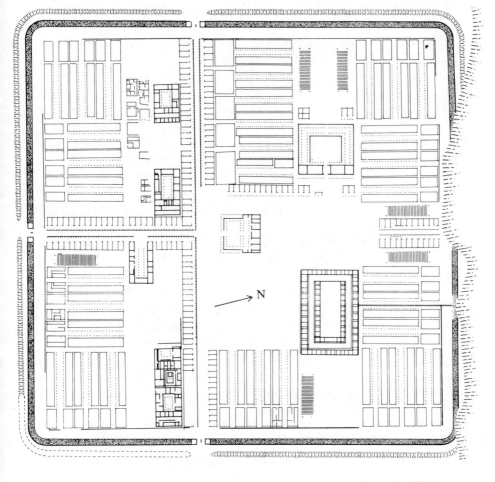

L____I 50 m

23 Incomplete legionary fortress at Inchtuthil (after Richmond) (by permission of Edinburgh University Press)

216), nor apparently had all the cooking ovens inside the fortress (Ogilvie and Richmond 1967, 71 *contra* Pitts and St Joseph 1985, 200). It remains uncertain how long the construction of a 53.5-acre (21.7-ha) timber legionary fortress would have taken, but probably considerably less than the minimum three or four years between the departure of Agricola and the abandonment of the site. By extrapolating from experimental reconstruction work at Baginton, a period of only two weeks was suggested for the construction of the rampart around a legionary fortress if half its garrison, some 2500–3000 men, had been employed (Hobley 1971, 31). The addition of a five feet (1.5 m) wide stone wall at Inchtuthil will obviously have increased the time taken but not excessively, for stone was quarried only two miles (3.2 km) away at Gourdie among other places. The speed at which the internal timber buildings would have been erected is more problematical. It has long been assumed that the timber was converted and stockpiled in advance, the buildings possibly even pre-fabricated. If true, very rapid assembly might have been achieved on site, as was demonstrated by the experimental reconstruction of a gateway and a granary at Baginton (Hobley 1974). Unfortunately this hypothesis is no longer tenable (Hanson 1978c and 1986a). On the other hand, local extraction and conversion of suitable timber and the fabrication of buildings on site need not have delayed the construction excessively. Even with only half the legion employed the whole process is likely to have taken months rather than years. Indeed, it was this very requirement of speedy erection which largely dictated the choice of building materials employed.

The auxiliary forts which skirt the Highlands north and south of Inchtuthil are generally seen as contemporary because they appear to form such a coherent strategic disposition of forces that the discovery of missing elements was predictable with some degree of accuracy. In 1967 Ogilvie and Richmond postulated at least two further forts to the south of Bochastle (1967, 67) and, indeed, two were subsequently discovered by aerial reconnaissance at Malling (pl 15) and Drumquhassle (Maxwell 1983a, 168–72). The forts are all located at the mouths of glens emanating from the Highland massif: Fendoch in the Sma' Glen (pl 16), Dalginross at the head of Strathearn, Bochastle by the Pass of Leny, Malling (Mentieth) at the head of the Forth and Drumquhassle at the south-east end of Loch Lomond covering Strathblane. Hence they are frequently referred to as the glen-blocking forts. The examples to the north of Inchtuthil, however, do not fit this generic description quite so well. The large forts in Angus at Cardean and Stracathro, both *c.* 6.5 acres (2.4 ha) in area, are situated in the centre of Strathmore and might better be seen in strategic terms as a continuation of the inner line of forts. But the recently discovered small fort between them at Inverquharity (*c.* 1.3 acres; 0.5 ha) (pl 17), whose Flavian date is implied by its proximity to a Stracathro-type camp, is ideally located to control the mouths of Glen Prosen and Glen Cova, which may indicate that the double line of forts attested to the south of Inchtuthil also continued northwards (Frere 1984, 274).

The function that the Highland line forts were intended to perform has also been a subject of debate in recent years. Their earlier classification as glen-blocking forts carried with it an assumption of a defensive role, to prevent egress from the Highland massif into the more fertile lowland fringe (Ogilvie and Richmond 1967, 74). Recently this view has been challenged and an offensive role postulated, the forts supposedly intended as a spring-board for further advance by Agricola's successor (Breeze and Dobson 1976, 128; Breeze 1982, 55–6). Such a debate is not readily resolved, but may in any case be irrelevant. The location of the legionary fortress at the very limit of the occupied area is paralleled by the early establishment of a fortress in South Wales at Usk (Manning 1981, 31–8) and is almost certainly indicative of an intention to continue campaigning in the north, though there seems no real justification in categorising it as a special form of campaigning fortress (Frere 1980b *contra* Petrikovits 1975, 119–20). Auxiliary forts, however, were not located with such considerations in mind. They were usually placed on strategic routes to control movement and police the local area. When further campaigns of conquest were to be undertaken, troops would be assembled from a number of forts to accompany one or more legions. Such a requirement would not be readily facilitated by deploying the auxiliary troops in forts not directly linked by road and dispersed over a distance of some 85 miles (137 km). The consistent topographical location of the Highland line forts does suggest that they were intended primarily to control movement through the glens, an interpretation further supported at Fendoch where the watchtower to the west of the fort is ideally situated to warn of any such activity. As to the direction of this traffic, whether into or out of the Highland massif, we have no evidence.

Further campaigns may have been conducted, but after the recall of Agricola Tacitus' biography is concerned with affairs at Rome, and the relevant portion of his *Histories*, which might have shed some light on the question, does not survive. As yet, however, no marching camps have been found up the glens, though the larger Stracathro-type camps adjacent to some of the Highland line forts could as easily relate to operations at this time as during Agricola's governorship. Whatever action was taken, it was only short-lived. Having carefully charted the Roman advance into Scotland we must now retrace our steps, for within twenty or twenty-five years of Agricola's recall all his conquests in Scotland had been abandoned. All the forts north and west of the inner road line which have been examined show only one period of occupation. It was this very fact which allowed the reconstruction of virtually the complete plan of the fort at Fendoch (fig 24) on the basis of only very limited sampling. Hints of a second period of occupation at Dalginross and Bochastle may be dismissed. The outer rampart at the former (pl 12) is more likely to demarcate an annexe to the $c.3.5$-acre (1.5-ha) fort rather than a larger establishment of different date, for such features are commonly associated with Flavian forts, and trial excavation suggested that the outer enclosure was not permanently occupied (Robertson 1963, 196–8). At Bochastle the discrepancies in levels noted during excavation within the fort (Anderson 1956, 61) are best explained as the result of partial flooding at the site.

Extensive excavations at Inchtuthil, Fendoch and Cardean have demonstrated quite graphically the systematic demolition and evacuation of these establishments after only a short period of

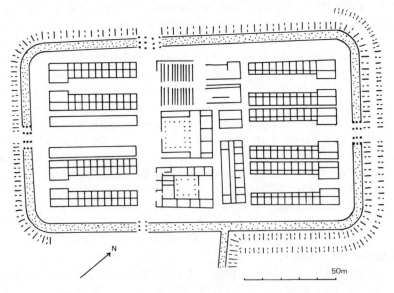

24 Plan of the auxiliary fort at Fendoch (after Richmond and McIntyre)

occupation. At Inchtuthil the massive gate timbers and the smaller posts of the internal buildings were pulled out leaving a scatter of bent nails of all sizes, the wattle and daub infilling from the latter being collected together and burnt in bonfires (Taylor 1954, 84–5; Pitts and St Joseph 1985, 52). Glass and pottery from store rooms along the main road in the fortress, the *via principalis*, was thrown into the gutter of the colonnade which bordered that road, while iron wheel tyres and nearly 10 tons of mainly unused nails were buried in a huge pit in the front range of the workshop (Pitts and St Joseph 1985, 109–12, 180 and 280). At Fendoch the timbers of the gates and internal buildings were dug out of their pits and construction trenches, the backfill of the latter containing broken and twisted nails, and even a discarded sword (Richmond and McIntyre 1939, 140–2). The buildings at Cardean revealed a similar picture with broken glass and pottery neatly disposed of in the ditch-ends (Robertson 1975b, 9). This clear evidence of deliberate evacuation is usually extrapolated to the remaining forts of the Highland line, though examination of the other sites has not been sufficiently extensive to confirm this.

The date of this abandonment is quite well fixed. Low-denomination bronze coins, *asses*, of AD 86 have been recovered from Stracathro, Dalginross and the legionary fortress at Inchtuthil (pl 18), and provide a *terminus post quem*, though one coin from the last may date from the following year. The presence of all four main reverse types issued in AD 86 would suggest that the date of the arrival of the coins was no earlier than the latter half of the year, probably in a shipment direct from Rome to pay the troops, perhaps linked to Domitian's raising of legionaries' pay (Robertson 1968, 61–3; 1977, 72–3). All the coins are in virtually mint condition and as such are unlikely to have been long in circulation before being lost. We may reasonably suggest, therefore, that the withdrawal from these Highland line forts took place some time in AD 87.

That this was a deliberate decision and, moreover, a clear reversal of policy, is self evident. There is no question of the Romans being expelled from the north. No excavation has revealed any signs of enemy action against Roman installations, nor of a particularly hasty departure by their occupants. The demolition was orderly and methodical. Work of consolidation was still under way as the unfinished fortress at Inchtuthil makes clear. Moreover, the huge cache of unused nails from the site implies that further auxiliary fort construction was envisaged for the number of nails, over three-quarters of a million, seems far too great solely for the construction of the rest of the fortress (*contra* Angus *et al.* 1962, 956–7). A context for this change of plan is not far to seek in military actions elsewhere in the empire. Domitian himself had begun campaigning against the Chatti in northern Germany in AD 83 and, as has already been noted (above, p 135), had called for vexillations from all the British legions even before Agricola had reached Mons Graupius. This war was concluded successfully, but major problems arose along the Danube. Serious incursions by the Dacians, occupying modern Rumania, occurred in AD 85. A punitive expedition sent into their territory met with disaster: the general Oppius Sabinus, was killed and many troops lost. A second expedition, probably in AD 86 also ran into trouble and its leader, Cornelius Fuscus, met his death in battle. Eventually in AD 88 after careful preparations Tettius Julianus achieved victory on Dacian soil at Tapae (Garzetti 1974, 287–90). The need to avenge two major defeats with their consequent troop losses will have necessitated the transfer of forces from other provinces. We know that *legio II Adiutrix*, stationed at Chester under Agricola, was involved in these actions, for one of its centurions was decorated in the Dacian war (*I.L.S.* 9193) probably in AD 88. Nor would the legion have been sent unaccompanied. *Cohors II Batavorum* and an unnamed unit containing at least two British soldiers are among those whose dead are commemorated on the famous altar at Adamclisi in Moesia (*I.L.S.* 9107), though exactly when they were transferred from Britain is unclear for it remains uncertain whether this monument records those killed under Oppius Sabinus or Cornelius Fuscus or in Trajan's Dacian wars. In addition troopers of *ala I Pannoniorum Tampiana* and *ala I Tungrorum*, both part of the British army, are recorded on tombstones at Carnuntum in Pannonia (*C.I.L.* 4466 and 6485). Such troop withdrawals cannot but have pushed the already stretched army in Britain to the limit. The need to fill the important strategic base at Chester, where rebuilding is attested at about this time (McPeake 1978, 16), meant the withdrawal of the legion from Inchtuthil, probably the XXth, while the removal of auxiliary units must have necessitated the giving up of some of the territory already garrisoned. Britain was, after all, a remote peripheral province: the Danube was closer to the heart of the empire.

The Romans did not, it seems, intend to cast off their recent conquests entirely. The logical point at which to draw a line, across the isthmus, had already been so employed a few years earlier. Beyond it the road from Camelon to Bertha may still have been held, for unlike the forts of the Highland line those along the road tend to provide hints of two phases of occupation. It has been suggested above (above, pp 120–1) that the first phases at Ardoch, Strageath and perhaps the fort at Cargill indicated their employment as outpost forts during the temporary halt on the isthmus in Agricola's fourth campaign. Subsequently, unless they continued to be held in order to control the road line, they may have been left unoccupied while the Highland line forts were in use, for their close proximity would otherwise make contemporary occupation largely superfluous, as was noted at the beginning of this chapter. Thus, the second phases of occupation in the road forts might best seem to relate to this primary withdrawal.

It is into this context, when the road line was serving as the northernmost limit of Roman occupation, that the series of timber towers between Ardoch and Bertha would seem to fit, for they provide clear evidence that the line was functioning as part of a frontier. As such they are not relevant to the fluid situation which prevailed during Agricola's campaigns, unless they relate to the earlier halt on the isthmus.★ Unfortunately they cannot be dated more precisely than to the Flavian period and even this attribution is based on only two fragments of pottery, one found during excavations at Gask House (Robertson 1974, 20–1) the other from recent work at Westerton (Friell and Hanson forthcoming). Several of the more northerly posts have long been known for they still survive as earthworks (pl 19). They are located on a low ridge running east–west between Strageath and Bertha, the Gask ridge, which has given its name to the system. Air reconnaissance his filled out the original line at both ends and demonstrated that it continued at least as far south as Ardoch and probably beyond[1] (fig 25) bringing the total of towers known at present to fifteen or possibly sixteen if a further example recently noted from the air in the vicinity of Huntingtower is confirmed (information from Mr G.S. Maxwell).

Each of the sites consists of a square or rectangular timber tower some 2.5–3.5 m in dimension, surrounded by a small bank or rampart set within a circular ditch some 15 m in internal diameter (fig 26). That this was intended to provide at least a measure of protection is suggested by the provision of a second ditch around the most southerly examples. The size of the posts, where traces survive, and of the pits into which they were set indicates that the towers

[1] Aerial reconnaissance in 1986 revealed a further tower between Ardoch and the fortlet at Glenbank and confirmed that in the vicinity of Huntingtower (information from G.S. Maxwell). This brings the total up to seventeen and suggests that the system may well have continued at least as far south as the crossing of the river Forth.

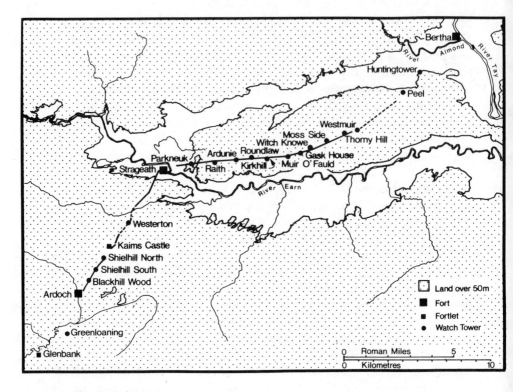

25 The Gask frontier

would have been at least two storeys high. Though often described as signal towers, this presumed function is likely to have been only secondary. If the primary intention had been to facilitate the relay of information down the line to the fort garrisons, then the number of intermediate posts would have been kept to a minimum, both to reduce the risk of human error and maximise the speed of transmission. In such circumstances the towers need not be evenly distributed, the only criterion for their location being ready intervisibility between adjacent examples. If we take the most completely known section along the Gask ridge, the spacing between the eleven towers is quite close and does not exceed one mile (1.6 km) (table 4). This indicates that they were intended primarily as watch towers, presumably to oversee movement across a cleared strip of land on either side of the road by which they lay. As such they clearly demarcate a precise boundary, an interpretation also supported by the further reduction of the already close spacing between the garrison forts with the addition of a fortlet at Kaims

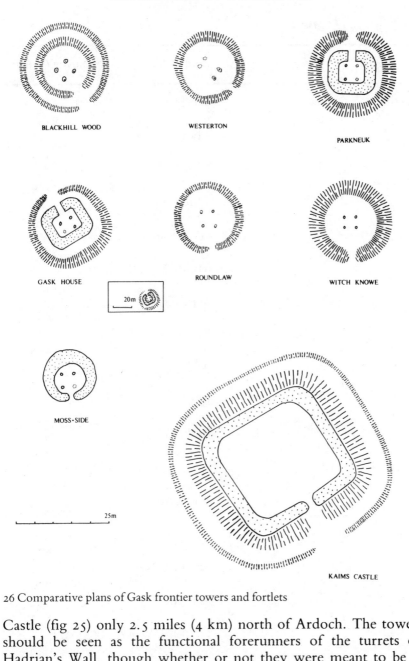

26 Comparative plans of Gask frontier towers and fortlets

Castle (fig 25) only 2.5 miles (4 km) north of Ardoch. The towers should be seen as the functional forerunners of the turrets on Hadrian's Wall, though whether or not they were meant to be as regularly distributed is uncertain, for there is no consistent pattern in their spacing (table 4). The three most southerly examples are quite evenly spaced, an impression confirmed by the inclusion of the

Table 4   *The Gask Frontier*

Fort/fortlet	Spacing in miles	Watchtower	Spacing in metres
Bertha		Westmuir	
			c.915
		Thorny Hill	
			1400
		Moss Side	
			1120
		Witch Knowe	
			800
		Gask House	
			870
	13.6	Muir O' Fauld	
			1440
		Kirkhill	
			960
		Roundlaw	
			1110
		Ardunie	
			1510
		Raith	
			1520
		Parkneuk	
			1750
Strageath			
			c.4200
	3.9	Westerton	
			2300
Kaims Castle			
			875
		Shielhill N.	
			950
	2.3	Shielhill S.	
			875
		Blackhill Wood	
			900
Ardoch			
	3.1		
Glenbank			

distance to the north gate at Ardoch at one end and to the fortlet at Kaims Castle at the other. But the distances separating those along the Gask ridge proper are rather more variable. The underlying measurement may have been the Roman mile (1480 m), or fractions thereof; several are close to that distance apart and two of the posts, Parkneuk and Gask House, are exactly 5 Roman miles apart (Rivet 1964, 197). However, there is no certainty that even in the best preserved section all the examples have been found. Clearly the system is not complete between Strageath and Kaims Castle or beyond Westmuir. The discovery from the air of a fortlet at Glenbank some three miles (4.8 km) south of Ardoch may hint at the continuation of the line even further south. The best parallel for the Gask frontier is provided by the Taunus–Wetterau *limes* in Germany which was almost exactly contemporary in its construction. Here a line of forts was supplemented by watchtowers normally at intervals of 500–600 m, but up to 1000 m apart on level ground (Schönberger 1969, 159).

The demarcation of a frontier along this line may at first seem rather strange, for the choice is not an obvious topographical one. However, the position is ideally situated to control movement across Strathearn either from the west or the north and there can be little doubt that this desire was determined by the political geography of the area. The question of the allegiance of the Venicones in Fife, Kinross and Clackmannan has already been raised (above, p 120) and it is difficult to avoid the conclusion that this frontier was intended to define what might be termed a protectorate; to keep control of an area which had the dual advantages of being both agriculturally wealthy and politically pro-Roman.

The policy was short-lived. After examination of the samian pottery from all the forts north of the Forth–Clyde isthmus, it was concluded that none could have continued in occupation after *c.* AD 90 because of the absence of the work of particular known and well-dated potters (Hartley 1972, 13–14). Once again the withdrawal seems to have been a policy decision. There are no signs of destruction in the forts or towers examined, on the contrary the evidence is of deliberate demolition. At Shielhill North (St Joseph 1973, 218), Sheilhill South (St Joseph 1977, 138) and Westerton (Friell and Hanson forthcoming) disturbance of the postholes indicated that the timber uprights forming the main structure of the watch tower had been dug out. The fort at Strageath had also been systematically demolished: the discarded wattle-and-daub wall fabric had been collected into heaps and burnt, the lining of the large water tank in the *principia* (headquarters building) had been removed and the hole backfilled with turf and clay (Frere 1979, 39–41).

The geographical extent of this stage of withdrawal is uncertain (fig 27). The isthmus might seem the logical line to have held, but apart from one piece of Flavian-Trajanic samian from the Antonine Wall fort at Castlecary, which is unlikely to have survived to be discarded during the Antonine occupation, there is a lack of supporting evidence. Moreover, limited examination of Elginhaugh at the northern end of Dere Street just south of the Firth of Forth suggested only one period of occupation before the fort was deliberately demolished (Maxwell 1983a, 174), a conclusion which subsequent large-scale work has confirmed, with only one phase of construction evident in the buildings examined (pl 20). In contrast, those sites south of the isthmus where occupation after AD 90 has been identified all reveal a second structural phase. Similarly the forts at Castledykes (Robertson 1964, 103–19), Easter Happrew (Steer 1957, 97) and Crawford have demonstrated only one period of Flavian occupation. Only in the latter case, however, was the evidence sufficient to confirm that the internal buildings had been deliberately demolished, a slightly worn *as* of AD 86 providing a useful *terminus post quem* for abandonment of the site (Maxwell 1972, 167–9). The excavator of the fort at Castledykes suggested that it may have been burnt down (Robertson 1964, 264), but the traces of burnt daub and charcoal recovered from the very limited trenching of the internal buildings could be just as readily interpreted as the remains of demolition bonfires. Moreover, the parallel examples quoted to support the interpretation, Newstead and Glenlochar, are open to a similar challenge and in any case relate to the next phase of withdrawal, for the occupation of Castledykes was dated too late by its excavator (Frere 1966 *contra* Robertson 1964, 261). It is necessary to return well to the south of the Forth–Clyde isthmus before there are clear signs of Roman occupation after *c.* AD 90.

The occupation of Lowland Scotland seems to have undergone a major process of rationalisation and re-organisation at about this time (fig 27). The key sites at Newstead and Dalswinton, already large forts, were further enlarged. The unique fort at Newstead (fig 14) was demolished and a more regular fort of some 13 acres (5.3 ha) was constructed on the same site to hold a garrison containing probably both legionary and auxiliary troops. A *terminus post quem* for this rebuilding is provided by two bronze coins of AD 86 in almost mint condition found within the infilled ditches of the earlier fort (Richmond 1950, 7–11). At Dalswinton the reconstruction was

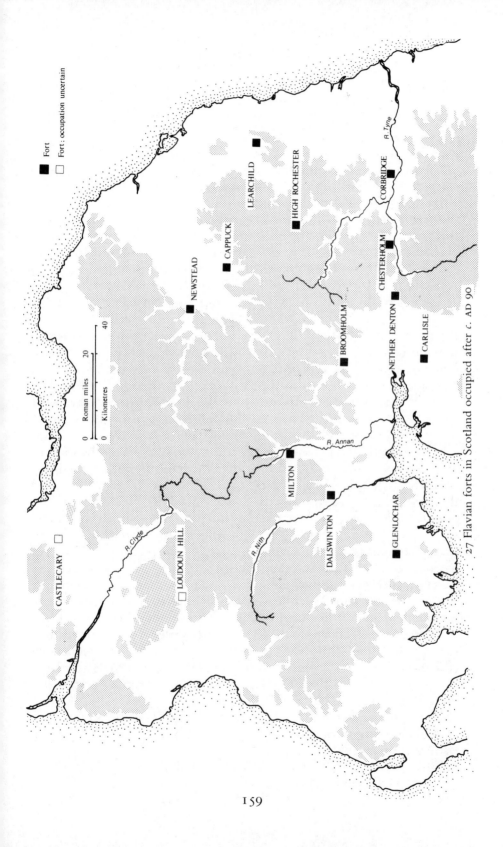

27 Flavian forts in Scotland occupied after c. AD 90

Fort

Fort : occupation uncertain

LEARCHILD

HIGH ROCHESTER

CORBRIDGE

R. Tyne

CAPPUCK

CHESTERHOLM

NEWSTEAD

BROOMHOLM

NETHER DENTON

CARLISLE

Roman miles
0   20   40

Kilometres
0

R. Annan

MILTON

DALSWINTON

GLENLOCHAR

LOUDOUN HILL

R. Nith

CASTLECARY

R. Clyde

superficially less dramatic, with a simple extension of the north-east rampart of the fort, increasing the area by some 25 per cent (pl 11). But the whole interior was revamped, the buildings turned through 90 degrees, the ditches remodelled and a new annexe added to the eastern side (Richmond and St Joseph 1956). Because of the large size of the fort the excavators suggested that its garrison may have been *ala milliaria Petriana*, the largest auxiliary cavalry unit known in Britain, but it is debateable whether the unit had been increased to this size as early as the reign of Domitian, so that a combination of the two unknown units of quingenary strength (500 men) is more probable (Birley 1957). The unusually shaped fort at Milton was also replaced by a fort of more normal outline on the same site, but the resultant increase in its size was only marginal (Clarke 1947, 22–30).

Elsewhere the evidence is less dramatic and in some cases less conclusive. There is structural evidence of a second Flavian occupation at Loudoun Hill (Taylor 1949, 98), but the site remains unpublished in any detail. Moreover, it would have been somewhat out on a limb if, as suggested above, Castledykes was abandoned. The situation at Oakwood is similarly uncertain. Remodelling of the defences after only a short time was suggested by the excavators (Steer and Feachem 1952b, 97), but the structural evidence of a second period of use lacks the support of sufficiently late dated samian from the site (Hartley 1972, 10). In the south-west the fortlet at Gatehouse-of-Fleet demonstrates only a single period of occupation whose end came in an orderly manner (St Joseph 1983, 232), but the fort at Glenlochar may have continued in use. Excavation revealed a Flavian fort, beneath the later Antonine one on the same site, which was thought to represent military occupation secondary to that on an as yet unidentified adjacent site (Richmond and St Joseph 1952, 12). On the other hand, the samian pottery recovered was insufficient to support the suggestion that occupation continued beyond AD 90. At Broomholm, however, the second period of building evident in the defences (Wilson 1965, 202) is confirmed by the presence of Flavian-Trajanic samian (Hartley 1972, 10). In the east, the defences of the small fort at Cappuck were also remodelled (Richmond 1951, 145) and again samian pottery of appropriately late date is known from the site (Hartley 1972, 9). A similar pattern is indicated at High Rochester (Richmond 1936, 175–9) and Learchild (Birley 1961, 245), but the suggestion of Flavian-Trajanic occupation at Blakehope rests on very little pottery from limited excavation (Birley 1961, 241–2).

What prompted this major reshaping of the northern frontier is uncertain. However, AD 89 saw a serious revolt in Germany and further problems arose in Pannonia with the beginning of the Sarmatian war in AD 92 (Garzetti 1974, 271–2 and 230). We have no direct evidence of further troop withdrawals at this time, with the possible exception of the *pedites singulares Britannici*, the governor's guards, who are first attested in Moesia in *c.* AD 103. Their removal from Britain may have been an isolated event connected with the demise of the governor, Sallustius Lucullus, executed by Domitian in AD 89 supposedly on no graver charge than having a lance named after him (Birley 1953, 22). If the earlier removed of *legio II Adiutrix* had been intended only as a temporary measure, the resurgence of trouble on the Danube would almost certainly have prevented its return; indeed the legion was once more in the thick of the fighting, for one of its tribunes was decorated for his actions in the Suebo-Sarmatian war (*I.L.S.* 2719). On the other hand the withdrawal from Scotland coincides with the construction of further auxiliary forts in northern England, so many of the troops released from garrison duties in the far north seem to have been rapidly redeployed elsewhere in Britain. It is unclear whether this was in reaction to local unrest, or simply recognition that the original dispositions in northern England were rather thin, though as we shall see shortly there are hints of trouble in Britain by the beginning of the second century AD. Nor was the reorganisation limited to Scotland. There are slight signs of a contemporary reduction in the strength of the garrison in Wales with the abandonment of the forts at Pen Llystyn, possibly Forden Gaer, Gelligaer and Cardiff (Davies 1980a, 264–5).

It was around this time that a permanent Roman presence is first seen in the Lake District (fig 8). A late Flavian foundation date for the supposedly Agricolan fort at Ambleside was suggested some years ago on the basis of the samian pottery from the site (Hartley 1966, 12). More recently the coins, samian and coarse pottery from Watercrook fort have confirmed a similarly late date for its establishment (Potter 1979, 176–7). These two seem likely to carry with them the forts at Papcastle, Old Carlisle and Troutbeck, where little investigation has taken place. The limited dating evidence from Caermote does not seem to support the postulated Agricolan foundation there (Shotter 1984, 22), while examination of the *vicus* or civil settlement outside the fort at Old Penrith suggested that the earliest occupation may have been as late as the reign of Trajan (Goodburn 1978, 424–5). Similarly the fort at Kirkbride, once proposed as an Agricolan site, is now dated to the Trajanic period

(Bellhouse and Richardson 1982, 47), though a late Flavian date would fit the evidence just as well. Indeed, once the decision to occupy the area had been made, a fort on the coast with suitable harbourage facilities would surely have been essential. Other than Kirkbride the known coastal forts appear to be Hadrianic or later in date.

The number of forts along the roads which subdivided the remaining territory of the Brigantes may also have been increased at about this time, particularly on trans-Pennine routes away from the main lines of communication. At Bainbridge the known fort is of Flavian-Trajanic date, though there are traces of some form of earlier activity beneath it (Wilson 1969, 207). That at Greta Bridge is probably of similar date, though here the evidence relates to the *vicus* rather than the fort (Hartley 1971, 58). Further south the fort at Brough-on-Noe has been variously referred to as Flavian or Flavian-Trajanic in the interim reports, which may indicate a foundation date around this time (Jones and Wild 1969, 99–100). Finally, the number of forts on the Stanegate, the road linking Carlisle and Corbridge may also have been increased around AD 90. The Agricolan base at Red House was demolished, the timber uprights of its internal buildings being removed and the wattle and daub infill collected and burnt (Hanson *et al.* 1979, 24), and a normal auxiliary fort constructed three-quarters of a mile (1.2 km) away at Corbridge. The well-known fort at Vindolanda (Chesterholm) some 13.2 miles (21.2 km) to the west appears on the basis of pottery evidence to have been founded in the late Flavian period (Hird 1977, 3–4 *contra* Birley 1977, 108) and a similar foundation date would not be out of keeping with the pottery and coins recovered from early excavations at Nether Denton 10.9 miles (17.5 km) further west along the Stanegate (Birley 1961, 141–2). As yet, however, there is no hint of the closer spacing of garrisons and the provision of surveillance facilities which were later to demarcate a frontier along this line.

Thus, within less than a decade of Agricola's recall, territory directly controlled by Rome had been pulled back some 85 miles (137 km) south from the North Esk in Angus to the Tweed in Roxburghshire. It is arguable that the distance would have been even greater since the defeat of the tribes assembled at Mons Graupius should have brought with it the primary control of tribal territory even further north. Perhaps it was this realisation which prompted Tacitus' famous comment at the beginning of his *Histories* (1, 2):

perdomita Britannia et statim missa (Britain was subdued and immediately let go).

This single line judgement on the conquest of north Britain was written towards the middle of the reign of Trajan, probably at some time between AD 104–109. Thus it may be a reflection upon the more immediate situation, for it was about this time that the Romans withdrew completely from the area north of the Tyne–Solway line. The dating of the samian pottery from the two major forts at Newstead and Dalswinton suggests that they did not continue to be occupied for more than five years after the turn of the century (Hartley 1972, 14–15). Excavation at Corbridge has provided further confirmation of this date. This key site, founded at the time of the reorganisation of the frontier in the early 90s AD, was totally rebuilt at some time after AD 103, the date provided by a coin recovered from a construction trench in one of the barracks of the period II fort (Gillam 1977, 60).

The nature of this second withdrawal is much disputed. For many years some scholars have maintained that hostile native action precipitated this abandonment of Agricola's conquests (e.g. Clarke 1958, 58; Daniels 1970, 93–4), but recently others have argued that this was simply another strategic retreat dictated by events elsewhere in the empire (Breeze and Dobson 1976, 133). The crucial evidence is the burning attested at a number of forts in Lowland Scotland and northern England. This has usually been interpreted as the result of destruction by fire at the hands of hostile locals, but the equation between burning and enemy destruction is too simplistic and requires careful consideration. Roman military timber buildings were no less prone to accidental fires than any other wood structures, though a rash of such fires would be rather suspicious. More importantly, there is growing evidence that fire was part of the process of deliberate demolition of forts by the Romans on evacuation (Hanson 1978c, 302–4): the wattle and daub panels, and perhaps many other timbers for which an alternative use could not be found, were collected into piles and burnt. This is most graphically attested at Carlisle where the end of the fort's life at around this time was marked by extensive burning, yet examination of the surviving timbers of the gateway made clear that it had first been demolished (Charlesworth 1980, 208) (pl 21).

If we are to distinguish between burning as part of the demolition process and that caused by enemy attack, meticulous observation of the archaeological remains is necessary over as wide an area as possible. Unfortunately, at four of the sites where burning has been recorded, namely Glenlochar (Richmond and St Joseph 1952, 8–10), Cappuck (Richmond 1951, 143), High Rochester (Richmond 1936, 179) and Blakehope (Birley 1961, 241), its significance must remain uncertain because of the very limited extent of the areas subject to investigation. At two other forts, however, the recorded burning has no historical significance whatsoever. At Dalswinton traces of burning interpreted as the result of enemy action were referred to in a summary account (Taylor 1955, 128) but do not figure in the final report (Richmond and St Joseph 1956). This discrepancy would seem to have been caused by the failure to recognise at first that the abundant traces of burnt material in one trench came from an oven or hearth at the rear of the rampart. At Oakwood, on the other hand, there is no evidence of burning at all. Confusion this time was caused by the state of the surviving stumps of the gate timbers. Their pointed tops, in fact caused by the natural process of decay, were incorrectly interpreted by the excavators as the result of fire damage (Steer and Feachem 1952b, 97 and 105).

At two important forts, however, the evidence is more extensive. The presence in a number of pits at Newstead of military equipment, smith's and carpenter's tools and even human heads would seem to provide quite graphic evidence of an orgy of destruction (Curle 1911, 119–21 and 128–9). But a reconsideration of the contents of these pits has led to the suggestion that they were filled as part of the clearing up process by the Romans on evacuation of the site (Manning 1972, 244–6). It has been plausibly argued that the military equipment and tools were damaged or surplus stock discarded because it could not be readily transported by the retreating garrison and buried, like the nails and iron tyres at Inchtuthil, to prevent it falling into enemy hands. The human skulls could have been discarded trophies, such as those displayed outside one Roman fort depicted on Trajan's Column (pl 22). Indeed, if the human deaths had resulted from an enemy attack, the head-hunting Celts would hardly have removed the bodies and left behind the heads. All too often it is forgotten that Roman auxiliary troops were frequently recruited from among the Celtic tribes of Europe and may not have been discouraged from continuing their traditional treatment of defeated foes as a form of deterrent. There is some evidence of burnt daub from the site in the levels which mark the end of period II (Richmond 1950, 11), but this derives from very limited trenching and is entirely commensurate with the burning of wattle panels as part of the demolition process. The evidence from Corbridge, however, is not so readily dismissed.

The burning of timbers *in situ* is attested and this destruction has been noted in numerous excavations over the years in various parts of the site (Gillam 1977, 55). Although the fort was rapidly rebuilt, it is hard to understand why it was necessary to burn down all the buildings in order to facilitate this, rather than demolish them in orderly manner as seems to have been the norm elsewhere. An accidental fire is, of course, a possibility, but failure to recover the famous hoard of ironwork and other miscellaneous items buried beneath the floor of the workshop (previously identified as a hospital), whether it represents the hurried burial of valuables as the excavator suggested (Daniels 1968, 126) or a hoard of personal belongings (Manning 1972, 242), speaks eloquently of a rather hasty evacuation. The best analogy would seem to be provided by the actions of the commanders of two auxiliary forts in Germany who, on realising that they could not hold their positions in the face of the Batavian revolt, fired their own forts after evacuation so that they could not be used by the rebels (Tacitus, *Hist.* 4, 15).

On the subject of Britain at this time the literary sources are silent. This fact has been taken to support the view that the total withdrawal from Scotland was not precipitated by enemy action. Had it been so, the argument goes, it is unthinkable that the Romans would not have retaliated (Frere 1978, 144). But it is dangerous to place too much weight upon the absence of any reference to a punitive campaign when the literary sources for the period are so meagre. All the more so when the emperor, Trajan, was fully occupied in Dacia at the time. He would have had little opportunity, or perhaps inclination, to concern himself with a minor problem on the remote northern frontier. Any small-scale campaign by the governor, probably Neratius Marcellus' unknown successor, is unlikely to have figured prominently in the contemporary historical accounts when the emperor himself was so actively engaged in warfare for much of his reign. Nor can we argue, as some do, that the inhabitants of north Britain were never able to present any serious threat to Rome. The concentration of troop dispositions in Annandale and Nithsdale in the mid-second century AD would seem to indicate that the area was judged to be a potential source of trouble, while the subsequent history of the northern frontier suggests that the tribes north of the Forth–Clyde isthmus, at least, were a persistent thorn in the side of Rome (Breeze 1982, 125–31).

More specifically, there is both literary and epigraphic evidence for serious fighting in the area only a decade or so later. Fronto compares the losses in Britain during Hadrian's reign with those sustained in the Jewish rebellion of AD 132–5 (*Letters*, On the Parthian war). A tombstone from Cyrene in North Africa records the death of a legionary tribune who, while prefect of *cohors II Asturum*, had been decorated in a British war at some time between AD 89 and 128 (Birley 1953, 23–4). If the northern frontier could be deemed uncontrollable by the beginning of Hadrian's reign (*S.H.A.* Hadrian 5), it seems not unreasonable to argue that it may have been troublesome some twelve years earlier. This is not to say that the Romans were expelled from Scotland nor faced with a situation with which they could not cope, for less than forty years later the re-occupation of Lowland Scotland was achieved with consummate ease. The difference was one of will. Antoninus Pius needed a successful conquest largely for political propaganda purposes and Britain was the ideal place to achieve it (Breeze and Dobson 1976, 134). Trajan had no such need. His energies and, more importantly, his military resources were concentrated elsewhere. Whether or not further troops were withdrawn from Britain to serve in Trajan's Dacian Wars is unattested, though possible candidates have been put forward on rather circumstantial evidence (Holder 1982, 16–17). *Cohors I Cugernorum* certainly won its honorific titles *Ulpia Traiana civium Romanorum* under Trajan, but there is no positive evidence that it had to leave Britain to do so.

It seems ironic that it was Trajan, the most expansionist ruler that the empire had seen since its establishment, who was responsible for the abandonment of the last of what might legitimately be claimed as Agricola's conquests in Britain. But it serves to emphasise the relative strategic importance of an insular province at the northern limit of Roman territory. The Dacians across the Danube and subsequently the Parthians across the Euphrates represented a greater threat to the empire and, accordingly, were of more immediate concern to Trajan.

Thus Britain north of Tyne–Solway isthmus had remained under Roman control for only a quarter of a century. It is perhaps apposite at this point, therefore, to consider the effects that the brief presence of an imperial power had upon the indigenous population.

Obviously the primary impact was military. Inevitably a large number of men of fighting age would have been killed: Tacitus suggests 10,000 at Mons Graupius alone (*Ag.* 37). Other skirmishes and executions would have accounted for more. Even if we accept what is probably an exaggerated figure for Mons Graupius, this represents only one third of those assembled for the battle and we have no evidence for any other encounters of similar magnitude. We have no idea what percentage of the total population may have lost their lives during Agricola's five years in Scotland, but it is unlikely to have been high. Not all tribes were uniformly hostile to the Romans and, if Celtic scholars are correct (Powell 1980, 127), not all strata of society would have been involved in the fighting. In any case the effects would have been relatively short-term until the next generation reached manhood. In areas of hostility there may have been some further slight effects on population numbers as the result of the taking of hostages (*Ag.* 49) or even captives for slavery. It had also become common practice to recruit from recently conquered areas into the auxilia of the Roman army. British recruits are attested in the first century AD and some were actually involved at Mons Graupius (Dobson and Mann 1973, 198–9), but we have no certain evidence of any from the north at this stage.

The presence of Roman garrisons is likely to have precipitated a certain amount of settlement dislocation, though at present this is difficult to quantify. Some settlements may have been abandoned, their inhabitants fleeing like refugees to areas not under Roman control. Others may have been deliberately cleared by the Romans either because they represented centres of resistance, as is usually assumed at Eildon Hill North, or because the site was required by the army. The evidence of native settlements beneath or immediately adjacent to first century AD Roman forts or camps continues to grow. At Broomholm the Flavian fort replaced a native enclosure whose ditches had been filled with turf and stones (information from Mr C.M. Daniels). At Cappuck the palisade trench of a native settlement had been deliberately packed with clay prior to the construction of the fortlet on the site (Richmond 1951, 142–3). A similar sequence has recently been recorded slightly further north at Elginhaugh, though there the native site may well have been abandoned long before the Roman arrival (Maxwell 1983a. 174–6).★ The recovery of quite large quantities of Iron Age pottery during excavations at Cardean points to the presence of a native settlement beneath the Roman fort, but no structural remains were noted (Robertson 1977, 71–2). Air reconnaissance indicates that the labour camps adjacent to the legionary fortress at Inchtuthil overlie an enclosure of possible Iron age date (Pitts and St Joseph 1985, 261), while the small Flavian camp at Dun on the northern shore of the Montrose Basin is located in an area of dense native settlement (pl 23). The problem posed by this evidence is highlighted by the last examples: it is difficult to be certain that the settlements concerned were actually in use at the time of the Roman arrival.

A similar problem arises with the evidence for the apparently beneficial effects of the *pax Romana*, though this is usually referred to in the context of later Roman occupation. Recognition that a distinctive form of stone-built enclosed settlement in northern Northumberland was occupied during the Roman period, and that a large number of examples succeeded hillforts (Jobey 1965, 56–8), is not sufficient to establish a causal relationship. Indeed, there is growing evidence that the move to less defensive forms of settlement may have occurred before the Roman arrival on the scene. At Broxmouth in East Lothian the carbon–14 dates linked with the sequence of defences indicate that the hillfort had reached its final form long before the Roman period and had probably ceased to be maintained as a defended site (Hill 1982, 185). Similarly at Burnswark in Dumfriesshire the rampart of the large hillfort was no longer standing at the time that it served as target practice for the Roman army in the mid-second century AD and had probably not been defended for some long time before that (Jobey 1978, 67 and 98). At Belling Law the rectangular stone-walled enclosure was certainly occupied in the Roman period, for a jar of second century date was found sealed beneath the wall of one of its stone-built houses, but the settlement succeeded a timber-built example of similar form from which was obtained a carbon–14 date of 160 ± 80 b.c. (Jobey 1977, 32–4). Thus here at least the move to a less defensive form of settlement cannot have had anything to do with the arrival of Roman forces in the area.

Despite the words that Tacitus places in the mouth of Calgacus (*Ag.* 30), the Romans did not set out to create desolation in the areas that they overran. Rather they were concerned to control them efficiently and, of course, tax them effectively. The subject of taxation features several times in the *Agricola*. Though there is obviously no need to take the words that Tacitus attributes to Calgacus as indicating that the prospect was a particular stimulus to resistance (*Ag.* 31–2), clearly they do confirm that it was normal practice to levy taxes from the recently subjugated population. The main sources of revenue were a tax on land productivity (*tributum soli*) and a poll tax (*tributum capitis*) (Jones 1974, 164–5). In exactly what form these taxes were paid in the north and how that payment was organised is unknown. The existence of the essential prerequisite, a land and property census, is implied by the presence in the north of a British census official, though this record dates from the latter part of Trajan's reign (*I.L.S.* 1338). His title, *censitor Brittonum Anavion[ensium]*, ought to indicate that the area concerned was

Annandale in Dumfriesshire (Rivet 1982), though this has been disputed on the grounds that the Romans had only recently withdrawn south of that area to the Tyne–Solway line (Frere 1978, 246). The taxes may have been collected in kind, as was apparently the case in the Netherlands where the Frisii were assessed in ox-hides because of their poverty (Tacitus, *Annals* 4, 72). Usually, however, taxes were payable in coin. Since there was no pre-existing monetary system in operation in the north into which the Roman coinage could have been tied, coin must have been obtained in exchange for the provision of goods or services. The foodstuffs requisitioned from the locals for army use, a system whose abuse in relation to grain has been discussed above (pp 71–2), would have provided a convenient source of coin by which taxes might then have been paid. Further coin may, of course, have been obtained by trade but there are insufficient first-century AD coin finds from native sites to argue convincingly that the Romans introduced a monetary economy during their brief presence in the north (fig 28). Nor does it seem likely that Roman tax collectors would have toured around all the scattered settlements collecting their dues. It had become common practice for the collection of taxes to be farmed out to independent syndicates (*publicani*) or the liability imposed on local urban magistrates (Stevenson 1939, 148–9). In areas still under military control the latter pattern could easily have been translated to work within the context of the local tribal structure. Once an assessment had been reached, demand for payment could have been made to the tribal leaders. It was up to them how this sum was then recouped from the wider population.

The economic demands of the army would have been consider-able. It was standard practice for ancient armies to live off the land while on campaign, so the presence of a force of between 25,000 and 30,000 men would have put considerable pressure on local food supplies even if these had been augmented by seaborne supply from the south. With the establishment of a permanent garrison the number of troops would have been reduced to a maximum of somewhere in the region of 20,000. Since all of them would have been present throughout the year, whereas not all of the troops on campaign would have over-wintered in Scotland, the total demand for foodstuffs would have stayed much the same, though its effects would have been less devastating since they were more widespread. Because of the high cost of overland transport bulk supplies such as grain were obtained locally whenever possible (Manning 1975). Indeed, this dependence on local resources may even have been a factor in the location of forts in relation to areas of good arable land (Higham 1982, 108–10). On the other hand the needs of a permanent garrison were not restricted to grain and meat. Animals were also required for transport, both as mounts and beasts of burden, while the demand for leather for clothing, shoes, horse gear and even tents was considerable (Breeze 1983b, 269–72).

To what extent the combination of taxation and these various military demands stimulated local agricultural production is uncertain. We have already noted (above, p 128) that in some areas the provision for storage in large underground passages or souterrains implies the ability to produce a considerable surplus, so that the additional demands of the local garrison might not have had as much impact as is usually assumed. On the other hand Roman food preferences may well have differed from those of the local population in terms of both meat (King 1984) and grain (Groenman-van Wateringe 1986) and resulted in pressure for change. Not until we have obtained environmental evidence in sufficient quantities for meaningful comparisons to be made between pre-Roman Iron Age sites, Romano-British settlements and Roman forts will answers to this question being to emerge.

An alternative way of looking at the environmental impact of the Roman presence is to consider the evidence of forest clearance. A number of dated regional pollen diagrams from the north-east of England seem to indicate that quite widespread forest clearance was well under way before the Roman arrival (Turner 1979), although the wide range of the carbon–14 dates when expressed at a probability level of 95 per cent make this conclusion less certain. On the other hand there is growing archaeological evidence that large areas of land in Scotland were already under cultivation by the later Iron Age if not before. Field systems and pit alignments, a form of land division, continue to be found in association with settlement sites (Halliday et al. 1981), while evidence of arable farming is also becoming more common (Hanson and Macinnes 1980, 109). One immediate Roman requirement would have been building timber. The construction of over forty auxiliary forts or fortlets and a legionary fortress in the area north of the Tyne–Solway line would have required in the region of 30,000 cubic metres of structural timber. Assuming that this was obtained locally rather than imported from stock-piles in the south (Hanson 1978c), it represents clearance of between 830 and 1470 acres (335 and 595 ha). Yet when this is set against the timber requirements of indigenous settlements, allowing for the smaller individual needs of most sites but their far greater numbers, the Roman impact in terms of forest clearance is put into some perspective (Hanson and Macinnes 1980, 108–10). Indeed, it is far too easy to overestimate the impact that the Roman presence would have had upon the environment.

One positive way in which we can make some assessment of the influence of Rome upon the indigenous population is by tracing the extent to which Roman artefacts found their way on to native sites. The basic work has been done for Scotland (Robertson 1970), but not yet for northern England. Even though based on stray finds and very limited sampling by excavation, the distribution is noticeably restricted, though it does correspond broadly with the areas of direct Roman occupation (fig 28). Only one or two fragments of pottery are found at most sites, but some produce more extensive remains. What is noticeable is that it is the larger or less common types of site, such as the large hillfort at Traprain Law, the crannog at Hyndford or the broch at Torwoodlee which seem to have greatest access to Roman goods (Macinnes 1984, 241–2). In order words, Roman material fails to progress far down the social hierarchy. The mechanism by which it found its way to these sites is uncertain. The method which first comes to mind is trade. Coin obtained from the requisition of foodstuffs which was left over after payment of taxes might have been used to purchase items in the settlements which began to grow up alongside forts; the goods could have been obtained by straightforward exchange or barter, for artefacts of native manufacture are found in Roman forts (Robertson 1970, 201–2); or Roman merchandise may have been distributed to individuals or groups by the Roman authorities by way of gifts to cement good relations. At the other extreme items could have been looted from abandoned forts (Gillam 1958, 77). Though it might reasonably be felt that this was a less likely means of obtaining the more mundane or fragile material such as pottery or glass, the very fact that the Romans buried the huge cache of nails on the abandonment of Inchtuthil suggests concern over the fate of ironwork, if only to prevent it being forged into weapons.

In conclusion, though the immediate impact of a large body of foreign troops was bound to have been considerable at a local level, the longer-term effects, particularly when viewed against a regional background, were probably more limited. If the disposition of Roman garrisons in Scotland is seen against the background of settlements of probable Iron Age date, using hillforts as a conveniently identifiable indicator, it becomes apparent that a concentration of population was not the only criterion for the location of a Roman

28 First-century Roman artefacts from native sites in Scotland

◆ COINS
● POTTERY & GLASS

R. Don
R. Dee
R. North Esk
R. South Esk
R. Tay
R. Earn
R. Forth
R. Clyde
R. Tweed
R. Nith
R. Annan
R. Tyne

post (Hanson and Macinnes 1980, 105–8). Control of strategic communications was arguably more important that local policing. Thus large areas may never have seen a body of Roman troops. Even if they did so, interaction is likely to have occurred mainly between the Romans and the tribal aristocracy. The extent to which Roman interference subsequently undermined the political and social structure of these tribal groups remains a matter of debate.

· 8 ·

ASSESSMENT AND RE-ASSESSMENT

THE logic of the narrative has taken us some way from the main focus of this work and it is now time to return to Agricola and attempt to assess his character, abilities and impact in the light of what has gone before. No one reading Tacitus' biography can fail to notice its eulogistic tone. In Tacitus' eyes Agricola seems to have been a paragon of virtue: honest, fair-minded, honourable and modest in character, an outstanding military strategist and tactician and a humane and compassionate civil administrator. This assessment, frequently followed (e.g. Todd 1981, 103) or even amplified and augmented (e.g. Richmond 1944; Frere 1978, 132–7) by modern scholars, requires closer examination.

First and foremost Agricola is seen as a great general. His achievements are seemingly self-evident, for during his governorship Roman arms advanced from Wales to northern Scotland. Yet three factors must be borne in mind which should serve to temper overenthusiastic praise. Firstly, his achievements in Wales and northern England, much enhanced by Tacitus' wilful vagueness, were in reality little more than the suppression of a minor insurrection and the completion of the consolidation process which followed the main conquest of those areas by his predecessors (above chapter 3). Secondly, in Lowland Scotland, at least in the east, Agricola seems to have met little resistance and perhaps benefited from earlier campaigns in the north by Cerialis or Frontinus and the pro-Roman stance of the Votadini and Venicones. Finally, his period of office was exceptionally long, approaching twice the norm (Birley 1981, 397). Given that a forward policy in general was favoured by the Flavian emperors, failure to make such gains would have been cause for serious criticism. Once such support was withdrawn, for whatever reason, retrenchment was not far away; but those responsible for strategic retreat, no matter how skilfully achieved, rarely receive praise.

Twenty-five percent of the *Agricola* is devoted to a single battle and its immediate preliminaries. It seems not unreasonable to assume, therefore, that this particular engagement was seen as the pinnacle of Agricola's success in Britain and his main claim to fame as a general. Yet the outcome of the battle can hardly have been in question. It required only adherence to textbook tactics to ensure victory, for the sides were fairly evenly balanced numerically and Roman superiority in weaponry, training and organisation was so great as to promise success in open battle even against apparently overwhelming odds. To suggest, as some have (Richmond 1944, 42–3; Ogilvie and Richmond 1967, 66), that Agricola invented some new tactic because he achieved victory using only auxiliary troops is neither justified nor particularly praiseworthy. If the intention was to save *Roman* manpower at the expense of the non-citizen auxiliary as Tacitus implies (*Ag.* 35), this is hardly commensurate with the picture of Agricola as humane and compassionate in his treatment of provincials. But the tactic of plannning the battle in stages and keeping fresh troops in reserve already had a long history (Rainbird 1969). More specifically, Cerialis had also kept his legionaries in the second rank when facing Civilis in AD 70 (Tacitus *Hist.* 5, 16). That he was obliged to employ them, while Agricola was not, merely reflects the relative weakness of the opposition at Mons Graupius. Over twenty years earlier Ostorius Scapula had faced and defeated the rebellious Iceni in a set-piece battle with only auxiliary troops (Tacitus, *Annals* 12, 31). No new principles of warfare were employed by Agricola.

The same applies to his use of the fleet. It has been suggested that this was employed in an unprecedented manner (Burn 1969, 54), revealing once more Agricola's supposed innovatory tactical genius. While the tactic of naval support for the campaigns in Scotland was an eminently sensible one, it was in no way innovatory. It had become standard practice to transport troops and supplies by water, and fleets were established for this purpose in all the frontier provinces of the western empire. The benefits of coastal reconnaissance were also well appreciated and had been employed at an early stage of the Roman advance into Germany (Pliny *Nat. Hist.* 2, 167). Sea-borne raiding was a logical concomitant whose effectiveness Agricola had personal cause to regret, for it had resulted in the death of his mother (*Ag.* 7). Combined operations between the fleet and land-based forces are well attested during the German campaigns of Drusus, Tiberius and Germanicus (Starr 1941, 141–4). Though the coming together of army and navy in remote locations well beyond the limits of Roman held territory was usually intended to facilitate the collection or supply of the former, independent operations by the latter are also attested (Velleius Paterculus 2, 106).

In similar nautical vein Tacitus credits Agricola with being the first to establish that Britain was an island by its circumnavigation (*Ag.* 10), one of the few facts subsequently noted by Dio (66, 20). But it was already well known that Britian was an island: both the geographer Pomponius Mela and Pliny the Elder refer to it as such, the former writing over forty years earlier in the reign of Gaius, and both identify the Orkneys and other islands off the north coast (Mela 3, 6, 54; Pliny *Nat. Hist.* 4, 103). Agricola may have been responsible for the first formal circumnavigation of the island, but even here some of the attached kudos is lost because of the accidental circumnavigation achieved by a cohort of Usipi after their mutiny. Tacitus places this episode only a year before Agricola's fleet achieved the same feat in AD 83 (*Ag.* 28), though Dio dates it some four years earlier (66, 20).

Examples of Agricola's supposedly excellent generalship are surprisingly rare. His speedy reaction to the uprising in North Wales at the very beginning of his governorship is highly commendable, but despite Tacitus' attempt to make the most of the episode it seems to have been no more than a limited mopping up exercise. Perhaps more worthy of praise was his subsequent impromptu extension of the action against Anglesey where use of lightly armed troops to swim the Menai Strait gained the benefit of surprise (*Ag.* 18), though once again there was little or no opposition to test his abilities further. Some other episodes, however, are distinctly unimpressive. Having divided his army late in his sixth campaign to avoid encirclement by the enemy, a sensible precaution, Agricola does not seem to have taken sufficient care to avoid the obvious counter measure, a lightning strike against the weakest point. The IXth legion had been particularly affected by the removal of vexillations to Germany before AD 83 to serve in Domitian's war against the Chatti. Detachments from nine legions including all four British units were serving under a senior centurion there (*I.L.S.* 9200), but in addition a separate vexillation from *IX Hispana* was present under its senior tribune (*I.L.S.* 1025). Identifying this potential weakspot, the Caledonians massed for a night attack on the encamped legion. After a forced march through the night Agricola brought help just in time. Tacitus does his best to paint it as a triumph of Agricola's generalship (*Ag.* 26), but it was a very close call and could have been disastrous.

An important insight into Agricola's military thinking relates to Ireland. Within sight of it during his fifth campaign, when his forces were assembled probably in Galloway, Agricola seems to have considered it a potentially easy prize, for even in his retirement he continued to maintain that it could have been conquered and held by one legion and a reasonable complement of auxiliaries (*Ag.* 24). Even with the anticipated help of an exiled Irish prince, this seems a rather gross underestimate of the forces that the task would have required, and with northern Scotland still unconquered it was a distinctly inopportune moment at which to consider such involvement. The overestimation of the strategic significance of Ireland, however, is not to be laid entirely at Agricola's door for it rested upon what appears to be a general geographical misconception of the position of the island in relation to Britain and Spain (Pliny *Nat. Hist.* 4, 102).

Particular store has been set by Agricola's appreciation of topography at both the strategic and tactical level, that is in determining both the overall pattern of the deployment of troops and the detailed location of their encampments. He is especially praised by Tacitus for his personal skill in the selection of the sites of forts and camps:

> It has been observed by experts that no general had ever shown a better eye for ground than Agricola. No fort of his was ever stormed, ever capitulated or was ever abandoned. (*Ag.* 22)

What truth there is in this claim is open to question, for such praise was evidently part of the stock description of a good general (Ogilvie and Richmond 1967, 230–1). While Agricola *may* have taken a particular interest in the location of forts and camps, this would hardly have been possible in every case: when his forces were split in the sixth campaign he could not have been in three places at once, and the subsequent process of fort construction would have been much delayed if his presence in person were necessary to approve each location. Where there is literary evidence of fort or camp construction the responsibility seems to have rested either with a senior tribune (Polybius 6, 26 and 41) or the *praefectus castrorum* (camp prefect), the third in command of the legion (Tacitus *Annals* 12, 38; Vegetius 2, 10). However, if we accept that Agricola had a hand in the selection of fort sites, what of the claim for the excellence of their siting? Many, it is true, were extremely well situated, as their subsequent re-use in the Antonine period testifies, but others were moved or replaced. Thus, discounting the effect of the different strategic requirements in the first as opposed to the second century on the location of forts across the Forth–Clyde isthmus, the Roman army did not return to Dalswinton, Easter Happrew, Barochan or Elginhaugh in the Antonine period, but established forts at alternative sites a few miles away in each case at Carzield, Lyne, Bishopton and Inveresk respectively. Similarly, at Ardoch and Red House, Corbridge the probable Agricolan works were replaced later in the Flavian period by forts on adjacent sites.

Modern writers have further inflated this praise of Agricola's prowess, sometimes to ludicrous proportions. He has, for example, frequently been credited with the establishment of sites which were subsequently to dictate the line followed by the Antonine Wall almost as if imbued with some prescience of the future (Ogilvie and Richmond 1967, 323–4), an assertion now shown to be misguided (Hanson 1980a). Agricola is also seen by many as an innovator in fort and camp design because of the unusual features sometimes exhibited on sites of the Flavian period, in particular the provision of inturned ramparts at fort gateways (Jones 1975, 118) and the use of the unique clavicula with oblique traverse in temporary camp entrances, the so-called Stracathro-type gateway. Two forts of Agricolan date, Newstead and Milton, indeed are unique in form (fig 14), but the very rarity of their appearance surely argues against an innovation emanating from the governor, for its more widespread application might then have been anticipated. More common is the provision of a simple inturned rampart as at Elslack, Elginhaugh, Caermote, Oakwood, Cardean, Bochastle and Strageath. The same feature is sometimes seen on aerial photographs of unexcavated sites reflected in the ditch system, its shape vividly evoked by the descriptive term 'parrot's beak', as at Malling (pl 15). While all these forts are certainly Flavian in date, it has been argued above (pp 148–9, 161) that at least three or possibly four (Caermote, Bochastle, Malling and possibly Cardean) are likely to post-date Agricola's governorship, so that it is difficult to attribute this design feature to him. Similar objections apply to the other minor innovations in fort design which are broadly Flavian in date (Breeze 1980, 18–19). The Stracathro-type camp entrance (fig 20) is unique to Scotland (Lenoir 1977, 702) and its Flavian date seems secure. While the most northerly examples are likely to relate to campaigning under Agricola, those adjacent to the forts at the mouths of the Highland Glens seem to fit into a later context (above, pp 125–6). Moreover, the very limited number of such camps known again argues against their design having originated with the governor, but suggests that they were probably the work of one particular legion (Breeze 1980, 17–18).

Tacitus succinctly describes the method Agricola employed to control tribes living in mountainous regions: *praesidiis castellisque circumdatae* (a ring of garrisoned forts was placed around them) (*Ag.*

20). As a result there has been a tendency amongst modern authors to give praise to Agricola as if he had developed some new approach to this problem (Ogilvie and Richmond 1967, 56–7). If any credit is due for the invention of such a system, rather than seeing it as a gradual evolution over a period of time, it should surely go to Agricola's predecessor, Frontinus, who was primarily responsible for its application to the rugged terrain of Wales. Similarly, the process of blocking up the glens, assuming that that is the correct interpretation of the function of the Highland line forts, has also been seen as indicative of Agricola's excellent strategic insight (Dorey 1969b, 7). Once again the principle is paralleled in Wales (Manning 1981, 43–4) and in any case it seems most unlikely that the Scottish forts were actually constructed at Agricola's behest (above, pp 146–9).

Even greater praise has been heaped upon Agricola for his 'administrative genius' in organising the supply of his large and scattered force of occupation (Frere 1978, 135). Two aspects tend to be stressed: the supply of building materials for so many forts and their provisioning over winter. Both rest on a general misunderstanding of Roman military logistics. If, as Richmond hypothesised, the building of Roman turf and timber forts required the supply of pre-cut and seasoned timber, then the advance organisation necessary to make this available in the quantities required for the large number of forts built in northern Britain during Agricola's governorship would indeed have been a considerable task (Ogilvie and Richmond 1967, 80).However, a recent detailed study makes clear that wherever possible timber growing locally would have been utilised (Hanson 1978c). This was abundantly available and its seasoning, which is simply a drying process, was an unnecessary extravagance since the posts were then to be placed in the ground where they would immediately regain the moisture previously removed. The same principle applies to the provisioning of forts. Wherever possible local sources were tapped, particularly for the staple diet of grain (Manning 1975). This would have been more widely available than has previously been supposed as evidence for arable cultivation in northern England and Scotland in the pre-Roman Iron age increases (e.g. Wilson, D. 1983, 45–6). Tacitus lays great stress on the importance of the supplies being stored over winter so that the garrison was secure against siege and did not lose ground gained in the summer (*Ag.* 22). He does not suggest that this was a feature exclusive to Agricolan foundations as seems to be implied by some modern authorities (Salway 1981, 144). Indeed, the archaeological manifestation of this policy, the presence within forts of granaries, buildings readily identified by their artificially raised floors, is so widespread that it was clearly standard practice to make such provision. Thus Agricola was doing no more than following normal military routine.

One of the major stumbling blocks in Tacitus' attempt to portray his father-in-law as a great man and an outstanding general is the failure of his career to progress after the governorship of Britain. On his return to Rome, though honoured with a statue and *ornamenta triumphalia* (triumphal decorations), the nearest thing to a triumphal procession permissible for those who were not members of the imperial family, Agricola found no further employment. Given the various threats to the security of the empire in the European frontier provinces in the latter years of Domitian's reign, and in particular the death in battle of two generals sent against the Dacians (above, p 152), its seems strange that someone with Agricola's supposed military talents should not have been called into service. Yet despite alleged public clamour for Agricola to take command (*Ag.* 41), the remaining nine years of his life were spent in quiet retirement. He did not even go on to attain the proconsulship of Africa or Asia, the supreme accolade and crowning achievement of a successful senatorial career, and a distinction certainly attained by two of his three immediate predecessors in Britain, Vettius Bolanus and Julius Frontinus (Birley 1981, 399). Clearly Tacitus recognised this evidence of failure. His solution was to blame the emperor. Domitian is, therefore, portrayed as a tyrant who felt both envious of and threatened by the military success of Agricola and thus deliberately stood in the way of his further employment. Can such an explanation reasonably be justified?

Domitian's jealousy supposedly stems from the contrast between Agricola's military achievements in Britain and his own in Germany:

> He (Domitian) was bitterly aware of the ridicule that had greeted his sham triumph over Germany, when he had bought up slaves to have their dress and hair made up to look like prisoners of war. But now came a genuine victory on the grand scale: the enemy dead were reckoned in thousands and the popular acclaim was imense. (*Ag.* 39)

Tacitus is here unreservedly hostile to Domitian, his attitude described by one scholar as 'ignorance coupled with malevolence' (Wellesley 1969a, 269). But Frontinus, himself a man of considerable military experience, gives a much more favourable account of the emperor's involvement in the war against the Chatti (*Strat.* 2, 3, 23;

2, 11, 7) and indicates that it produced positive results (*Strat.* 1, 3, 10), a fact confirmed by archaeology (Schönberger 1969, 158–9). Similarly, despite very serious setbacks on the Danube frontier, Domitian did avenge Roman dishonour and achieved an uneasy peace when faced with serious problems elsewhere. Indeed, modern scholarship credits Domitian with a responsible policy, probably continuing that of his father, which focussed attention upon points of real danger (Garzetti 1974, 286–91). In contrast, Agricola's successes, though well earned, were relatively peripheral to the general welfare and military security of the empire. Thus Domitian had no cause to be envious. Moreover, he did not exhibit the same characteristic in relation to other successful generals, as the careers of Julius Frontinus, Tettius Julianus, Verginius Rufus and Trajan serve to testify (Dorey 1960, 69).

The evidence which Tacitus adduces to support his case is largely circumstantial: it is mainly the manner of its telling which achieves the desired effect. First of all Tacitus refers to a rumour that a freedman was sent to meet Agricola with instructions to offer him the governorship of Syria, but only if he was still in Britain. Tacitus admits that the story may have been invented (*Ag.* 40), but its telling is sufficient to plant the seed of doubt in the reader's mind about Domitian's motives. It is hardly credible that Domitian would have felt that Agricola required some inducement to quit his province when Tacitus consistently describes his father-in-law as a model of moderation and obedience to the state (Ogilvie and Richmond 1967, 289; Dorey 1969b, 6). To accept such a rumour would be to challenge Tacitus' own characterisation of Agricola, unless we believe that Domitian was totally paranoid. Nor, indeed, might Agricola legitimately have expected to be offered the post in Syria, for his appointment to another major governorship after a double-length tenure of Britain would have been unprecedented (Dobson 1980, 11).

Similar doubts have been expressed about the veracity of Tacitus' account of the ballot for the proconsulship of Africa or Asia in *c.* AD 90. When it was his turn as one of the two senior proconsulars to be awarded one or other of these offices by lot, Agricola supposedly asked to stand down after being intimidated by the emperor's confidants, and Tacitus is quick to denounce Domitian for his hypocrisy in graciously granting what he had in fact decreed (*Ag.* 42). The motive for denying Agricola this post is not stated, but the offer was an honour in itself (Dobson 1980, 12). The implication is that Domitian feared Agricola, but the only explanation for this fear lies in Tacitus' unfavourable characterisation of the emperor. It was perfectly acceptable for a senator to seek the emperor's permission to excuse himself from these posts if there was some legitimate reason for so doing (Traub 1954). For example, Agricola may have been in poor health, in which case it would have been for his own good that he was dissuaded from assuming the burden of office (Dorey 1960, 70). That he was not awarded the salary by way of compensation was simply because he did not request it, an action perfectly in keeping with the honest and moderate character that Tacitus portrays. This re-interpretation has been rejected in favour of a literal acceptance of Tacitus' account because Agricola was relatively young – about fifty – and apparently still active. Tacitus makes no mention of any ill-health (Ogilvie and Richmond 1967, 294), though it would hardly have suited his purpose to have drawn attention to it. Yet Agricola died, almost certainly from natural causes rather than from human interference (see below), on 23 August only a few weeks after his fifty-third birthday (*Ag.* 44). Certain aspects of his personality have led some to suggest that he may have burnt himself out at such a relatively early age through overwork (Dorey 1960, 70). Reading between the lines of Tacitus' account Agricola seems to have been a stickler for detail and perhaps reluctant to delegate responsibility (*Ag.* 19 and 20), he suppressed his grief at the death of his son through hard work (*Ag.* 29), and was apparently subject to outbursts of violent temper (*Ag.* 22), frequently a sign of stress. With such character traits as these potential heart failure would not be an unreasonable prognosis.

Finally, Tacitus reports the rumour that Agricola met his death by poisoning, the implication being that the emperor was responsible (*Ag.* 43). Though he is careful to emphasise the lack of positive evidence to support this allegation, once more Tacitus succeeds in damning Domitian by the skilful introduction of scurrilous insinuation and innuendo, the effectiveness of the tactic confirmed by the subsequent acceptance of the story by Dio (66, 20). But if Domitian had been sufficiently jealous and afraid of Agricola to have him killed, it is strange that he should have waited nine years, during which Agricola lived in quiet retirement, before taking any action. Few now accept Tacitus' characterisation of Domitian. Indeed, so flagrant is the distortion when the emperor is defamed that it serves to raise further doubts about the superior qualities of his literary counterpoint, Agricola. If we examine the circumstances of Agricola's death without Tacitus' jaundiced eye, it is not unreasonable to put forward a diametrically opposed interpretation of the emperor's motivation. Domitian clearly showed concern during Agricola's illness and even sent the court physicians to his bedside; he wished to be kept appraised of Agricola's condition and expressed sorrow at his demise; finally even Tacitus admits that the emperor was delighted at the sincere compliment of being named co-heir in Agricola's will (*Ag.* 43). It is only because of Tacitus' colouring that these events are seen to indicate Domitian's hostility towards Agricola rather than genuine concern for the fate of a faithful servant and long-time supporter of the Flavian dynasty.

Moreover, there is other evidence that Agricola, rather than being a victim of Domitian, in fact enjoyed his personal favour. Despite having already held a command in Britain longer than any predecessor, Domitian still confirmed Agricola in office for a further two years enabling him to bring the Caledonians to battle and win the victory upon which much of his reputation seems to have depended. More significant is the imperial favour indicated by Tacitus' own public career (Dorey 1969b, 5). Of its early stages we know little, but he was elected praetor in AD 88 (Tacitus *Annals* 11, 11). The year is significant. It was the occasion of the Secular Games, officially held only once every century though in fact last celebrated by the emperor Claudius only forty years earlier. Accordingly, competition for the magistracies, and particularly the praetorship which was closely linked with the religious ceremonies involved, was likely to have been fierce. Moreover, Tacitus was already a member of one of the main priestly colleges, a lifetime appointment and a signal honour particularly at such an early stage in his career. He then spent four years away from Rome, presumably on imperial service, for neither he nor his wife was able to be at Agricola's bedside during his last days (*Ag.* 45). Exactly what task Tacitus was fulfilling during this time is uncertain, but the period seems too long for a legionary legateship alone. If he had also been serving as the governor of a minor imperial province, as various scholars have suggested (Syme 1958, 68; Ogilvie and Richmond 1967, 9), this hints at further imperial favour, for such posts were the most prestigious to which a man of praetorian rank might aspire (Campbell 1975, 16). Finally he achieved the consulship at the age of forty or forty-one, a not unreasonable achievement for a man who lacked senatorial antecedents. Although he held office in the second half of the year following Domitian's death in September AD 96, it is highly likely that he had already been nominated for the post by Domitian, for consular candidates seem to have been determined quite well in advance (Syme 1958, 70). We know, for example, that several who held office in AD 69 had actually been designated by Nero, who committed suicide in June the previous year (Tacitus *Hist.* 1, 77). If Agricola had been so feared and hated that the emperor curtailed his career and even caused his death, it seems very odd that Agricola's family did not suffer accordingly. On the contrary, the career of his son-in-law, Tacitus, under the same emperor was very successful with every sign of the imperial favour which stems largely from good family connections. There is no doubt that Tacitus' own qualities as an orator established his reputation and boosted his progress, but possession of such rhetorical talents would have been an excellent reason to suppress the career of someone who might have reasonable cause to bear a grudge.

If Domitian was not hostile towards him, why was it that Agricola spent his last nine years in retirement? The possibility that he suffered from ill-health has been raised, though this may only have applied to his last few years. The failure to employ him in Germany or on the Danube in the later 80s is more difficult to explain. One factor may have been the limited nature of Agricola's experience. Uniquely in our records of senatorial careers all his military expertise had been acquired in Britain: he had served as military tribune under Suetonius Paullinus, legionary legate of the *XXth* during the governorships of Vettius Bolanus and Petilius Cerialis and then governor of the province in his own right. We know of no other senator who served all of his military posts in one province (Birley 1981, 73). As a 'British specialist' his experience may have been deemed too limited for service elsewhere. On the other hand the very fact that the senatorial career did normally involve movement both between different types of posts and different parts of the empire, suggests that experience in one area was thought to be readily applicable to another. There remains the strong possibility, therefore, that Agricola's reputation as a general was rather more dependent on the assessment of Tacitus than any impression made on his military contemporaries and peers.

Agricola's second major claim to fame in modern assessments of his achievements is his enlightened policy towards the indigenous population. The various ways in which he encouraged the Britons to adopt the Roman lifestyle by building temples, houses and fora, and educating the sons of the aristocracy, have all been discussd in detail above (chapter 4). What is quite clear is that all of these actions have behind them sound pragmatism. They are all manifestations of the same desire to keep the peace and maintain control of a conquered people. Moreover, none can in any way be seen as Agricolan innovations: all have long pedigrees and in most cases were policies particularly encouraged by the Flavian dynasty. In his civil administration, therefore, Agricola was merely following precedent and probably direct instructions from Rome. There is every likelihood that he did so efficiently, but no more so than any of his immediate predecessors or successors. Once more Agricola is outstanding only insofar as we have precise information about his activities which we lack for others.

Finally, what was Agricola like as an individual? For any assessment of his personality we are almost solely dependent on Tacitus and there can be no doubt that the picture which he paints is heavily biased. Nonetheless, it remains possible to make some progress beyond Tacitus' idealised view. It has been suggested that Agricola's early flirtation with philosophy indicates an intellectual capacity above the common level of military men (Dorey 1969b, 10), but while there is no reason to doubt that he was an able man there are no indications of subsequent intellectual pursuits. More readily attested is his natural good sense, particularly in dealing with civilians (*Ag.* 9 and 19) with whom he may well have felt in sympathy because of his own provincial background. He was clearly an honest man at a time when corruption amongst imperial officials was not uncommon (*Ag.* 6 and 9). He is also recorded as exhibiting signs of personal bravery in battle: he led the advance against the Ordovices (*Ag.* 18) and joined the ranks on foot at the battle of Mons Graupius (*Ag.* 35). Since such gestures were expected of a 'good' general as represented in conventional rhetoric their credibility in this case is in some doubt (Ogilvie and Richmond 1967, 20). We need not doubt his diligence and propensity for hard-work: he took his first military appointment as a junior officer in a legion quite seriously in a way that others sometimes did not (*Ag.* 5), and is more than once praised for being everywhere at once (*Ag.* 20 and 37). Indeed, one begins to get the impression of someone who was inclined to get too involved in minutiae. He appears to have been humane and fair-minded in his treatment of others, whether as a civil administrator and judge (*Ag.* 9 and 19) or military commander (*Ag.* 22). Coupled with this there are hints that he was a stickler for discipline. He was appointed to a legionary command in Britain to restore discipline and ensure the loyalty of the *XXth* (*Ag.* 7), while his first reported action in his civil role as governor was to set his own house in order (*Ag.* 19). Some it seems found him overly harsh and even unpleasant (*Ag.* 22), and he may well have been particularly prone to loss of temper.

The characteristics to which Tacitus alludes most frequently by far are Agricola's sense of moderation and personal modesty. Tacitus often praises him for his modesty in understating his achievements. Thus while legionary legate during Cerialis' governorship, Agricola claimed no credit for his successes (*Ag.* 8), he played down the significance of his first military action as governor against the Ordovices (*Ag.* 18) and reported the results of his final Scottish campaign to Domitian in very moderate terms (*Ag.* 39), though in all three cases Agricola was probably being as honest as he was modest. Too often it seems Tacitus uses Agricola's modesty as a way of implying achievements greater than would otherwise be indicated. Though the return to Rome unannounced and by night, and the subsequent quiet retirement, support the picture of a modest, even shy man (*Ag.* 40), earlier in his career Agricola is said to have harboured ambitions, particularly for military renown *(Ag.* 5). His moderate stance in the execution of his judicial duties has already been noted, but the same approach can be seen in all his actions: it was the prominent trait of his character (Ogilvie and Richmond 1967, 144). While praetor in Rome responsible for organising the public games he steered a careful course between economy and excess (*Ag.* 6) and apparently had no great desire for personal wealth (*Ag.* 44). Even in his personal grief at the loss of his son he followed a middle road (*Ag.* 29). But this self-restraint may have been overdone. Indeed, there is sometimes an impression of a slightly too obsequious respect for authority, whether represented by the emperor (*Ag.* 42), or more immediate superiors earlier in his career:

> Agricola moderated his energy and restrained his enthusiasm, for fear of taking too much upon himself. He had learned the lesson of obedience and schooled himself to subordinate ambition to propriety. (*Ag.* 8)

He was a serious and slightly austere character who, despite Tacitus' protestations to the contrary (*Ag.* 9), probably found it difficult to drop the mask of authority when not on duty. Nowhere in Tacitus' biography is there any sign of a sense of humour, and whatever personal feelings Agricola had seem to have been suppressed or sublimated. Overall he comes across as a fairly colourless character who lacked strong feelings about anything. In Tacitus' own words:

> There was a lack of forcefulness in his features, but abundant charm of expression. There was no difficulty about recognising

him as a good man, and one could willingly believe him a great one. (*Ag.* 44)

The reservations expressed earlier about Agricola's generalship are not meant to suggest that he was in any way defective as a commander. But there is a considerable difference between honest competence and the brilliance with which he is so readily credited in modern sources. As a general Agricola cannot be equated with Caesar, for example, whose campaigns in Gaul reveal considerable military insight, ingenuity and guile. Nor, indeed, is there any justification in seeing Agricola's selection for the governorship of Britain as a reflection of any pre-established military reputation. The Roman empire did not depend upon great generalship for its strength; this would have been far too risky. The success of its army was built upon three basic tenets: training, organisation and discipline. Thus, victory could consistently be achieved almost regardless of the quality of leadership. Agricola's previous tasks gave him as much experience of administration as of military affairs, for he was expected to be able to conduct himself just as reasonably in one as in the other. This he did in a solid, sensible and unremarkable way like many hundreds of others of his class. He has, thus, reasonably been judged 'an outstanding example of moderation' to whom no extravagant genius is attributed (Woodhead 1948, 48), though the same author then goes on to claim paradoxically that he was a great man. Slightly less complimentary but in similar vein would be to describe him as a man of honest mediocrity. Tacitus himself implies that he did not make much impression upon his contemporaries, though he explains this in terms of Agricola's excessive modesty:

He was modest in his manner of life, courteous in conversation, and never seen with more than one or two friends. Consequently, the majority who always measure great men by their self-advertisement, after carefully observing Agricola, were left asking why he was so famous. Very few could read his secret aright. (*Ag.* 40)

The very fact that Tacitus felt obliged to write a biography of his father-in-law, and the whole tenor of the work, confirm that Agricola was not seen as an outstanding figure by contemporary Roman society, an impression further evidenced by his lack of impact on other sources of his day. But for Tacitus we would know virtually nothing of him. Nor is there anything in Tacitus' account of sufficient substance to reject the contemporary assessment of Agricola. He had followed quite a successful career, but one suspects it owed as much to his early adherence to the Flavian dynasty as to any particularly outstanding qualities in the man himself. Undoubtedly his greatest achievement was his choice of son-in-law, for the final words of Tacitus' biography are certainly true:

> With many it will be as with men who had no name or fame: they will be buried in oblivion. But Agricola's story is set on record for posterity, and he will live. (*Ag.* 46)

APPENDIX
Emperors and governors of Britain from Augustus to Antoninus Pius

Emperor and date of assuming title	Provincial governor and date of tenure of office	
Augustus	27 BC		
Tiberius	AD 14		
Gaius (Caligula)	37		
Claudius	41	A. Plautius	43–47
		P. Ostorius Scapula	47–52
Nero	54	A. Didius Gallus	52–57
		Q. Veranius	57–58
		C. Suetonius Paullinus	58–61
		P. Petronius Turpilianus	61–63
Galba	68	M. Trebellius Maximus	63–69
Otho	69		
Vitellius	69	M. Vettius Bolanus	69–71
Vespasian	69	Q. Petillius Cerialis	71–73/4
		Sex. Julius Frontinus	73/4–77
Titus	79	Cn. Julius Agricola	77–84
Domitian	81	Sallustius Lucullus	between 85 and 96
Nerva	96	P. Metillius Nepos	98
Trajan	98	T. Avidius Quietus	98–
		L. Neratius Marcellus	103
		M. Appius Bradua	
Hadrian	117	Q. Pomponius Falco	122
		A. Platorius Nepos	122–24
		Sex. Julius Severus	130–32
		P. Mummius Sisenna	135
Antoninus Pius	138	Q. Lollius Urbicus	139–42
		Cornelius Priscianus	
		Cn. Papirius Aelianus	146
		Cn. Julius Verus	158

Bibliography

ABBREVIATIONS

A.E. L'Année Epigraphique, Paris, 1888–
A.W. Archaeology in Wales, C.B.A. Group 2
C.I.L. Corpus Inscriptionum Latinarum, Berlin, 1863–
D.E.S. Discovery and Excavation in Scotland, C.B.A. Scotland
E.E. Ephemeris Epigraphica, Berlin, 1872–1903
I.L.S. Dessau, H. (ed.) *Inscriptiones Latinae Selectae*, Berlin, 1892–1906
P.I.R.² *Prosopographia Imperii Romani* (2nd. edn.), Berlin, 1933–
R.C.A.H.M.S. Royal Commission on the Ancient and Historical Monuments of Scotland, Edinburgh
R.I.B. R.G. Collingwood and R.P. Wright (eds.) *Roman inscriptions of Britain Vol. 1*, Oxford, 1965

Allen, D.F. 1963 *The coins of the Coritani*, London
Anderson, J.G.C. 1920 'When did Agricola become governor of Britain? *Class. Rev.* 34, 158–61
Anderson, W.A. 1956 'The Roman fort at Bochastle, Callander', *Trans. Glagow. Archaeol. Soc.* 15, 35–63
Angus, N.S., Brown, G.T. and Cleere, H.F. 1962 'The iron nails from the legionary fortress at Inchtuthil, Perthshire', *J. Iron Steel Institute* 200, 956–68

Balsdon, J.P.V.D. 1962 *Roman Women: their history and habits*, London
Barker, P. 1977 *Techniques of archaeological excavation*, London
Barrett, A.A. 1979 'The career of Tiberius Claudius Cogidubnus', *Britannia* 10, 227–42
Bellhouse, R.L. and Richardson, G.G.S. 1982 'The Trajanic fort at Kirkbride; the terminus of the Stanegate frontier', *Trans. Cumberland Westmorland Antiq. Archaeol. Soc.* 82, 35–50
Biddle, M. 1975 'Excavations at Winchester, 1971: tenth and final interim report. Parts 1 and 2', *Antiq. J.* 55, 96–126 and 295–337
Bidwell, P.T. 1979 *The legionary bath-house and basilica and forum at Exeter*, Exeter

Birley, A.R. 1973 'Petillius Cerialis and the conquest of Brigantia', *Britannia* 4, 179–90

Birley, A.R. 1975 'Agricola, the Flavian dynasty, and Tacitus', in Levick, B. *The Ancient Historian and his materials*, London, 139–54

Birley, A.R. 1976 'The date of Mons Graupius', *Liverpool Class. Monthly* 1.2, 11–14

Birley, A.R. 1981 *The Fasti of Roman Britain*, Oxford

Birley, E. 1953 *Roman Britain and the Roman army*, Kendal

Birley, E. 1957 'Dalswinton and the ala Petriana', *Trans. Dumfriesshire Galloway Natur. Hist. Antiq. Soc.* 35, 9–13

Birley, E. 1961 *Research on Hadrian's Wall*, Kendal

Birley, R. 1977 *Vindolanda: a Roman frontier post on Hadrian's Wall*, London

Blagg, T.F.C. 1984 'An examination of the connexions between military and civilian architecture in Roman Britain', in Blagg and King 1984, 249–63

Blagg, T.F.C. and King, A.C. (eds.) 1984 *Military and civilian in Roman Britain: cultural relationships in a frontier province*, Oxford

Bogaers, J.E. 1979 'King Cogidubnus in Chichester: another reading of R.I.B. 91', *Britannia* 10, 243–54

Boon, G.C. 1969 'Belgic and Roman Silchester : the excavations of 1954–8 with an excursus on the early history of Calleva', *Archaeol.* 102, 1–82

Boon, G.C. 1973 *Silchester the Roman town of Calleva*, London

Boon, G.C. and Brewer, R.J. 1982 'Two central Gaulish bottles from Pennal, Merioneth, and early Roman movement in Cardigan Bay', *Bull. Board Celtic Stud.* 29, 363–7

Braund, D.C. 1984 *Rome and the friendly king: the character of client kingship*, London

Breeze, D.J. 1979 *Roman Scotland: some recent excavations*, Edinburgh

Breeze, D.J. 1980 'Agricola the builder', *Scottish Archaeol. Forum* 12, 14–24

Breeze, D.J. 1982 *The northern frontiers of Roman Britain*, London

Breeze, D.J. 1983 'The Roman forts at Ardoch', in O'Connor, A. and Clarke, D.V. (eds.) *From the Stone age to the 'Forty-Five: studies presented to R.B.K. Stevenson*, Edinburgh, 224–36

Breeze, D.J. 1984 'Demand and supply on the northern frontier', in Miket, R. and Burgess, C. (eds.) *Between and beyond the Walls: essays on the prehistory and history of north Britain in honour of George Jobey*, Edinburgh, 264–86

Breeze, D.J. and Dobson, B. 1976 'A view of Roman Scotland in 1975', *Glasgow Archaeol. J.* 4, 124–43

Breeze, D.J. and Dobson, B. 1985 'Roman military deployment in north England', *Britannia* 16, 1–19

Brunt, P.A. 1960 'Charges of provincial maladministration under the early principate', *Historia* 10, 189–227

Buchanan, J. 1877 'Notice of the discovery of a Roman bowl in Glasgow Green and Roman remains found at Yorkhill', *Proc. Soc. Antiq. Scotland* 12 (1876–7), 254–8

Buckland, P. 1978 'A first-century shield from Doncaster, Yorkshire', *Britannia* 9, 247–69

Burn, A.R. 1953a *Agricola and Roman Britain*, London

Burn, A.R. 1953b 'In search of a battlefield: Agricola's last battle', *Proc. Soc. Antiq. Scotland* 87 (1952–3), 127–33

Burn, A.R. 1969 'Tacitus on Britain', in Dorey 1969a, 35–61

Bushe-Fox, J.P. 1913 'The use of samian pottery in dating the early Roman occupation of the north of Britain', *Archaeol.* 14, 295–314

Buttrey, T.V. 1980 *Documentary evidence for the chronology of the Flavian titulature*, Meisenheim

Campbell, B. 1975 'Who were the *viri militares*', *J. Roman Stud.* 65, 11–31

Campbell, D.B. 1986 'The consulship of Agricola', *Zeitschrift für Papyrologie und Epigraphik* 63, 197–200

Carr, E.H. 1961 *What is History?*, London

Casey, J. 1974 'The interpretation of Romano-British site finds', in Casey and Reece 1974, 37–51

Casey, J. and Reece, R. 1974 *Coins and the archaeologist*, Oxford

Chapman, J.C. and Mytum, H. (eds.) 1983 *Settlement in north Britain 1000 BC–AD 1000*, Oxford

Charlesworth, D. 1980 'The south gate of a Flavian fort at Carlisle', in Hanson and Keppie 1980, 201–10

Chevallier, R. 1976 *Roman roads*, London

Chilver, G.E.C. 1957 'The army in politics, AD 68–70', *J. Roman Stud.* 47, 29–35

Clarke, B. 1969 'Calidon and the Caledonian Forest', *Bull. Board Celtic. Stud.* 23, 191–201

Clarke, J. 1947 'The forts at Milton, Beattock (Tassiesholm)', *Trans. Dumfriesshire Galloway Natur. Hist. Antiq. Soc.* 25, 10–26

Clarke, J. 1958 'Roman and native, AD 80–122', in Richmond 1958, 28–59

Collingwood, R.G. and Myres, J.N.L. 1936 *Roman Britain and the English settlements*, Oxford

Collingwood, R.G. and Richmond, I.A. 1969 *The Archaeology of Roman Britain*, London

Collingwood, R.G. and Wright, R.P. 1965 *The Roman inscriptions of Britain*: vol. 1, Oxford

Collis, J. 1974 'Data for dating', in Casey and Reece 1974, 173–83

Cool, H.E.M. 1982 'The artefact record: some possibilities', in Harding 1982, 92–100

Coppock, J.T. 1976 *An agricultural atlas of Scotland*, Edinburgh

Crawford, O.G.S. 1949 *Topography of Roman Scotland north of the Antonine Wall*, Cambridge

Cunliffe, B. 1971 *Excavations at Fishbourne 1961–1969. Volume 1: the site*, London

Cunliffe, B. 1978 'Chichester: the first hundred years', in Down, A. *Chichester excavations III*, Chichester, 177–83

Curle, J. 1911 *A Roman frontier post and its people: the fort of Newstead in the parish of Melrose*, Glasgow

Curle, J. 1932 'An inventory of objects of Roman and provincial Roman origin found on sites in Scotland not definitely associated with Roman constructions', *Proc. Soc. Antiq. Scotland* 66 (1931–32), 277–400

Daniels, C.M. 1968 'A hoard of iron and other materials from Corbridge', *Archaeol. Aeliana*[4] 46, 115–26

Daniels, C.M. 1970 'Problems of the Roman northern frontier', *Scottish Archaeol. Forum* 2, 91–10

Davies, J.L. 1980a 'Roman military deployment in Wales and the Marches from Claudius to the Antonines', in Hanson and Keppie 1980, 255–77

Davies, J.L. 1980b *Aspects of native settlement in Roman Wales and the Marches*, unpublished Ph.D. dissertation, Cardiff

Davies, J.L. 1980c 'A Roman fortlet at Erglodd, near Talybont, Dyfed', *Bull. Board Celtic Stud.* 28, 719–29

Degrassi, A. 1952 *I Fasti Consolari dell 'Impero Romano*, Rome

Dixon, T.N. 1982 'A Survey of Crannogs in Loch Tay', *Proc. Soc. Antiq. Scotland* 112, 17–38

Dobson, B. 1979 'The *Rangordnung* of the Roman army', in Pippidi, D.M. (ed.) *Actes du VIIe congrès international d'épigraphie greque et latine*, Bucharest, 191–204

Dobson, B. 1980 'Agricola's life and career', *Scottish Archaeol. Forum* 12, 1–13

Dobson, B. and Mann, J.C. 1973 'The Roman army in Britain and Britons in the Roman army', *Britannia* 4, 191–205

Dorey, T.A. 1960 'Agricola and Domitian', *Greece and Rome* 7, 66–71

Dorey, T.A. (ed.) 1969a *Tacitus*, London

Dorey, T.A. 1969b 'Agricola' and 'Germania', in Dorey 1969a, 1–18

Duncan-Jones, R.P. 1985 'Who paid for the public buildings in Roman cities?', in Grew, F. and Hobley, B. (eds.) *Roman urban topography in Britain and the western empire*, London, 28–33

Edwards, B.J.N. and Webster, P.V. 1985 *Ribchester Excavations Part I: excavations within the fort*, Cardiff

Feachem, R.W. 1966 'The hillforts of northern Britain', in Rivet 1966, 59–87

Feachem, R.W. 1970 'Mons Graupius = Duncrub?', *Antiq.* 44, 120–4

Ferguson, R.S. 1893 'On a massive timber platform of early date uncovered at Carlisle and some sundry other relics connected therewith' *Trans. Cumberland Westmorland Antiq. Archaeol. Soc.* 12, 344–64

Février, P.A. 1973 'The origin and growth of the cities of southern Gaul to the third century AD: an assessment of the most recent archaeological discoveries', *J. Roman Stud.* 63, 1–28

Fox, C. 1946 *A find of the Early Iron Age from Llyn Cerrig Bach, Anglesey*, Cardiff

Frere, S.S. 1966 'Review of Robertson 1964', *J. Roman Stud.* 56, 269–70

Frere, S.S. 1972 *Verulamium excavations Volume I*, London

Frere, S.S. 1978 *Britannia: a history of Roman Britain* (2nd edn.), London

Frere, S.S. 1979 'The Roman fort at Strageath', in Breeze 1979, 37–41

Frere, S.S. 1980a 'The Flavian frontier in Scotland', *Scottish Archaeol. Forum* 12, 89–97

Frere, S.S. 1980b 'Hyginus and the first cohort', *Britannia* 11, 51–60

Frere, S.S. (ed.) 1983a 'Roman Britain in 1982: sites explored',*Britannia* 14, 280–335

Frere, S.S. 1983b *Verulamium excavations Volume II*, London

Frere, S.S. (ed.) 1984 'Roman Britain in 1983: I. Sites explored', *Britannia* 15, 265–332

Frere, S.S. (ed.) 1985 'Roman Britain in 1984: I. Sites explored', *Britannia* 16, 252–316

Frere, S.S. 1986 'The use of Iron age hillforts by the Roman army in Britain', in Unz 1986, 42–6

Frere, S.S. and St Joseph, J.K.S. 1974 'The Roman fortress of Longthorpe', *Britannia* 5, 1–129

Frere, S.S. and St Joseph, J.K.S. 1983 *Roman Britain from the air*, Cambridge

Friell, J.G.P. and Hanson, W.S. forthcoming 'Westerton: a Roman watchtower on the Gask Frontier', *Proc. Soc. Antiq. Scotland* forthcoming

Fulford, M. 1985 'Excavations on the site of the amphitheatre and forum-basilica at Silchester, Hampshire: an interim report', *Antiq. J.* 65, 39–81

Furneaux, H. and Anderson, J.G.C. 1922 *Cornelii Taciti de vita Agricolae* (2nd edn.), Oxford

Gallivan, P. 1981 'The *fasti* for AD 70–96', *Class. Quart.* 31, 186–220

Garnsey, P.D.A. 1978 'Rome's African empire under the principate', in Garnsey P.D.A. and Whittaker, C.R. (eds.) *Imperialism in the Ancient World*, Cambridge

Garzetti, A. 1974 *From Tiberius to the Antonines: a history of the Roman Empire AD 14–192*, London

Gillam, J.P. 1958 'Roman and native AD 122–197', in Richmond 1958a, 60–90

Gillam, J.P. 1970 *Types of Roman coarse pottery vessels in Northern Britain* (3rd edn.), Newcastle

Gillam, J.P. 1975 'Possible changes in plan in the course of the construction of the Antonine Wall', *Scottish Archaeol. Forum* 7, 51–6

Gillam, J.P. 1977 'The Roman forts at Corbridge', *Archaeol. Aeliana*[5] 5, 47–74

Goodburn, R. 1978 'Roman Britain in 1977: I. Sites explored', *Britannia* 9, 404–72

Goodburn, R. 1979 'Roman Britain in 1978: I. Sites explored', *Britannia* 10, 268–338

Goodyear, F.R.D. 1970 *Tacitus*, Oxford

Greene, K. 1978 'Apperley Dene 'Roman fortlet': a re-examination 1974–5', *Archaeol. Aeliana⁵* 6, 29–59

Greene, K. 1979 *Report on the excavations at Usk, 1965–76: the pre–Flavian fine wares*, Cardiff

Greene, K. 1983 *Archaeology: an introduction*, London

Groenman-van Waateringe, W. 1986 'Food for soldiers, food for thought' in Barrett, J.C., Fitzpatrick, A. and Macinnes, L. (eds) *Barbarians and Romans in north-west Europe*, Oxford

Halliday, S.P., Hill, P.J. and Stevenson, J.B. 1981 'Early agriculture in Scotland', in Mercer, R. (ed.) *Farming practice in British prehistory*, Edinburgh, 55–65

Hanson, W.S. 1978a 'Roman campaigns north of the Forth–Clyde isthmus: the evidence of the temporary camps', *Proc. Soc. Antiq. Scotland* 109 (1977–78), 140–150

Hanson, W.S. 1978b 'Corbridge and Croy Hill: recent work on Agricola's third and fourth campaigns', in Fitz, J. (ed.) *Limes: Akten des XI Internationalen Limeskongresses*, Budapest, 1–12

Hanson, W.S. 1978c 'The organisation of the Roman military timber supply', *Britannia* 9, 293–305

Hanson, W.S. 1979 'Croy Hill', in Breeze 1979, 19–20

Hanson, W.S. 1980a 'Agricola on the Forth–Clyde isthmus', *Scottish Archaeol. Forum* 12, 55–68

Hanson, W.S. 1980b 'The first Roman occupation of Scotland', in Hanson and Keppie, 1980, 15–43

Hanson, W.S. 1982 'Roman military timber buildings: construction and reconstruction', in McGrail, S. (ed.) *Woodworking Techniques before AD 1500*, Oxford, 169–86

Hanson, W.S. 1986a 'Building the forts and frontiers', in Breeze, D.J. (ed.) *The Frontiers of the Roman empire,* London, forthcoming

Hanson, W.S. 1986b 'Rome, the Cornovii and the Ordovices', in Unz 1986, 47–52

Hanson, W.S. and Campbell, D.B. 1986 'The Brigantes: from clientage to conquest', *Britannia* 17, 73–89

Hanson, W.S., Daniels, C.M., Dore, J.N. and Gillam, J.P. 1979 'The Agricolan supply-base at Red House, Corbridge', *Archaeol. Aeliana⁵* 7, 1–97

Hanson, W.S. and Keppie, L.J.F. (eds.) 1980 *Roman Frontier Studies 1979*, Oxford

Hanson, W.S. and Macinnes, L. 1980 'Forests, forts and fields: a discussion', *Scottish Archaeol. Forum* 12, 98–113

Hanson, W.S. and Maxwell, G.S. 1980 'An Agricolan *praesidium* on the

Forth–Clyde isthmus (Mollins, Strathclyde)', *Britannia* 11, 43–7

Hanson, W.S. and Maxwell, G.S. 1983 *Rome's north-west frontier: the Antonine Wall*, Edinburgh

Harding, D.W. (ed.) 1982 *Later Prehistoric settlement in southeast Scotland*, Edinburgh

Hartley, B.R. 1966 'Some problems of the Roman occupation of the north of England', *Northern Hist.* 1, 7–20

Hartley, B.R. 1969, 'Samian Ware or Terra Sigillata', in Collingwood and Richmond 1969, 235–51

Hartley, B.R. 1971 'Roman York and the northern military command to the third century AD', in Butler, R.M. (ed.) *Soldier and Civilian in Roman Yorkshire*, Leicester, 55–69

Hartley, B.R. 1972 'The Roman occupation of Scotland: the evidence of the Samian ware', *Britannia* 3, 1–55

Hartley, B.R. 1981 'The early Roman military occupation of Lincoln and Chester', in Anderson, A.C. and A.S. (eds.) *Roman pottery research in Britain and north-west Europe*, Oxford, 239–47

Hartley, B.R. and Wacher, J. (eds.) 1983 *Rome and her northern provinces*, Gloucester

Haselgrove, C. 1984 'The later pre–Roman Iron age between the Humber and the Tyne', in Wilson *et al.* 1984, 9–25

Hebditch, M. and Mellor, J. 1973 'The forum and basilica of Roman Leicester', *Britannia* 4, 1–83

Henderson, A.A.R. 1984 'From 83 to 1983: on the trail of Mons Graupius', *The Deeside Field* 18, 23–9

Henig, M. 1984 *Religion in Roman Britain*, London

Higham, N.J. 1982 'The Roman impact upon rural settlement in Cumbria', in Clack, P. and Haselgrove, S. (eds.) *Rural settlement in the Roman north*, Durham, 105–122

Hill, P. 1982 'Broxmouth hill-fort excavations, 1977–78: an interim report', in Harding 1982, 141–88

Hind, J.G.F. 1974 'Agricola's fleet and Portus Trucculensis', *Britannia* 5, 285–8

Hind, J.G.F. 1983 'Caledonia and its occupation under the Flavians', *Proc. Soc. Antiq. Scotland* 113, 373–8

Hind, J.G.F. 1985 'Summers and winters in Tacitus' account of Agricola's campaigns in Britain', *Northern Hist.* 21, 1–18

Hird, L. 1977 *Vindolanda V: the pre-Hadrianic pottery*, Hexham

Hobley, B. 1971 'An experimental reconstruction of a Roman military turf rampart', in Applebaum, S. (ed.) *Roman Frontier Studies 1967*, Tel Aviv, 21–33

Hobley, B. 1974 'The Lunt: reconstruction', *Current Archaeol.* 44, 276–80

Hogg, A.H.A. 1966 'Native settlement in Wales', in Thomas, C. (ed.) *Rural Settlement in Roman Britain*, London, 28–38

Hogg, A.H.A. 1968 'Pen Llystyn: a Roman fort and other remains',

Archaeol. J. 125, 101–92

Holder, P. 1977 'Domitian and the title Germanicus', *Liverpool Class. Monthly* 2.7, 151

Holder, P. 1982 *The Roman army in Britain*, London

Jarrett, M.G. 1964 'Excavations at Tomen-y-Mur, 1962', *J. Merioneth Hist. Record Soc.* 4 (1961–4), 171–5

Jarrett, M.G. (ed.) 1969 *The Roman Frontier in Wales* (2nd. edn.) Cardiff

Jarrett, M.G. and Mann, J.C. 1968 'The tribes of Wales', *Welsh Hist. Rev.* 4.2, 161–71

Jobey, G. 1965 'Hillforts and settlements in Northumberland', *Archaeol. Aeliana⁴* 43, 21–64

Jobey, G. 1973 'A native settlement at Hartburn and the Devil's Causeway, Northumberland', *Archaeol. Aeliana⁵* 1, 11–53

Jobey, G. 1976 'Traprain Law: a summary', in Harding, D.W. (ed.) *Hillforts*, London, 192–204

Jobey, G. 1977 'Iron Age and later farmsteads on Belling Law, Northumberland', *Archaeol. Aeliana⁵* 5, 1–38

Jobey, G. 1978 'Burnswark Hill', *Trans. Dumfriesshire Galloway Natur. Hist. Antiq. Soc.* 53 (1977–78), 57–104

Johnson, S. 1978 'Excavations at Hayton Roman fort, 1975', *Britannia* 9, 57–114

Jones, A.H.M. 1960 *Studies in Roman government and law*, Oxford

Jones, A.H.M. (ed.) 1970 *A History of Rome through the Fifth Century, Volume II: the Empire*, London

Jones, A.H.M. 1974 *The Roman Economy*, Oxford

Jones, B.W. 1984 *The Emperor Titus*, London

Jones, G.D.B. and Grealey, S. (eds.) 1974 *Roman Manchester*, Manchester

Jones, G.D.B. and Wild, J.P. 1969 'Manchester University excavations at Brough-on-Noe (Navio) 1969', *Derbyshire Archaeol. J.* 69, 99–106

Jones, M.J. 1975 *Roman fort defences to AD 117*, Oxford

Keppie, L.J.F. 1980 'Mons Graupius: the search for a battlefield', *Scottish Archaeol. Forum* 12, 79–88

Keppie, L.J.F. 1982 'The Antonine Wall 1960–1980', *Britannia* 13, 91–111

Kraay, C. 1960 'Two new sestertii of Domitian', *American Numis. Soc. Notes* 9, 109–16

Lacey, W.K. 1957 'Some uses of *primus* in naval contexts', *Class. Quarterly* 51, 118–122

Laing, L. 1969 'Medieval and other material in Linlithgow Palace museum', *Proc. Soc. Antiq. Scotland* 101 (1968–69), 134–45

Lenoir, M. 1977 'Lager mit claviculae', *Melanges de l'école Francaise de Rome: Antiquité* 89, 697–722

Lloyd-Jones, M. 1984 *Society and settlement in Wales and the Marches*, Oxford

Luttwak, E.N. 1976 *The Grand Strategy of the Roman Empire*, Baltimore

Lynch, F. 1970 *Prehistoric Anglesey*, Anglesey

McCarthy, M.R. 1984 'Roman Carlisle', in Wilson *et al.* 1984, 65–74

Macdonald, G. 1918 'Roman coins found in Scotland', *Proc. Soc. Antiq. Scotland* 52, (1917–18), 203–76

Macdonald, G. 1919 'The Agricolan occupation of north Britain', *J. Roman Stud.* 9, 11–138

Macdonald, G. 1934 *The Roman Wall in Scotland* (2nd edn.) Oxford

MacGregor, M. 1962 'The early Iron age metalwork hoard from Stanwick, N.R. Yorks.', *Proc. Prehist. Soc.* 28, 17–57

MacGregor, M. 1976 *Early Celtic art in north Britain: a study of decorative metalwork from the third century BC to the third century AD*, Leicester

Macinnes, L. 1982 'Pattern and purpose: the settlement evidence', in Harding 1982, 57–73

Macinnes, L. 1983 *Later prehistoric and Romano-British settlement north and south of the Forth: a comparative survey*, unpublished Ph.D. dissertation, University of Newcastle

Macinnes, L. 1984 'Brochs and the Roman occupation of lowland Scotland', *Proc. Soc. Antiq. Scotland* 114, 235–49

McPeake, J.C. 1978 'The first century AD', in Strickland, T.J. and Davey, P.J. (eds.) *New Evidence for Roman Chester*, Chester, 9–10

McPeake, J.C., Bulmer, M.A. and Rutter, J.A. 1980 'Excavations in the garden of No. 1 Abbey Green, Chester. 1975–77: interim report', *J. Chester Archaeol. Soc.* 63, 14–37

Mann, J.C. 1968 'Review of Ogilvie and Richmond 1967', *Archaeol. Aeliana*[4] 46, 306–8

Mann, J.C. 1985 'Two "Topoi" in the *Agricola*', *Britannia* 16, 21–4

Mann, J.C. and Penman, R.G. 1977 *Literary sources for Roman Britain*, London

Manning, W.H. 1972 'Ironwork hoards in Iron age and Roman Britain', *Britannia* 3, 224–50

Manning, W.H. 1975 'Economic influences on land use in the military areas of the Highland Zone during the Roman period', in Evans, J.G., Limbrey, S. and Cleere, H. (eds.) *The effect of man on the landscape of the Highland Zone*, London, 112–116

Manning, W.H. 1981 *Report on the excavations at Usk 1965–1976: the fortress excavations 1968–1971*, Cardiff

Marsden, P. 1978 'The discovery of the civic centre of Roman London', in Bird, J., Chapman, H. and Clark, J. (eds.) *Collectanea Londiniensia: studies in London archaeology and history presented to Ralph Merrifield*, London

Martin, R. 1981 *Tacitus*, London

Mattingly, H. 1948 *Tacitus on Britain and Germany: a translation of the Agricola and the Germania*, London

Maxfield, V.A. 1980 'The Flavian fort at Camelon', *Scottish Archaeol. Forum*

12, 69–78

Maxwell, G.S. 1972 'Excavations at the Roman fort at Crawford, Lanarkshire', *Proc. Soc. Antiq. Scotland* 104, (1971–72), 147–200

Maxwell, G.S. 1980a 'The native background to the Roman occupation of Scotland', in Hanson and Keppie 1980, 1–13

Maxwell, G.S. 1980b 'Agricola's campaigns: the evidence of the temporary camps', *Scottish Archaeol. Forum* 12, 25–54

Maxwell, G.S. 1983a 'Recent aerial discoveries in Roman Scotland: Drumquhassle, Elginhaugh and Woodhead', *Britannia* 14, 167–81

Maxwell, G.S. 1983b '"Roman" settlement in Scotland', in Chapman and Mytum 1983, 233–61

Maxwell, G.S. 1984 'New frontiers: The Roman fort at Doune and its possible significance', *Britannia* 15, 217–23

Merrifield, R. 1983 *London: city of the Romans*, London

Millar, F. 1967 *The Roman empire and its neighbours*, London

Millar, F. 1977 *The Emperor in the Roman world (31 BC–AD 337)*, London

Miller, N.P. 1969 'Style and content in Tacitus' in Dorey 1969a, 99–116

Miller, S.N. 1952 *The Roman Occupation of south–western Scotland*, Glasgow

Mocsy, A. 1974 *Pannonia and upper Moesia*, London

Mommsen, T. 1952 *Römische Staatsrecht, vol. 2* (2nd. edn.), Basel

Morris, J. 1964 '*Leges Annales* under the principate: 1 legal and constitutional', *Listy Filologicke* 87, 316–37

Morrison, I. 1985 *Landscape with lake-dwellings: the crannogs of Scotland*, Edinburgh

Newall, F. 1975 'The Romans and Strathclyde: the first century AD occupation', *The Western Naturalist* 4, 79–94

Ogilvie, R.M. and Richmond, I.A. 1967 *Cornelii Taciti de Vita Agricolae*, Oxford

Ordnance Survey 1978 *Map of Roman Britain* (4th edn.), Southampton

Petrikovits, H. von 1975 *Die Innenbauten römischer legionslager wahrend der Principatszeit*, Opladen

Philp, B.J. 1977 'The forum of Roman London: excavations of 1968–9', *Britannia* 8, 1–64

Piggott, S. 1958 'Native economies and the Roman occupation of north Britain', in Richmond 1958, 1–27

Pitts, L. and St Joseph, J.K.S. 1985 *Inchtuthil: the Roman legionary fortress*, London

Pococke, R. 1887 *Tours in Scotland 1747, 1750, 1760* (ed. D.W. Kemp), Edinburgh

Postgate, P.E. 1930 'Notes on Tacitus', *Proc. Cambridge Phil. Soc.* 8, 145–7

Potter, T.W. 1979 *Romans in north-west England: excavations at the Roman forts of Ravenglass, Watercrook and Bowness on Solway*, Kendal

Powell, T.G.E. 1980 *The Celts* (2nd. edn.), London

Rackham, H. 1942 *Pliny: Natural History. Volume II*, London
Rae, A. and Rae, V. 1974 'The Roman fort at Cramond, Edinburgh: excavations 1954–66', *Britannia* 5, 163–224
Rainbird, J.S. 1969 'Tactics at Mons Graupius', *Class. Rev.* 19, 11–12
Ralston, I.B.M., Sabine, K. and Watt, W. 1983 'Later prehistoric settlement in north-east Scotland: a preliminary assessment', in Chapman and Mytum 1983, 149–73
Rankov, N.B. 1982 'Roman Britain in 1981: I. Sites explored', *Britannia* 13, 328–395
R.C.A.H.M.S. 1929 *An Inventory of the monuments and constructions in the counties of Midlothian and West Lothian*, Edinburgh
Reece, R. 1974 'Numerical aspects of Roman coin hoards in Britain', in Casey and Reece 1974, 78–94
Reed, N. 1971 'The fifth year of Agricola's campaigns', *Britannia* 2, 143–48
Reed, N. 1976 'The Scottish campaigns of Septimius Severus', *Proc. Soc. Antiq. Scotland* 107 (1975–76), 92–102
Reynolds, N.D. and Wilson, N.G. 1974 *Scribes and scholars: a guide to the transmission of Greek and Latin literature* (2nd. edn.), Oxford
Reynolds, P.K. Baillie 1938 *Excavations on the site of the Roman fort of Kanovium at Caerhun, Caernarvonshire*, Cardiff
Richmond, I.A. 1936 'Excavations at High Rochester and Risingham, 1935', *Archaeol. Aeliana*[4] 13, 170–98
Richmond, I.A. 1944 'Gnaeus Julius Agricola', *J. Roman Stud.* 34, 34–45
Richmond, I.A. 1950 'Excavations at the Roman fort of Newstead, 1947', *Proc. Soc. Antiq. Scotland* 84 (1949–50), 1–38
Richmond, I.A. 1951 'Exploratory trenching at the Roman fort at Cappuck, Roxburghshire, in 1949', *Proc. Soc. Antiq. Scotland* 85 (1950–51), 138–45
Richmond, I.A. (ed.) 1958 *Roman and native in north Britain*, Edinburgh
Richmond, I.A. 1980 'The Roman fort at Inveresk, Midlothian', (ed. W.S. Hanson), *Proc. Soc. Antiq. Scotland* 110 (1978–80), 286–304
Richmond, I.A. and Keeney, G.S. 1937 'The Roman works at Chew Green, Coquetdalehead', *Archaeol. Aeliana*[4] 14, 129–50
Richmond, I.A. and McIntyre, J. 1934 'The Roman camps at Rey Cross and Crackenthorpe', *Trans. Cumberland Westmorland Antiq. Archaeol. Soc.* 34, 50–61
Richmond, I.A. and McIntyre, J. 1939 'The Agricolan fort at Fendoch', *Proc. Soc. Antiq. Scotland* 73 (1938–39), 110–54
Richmond, I.A. and St Joseph, J.K.S. 1952 'The Roman fort at Glenlochar, Kirkcudbrightshire', *Trans. Dumfriesshire Galloway Natur. Hist. Antiq. Soc.* 30 (1950–52), 1–16
Richmond, I.A. and St Joseph, J.K.S. 1956 'The Roman fort at Dalswinton', *Trans. Dumfriesshire Galloway Natur. Hist. Antiq. Soc.* 34 (1955–6),

1–21

Rickman, G. 1971 *Roman granaries and store buildings*, Cambridge

Rivet, A.L.F. 1964 'Gask signal stations', *Archaeol. J.* 121, 196–8

Rivet, A.L.F. (ed.) 1966 *The Iron Age in Northern Britain*, Edinburgh

Rivet, A.L.F. 1982 'Brittones Anavionenses', *Britannia* 13, 321–2

Rivet, A.L.F. 1983 'The first Icenian revolt', in Hartley and Wacher 1983, 202–209

Rivet, A.L.F. and Smith, C. 1979 *The Place-names of Roman Britain*, London

Robertson, A.S. 1963 'Miscellanea Romano-Caledonica', *Proc. Soc. Antiq. Scotland* 97 (1962–63), 180–201

Robertson, A.S. 1964 *The Roman fort at Castledykes*, Edinburgh

Robertson, A.S. 1968 'Two groups of Roman *asses* from north Britain', *Numis. Chron.* 8, 61–6

Robertson, A.S. 1970 'Roman finds from non-Roman sites in Scotland', *Britannia* 1, 198–226

Robertson, A.S. 1974 'Roman 'signal stations' on the Gask Ridge', *Trans. Perthshire Soc. Natur. Sci. Special Issue*, 14–29

Robertson, A.S. 1975a *Birrens (Blatobulgium)*, Edinburgh

Robertson, A.S. 1975b 'Agricola's campaigns in Scotland and their aftermath', *Scottish Archaeol. Forum* 7, 1–12

Robertson, A.S. 1975c 'The Romans in north Britain: the coin evidence', in Temporini, H. (ed.) *Aufstieg und Niedergang der römischen Welt II.3*, Berlin, 364–428

Robertson, A.S. 1977 'Excavations at Cardean and Stracathro, Angus', in Haupt, D. and Horn, H.G. (eds.) *Studien zu den Militärgrenzen Roms. II*, Cologne/Bonn, 65–74

Rüger, C.B. 1980 'Research on the *limes* of Germania Inferior (German part), 1974–79', in Hanson and Keppie 1980, 495–500

St Joseph, J.K.S. 1951 'Air reconnaissance of north Britain', *J. Roman Stud.* 41, 52–65

St Joseph, J.K.S. 1952 'Three Nithsdale sites', in Miller 1952, 117–123

St Joseph, J.K.S. 1969 'Air reconnaissance in Britain, 1965–68', *J. Roman Stud.* 59, 104–28

St Joseph, J.K.S. 1970 'The camps at Ardoch, Stracathro and Ythan Wells: recent excavations', *Britannia* 1, 163–78

St Joseph, J.K.S. 1973 'Air reconnaissance in Roman Britain, 1969–72', *J. Roman Stud.* 63, 214–46

St Joseph, J.K.S. 1977 'Air reconnaissance in Roman Britain, 1973–6', *J. Roman Stud.* 67, 125–61

St Joseph, J.K.S. 1978a 'A Roman camp near Girvan, Ayrshire', *Britannia* 9, 397–401

St Joseph, J.K.S. 1978b 'The camp at Durno, Aberdeenshire, and the site of Mons Graupius', *Britannia* 9, 271–87

St Joseph, J.K.S. 1983 'The Roman fortlet at Gatehouse-of-Fleet, Kirkcudbrightshire', in Hartley and Wacher 1983, 222–34

Salway, P. 1981 *Roman Britain*, Oxford

Schönberger, H. 1969 'The Roman frontier in Germany: an archaeological survey', *J. Roman Stud.* 59, 144–97

Seager, R.J. 1972 *Tiberius*, London

Sherwin-White, A.N. 1966 *The Letters of Pliny: a historical and social commentary*, Oxford

Sherwin-White, A.N. 1973 *The Roman Citizenship* (2nd. edn.) Oxford

Shotter, D.C.A. 1980 'The Roman occupation of north-west England: the coin evidence', *Trans. Cumberland Westmorland Antiq. Archaeol. Soc.* 80, 1–15

Shotter, D.C.A. 1984 *Roman north-west England*, Lancaster

Starr, C.G. 1941 *The Roman imperial navy 31 BC–AD 324*, New York

Stead, I.M. 1979 *The Arras Culture*, York

Steer, K.A. 1957 'The Roman fort at Easter Happrew, Peeblesshire', *Proc. Soc. Antiq. Scotland* 90 (1956–7), 93–101

Steer, K.A. and Feachem, R.W. 1952a 'A Roman signal-station on Eildon Hill north, Roxburghshire', *Proc. Soc. Antiq. Scotland* 86, (1951–2), 202–5

Steer, K.A. and Feachem, R.W. 1952b 'The Roman fort and temporary camp at Oakwood, Selkirkshire', *Proc. Soc. Antiq. Scotland* 86 (1951–2), 81–105

Stevenson, G.H. 1939 *Roman provincial administration till the age of the Antonines*, Oxford

Strickland, T.J. 1980 'First century Deva: some evidence reconsidered in the light of recent archaeological discoveries', *J. Chester Archaeol. Soc.* 63, 5–13

Sumpter, A.B. 1984 'The *vicus* of the Roman fort at Castleford', in Wilson *et al.* 1984, 83–6

Syme, R. 1958 *Tacitus*, Oxford

Talbert, R.J.A. 1984 *The Senate of Imperial Rome*, Princeton

Tatton-Brown, T.W.T. 1980 'Camelon, Arthur's Oon and the main supply base for the Antonine Wall', *Britannia* 11, 340–3

Taylor, M.V. (ed.) 1949 'Roman Britain in 1948: sites explored', *J. Roman Stud.* 39, 96–115

Taylor, M.V. (ed.) 1954 'Roman Britain in 1953: sites explored', *J. Roman Stud.* 44, 83–103

Taylor, M.V. (ed.) 1955 'Roman Britain in 1954: sites explored', *Roman Stud.* 45, 121–45

Taylor, M.V. (ed.) 1957 'Roman Britain in 1956: sites explored', *J. Roman Stud.* 47, 198–226

Tierney, J.J. 1959 'Ptolemy's map of Scotland', *J. Hellenic Stud.* 79, 132–48

Todd, M. 1981 *Roman Britain: 55 BC–AD 400*, Brighton

Traub, H.W. 1954 'Agricola's refusal of a governorship', *Class. Phil.* 49, 255–7

Turner, J. 1979 'The environment of north-east England during Roman times as shown by pollen analysis', *J. Archaeol. Sci.* 6, 285–90

Urban, R. 1971 *Historische Untersuchungen zum Domitianbild des Tacitus*, Munich
Unz, C. (ed.) 1986 *Studien zu den Militärgrenzen Roms III*, Stuttgart

Wacher, J.S. 1969 *Excavations at Brough-on-Humber, 1958-1961*, London
Wacher, J.S. 1975 *The Towns of Roman Britain*, London
Wacher, J.S. and McWhirr, A. 1982 *Cirencester excavations I: early Roman occupation at Cirencester*, Cirencester
Wainwright, F.T. 1963 *The souterrains of southern Pictland*, London
Walthew, C.V. 1975 'The town house and the villa house in Roman Britain', *Britannia* 6, 189–205
Watkins, T. 1980 'Excavation of a settlement and souterrain at Newmill, near Bankfoot, Perthshire', *Proc. Soc. Antiq. Scotland* 110, 165–208
Webster, G. 1978 *Boudica*, London
Wellesley, K. 1954 'Can you trust Tacitus?', *Greece and Rome* 23, 13–33
Wellesley, K. 1969a 'Tacitus as a military historian', in Dorey 1969a, 63–97
Wellesley, K. 1969b 'Review of Ogilvie and Richmond 1967', *J. Roman Stud.* 59, 266–69
Wellesley, K. 1975 *The long year AD 69*, London
Wheeler, R.E.M. 1954 *The Stanwick fortifications, North Riding of Yorkshire*, London
White, R.B. 1978 'Excavations at Brithdir, near Dollgellau, 1974', in Boon, G.C. (ed.) *Monographs and collections relating to excavations financed by her Majesty's Department of the Environment in Wales I: Roman sites*, Cardiff, 35–62
White, R.B. 1980 'Excavations at Aberffraw, Anglesey, 1973 and 1974', *Bull. Board Celtic Stud.* 28, 319–42
Wilkes, J.J. 1985 '*R.I.B.* 1322: a note', *Zeitschrift für Papyrologie und Epigraphik* 59, 291–6
Wilson, D. 1983 'Pollen analysis and settlement archaeology of the first millennium AD from north-east England', in Chapman and Mytum, 1983, 29–54
Wilson, D.R. (ed.) 1962 'Roman Britain in 1961: I. sites explored', *J. Roman Stud.* 52, 160–90
Wilson, D.R. (ed.) 1964 'Roman Britain in 1963: I. sites explored', *J. Roman Stud.* 54, 152–7
Wilson, D.R. (ed.) 1965 'Roman Britain in 1964: I. sites explored', *J. Roman Stud.* 55, 199–220
Wilson, D.R. (ed.) 1969 'Roman Britain in 1968: I. sites explored', *J. Roman Stud.* 59, 198–234
Wilson, D.R. (ed.) 1975 'Roman Britain in 1974: I. sites explored', *Britannia* 6, 221–83

Wilson, D.R. 1983 *Air Photo interpretation for archaeologists*, London

Wilson, D.R. 1984 'Defensive outworks of Roman forts in Britain', *Britannia* 15, 51–61

Wilson, P.R., Jones, R.F.J. and Evans, D.M. (eds.) 1984 *Settlement and Society in the Roman north*, Bradford

Woodhead, A.G. 1948 'Tacitus and Agricola', *Phoenix* 2, 45–55

Woodman, T. 1979 'Self imitation and the substance of history', in West, D. and Woodman, T. (eds.) *Creative imitation and Latin Literature*, Cambridge, 143–55

Wright, R.P. (ed.) 1965 'Roman Britain in 1964: II. Inscriptions', *J. Roman Stud.* 55, 220–28

Wright, R.P. and Hassall, M.W.C. (eds.) 1971 'Roman Britain in 1970: II. Inscriptions', *Britannia* 2, 289–304

Wright, R.P. and Richmond, I.A. 1955 *Catalogue of the Roman Inscribed and Sculptured stones in the Grosvenor Museum, Chester*, Chester

Addenda to the bibliography

Evans, J. and Scull, C. 1990 'Fieldwork on the Roman fort site at Blennerhassett, Cumbria', *Trans. Cumberland Westmorland Antiq. Archaeol. Soc.* 90, 127–37

Frere, S.S. and Wilkes, J.J. 1989 *Strageath: excavations within the Roman fort 1973–86*, London

Hanson, W.S. 1991 ''Tacitus' 'Agricola': an archaeological and historical study', in Haase, W. (ed.) *Aufstieg und Niedergang der römischen Welt II 33, 3*, Berlin, 1741–84

Hanson, W.S. and Yeoman, P.A. 1988 *Elginhaugh: a Roman fort and its environs*, Glasgow

Hobley, A.S. 1989 'The numismatic evidence for the post–Agricolan abandonment of the Roman frontier in northern Scotland' *Britannia* 20, 69–74

King, A.C. 1984 'Animal bones and the dietary identity of military and civilian groups in Roman Britain, Germany and Gaul', in Blagg and King 1984, 187-217

Index

Aberffraw, possible fort 51; fig 2
Abernethy, temporary camp 84, 127; figs 10, 11, 18
acta diurna 16
acta senatus 16
Adamclisi 152
aerial photography 27–8
Agricola, book
  literary genre 19
  manuscript tradition 22
  political purpose 19
Agricola, Cn. Julius
  administration of justice 69–70
  arrival in Britain 44–6
  birth 33
  consulship 40, 43
  daughter's marriage 44
  death 182–3
  early career 34–9
  family 35–7
  governorship of Aquitania 40, 44, 71
  military abilities 174–9
  personal characteristics 39, 49, 185–6
  proconsulship 180–2
  retirement 180–1, 184
  triumphal decorations 180
agriculture, native 48, 60, 170
ala Petriana 160
ala I Pannoniorum 152
ala I Tungrorum 152
Ambleside, fort 161; fig 8
Anglesey 47, 49–50, 176
Annan Waterfoot, temporary camp 95; fig 10
Aniensis, voting tribe 33
Antonine Wall 23, 108–12, 178
Apperley Dene, native settlement 102
Aquitania 40, 44, 71
Ardoch, fort 90, 121, 153, 156–7, 178; figs 15, 17, 19, 22, 25
  temporary camps 123, 126–7; figs 18, 19

army, Roman
  assistance in town building 81
  division into three 123
  effect on local population 166–73
  methods of controlling territory 51
  procedure on campaign 48, 50–1
  recruitment 70, 167, 183
asses, bronze coins 147, 151, 158; pl 18
Auchinhove, temporary camp 125, 136; figs 18, 20

Bainbridge, fort 162; fig 8
Balmuildy, fort 109
Bankhead, fortlet 104; fig 15
Bar Hill, enclosure 108–9
Barochan Hill, fort 110–11, 177; figs 15, 17, 22
Batavians, auxiliary troops 49, 137
Beattock, temporary camp 125; fig 10
Bellie, temporary camp 127; fig 18
Belling Law, native enclosure 168
Bennachie 134; pl 13
Bertha, fort 156; figs 15, 17, 22, 25
Binchester, fort 68, fig 8
Birrens, fort 102; fig 15; pl 9
Bishopton, fort 178
Blackhill Wood, watchtower 156; figs 25, 26
Blakehope, fort 160, 164
Bochastle (Callendar), fort 113, 148, 150, 178; fig 22
  temporary camp 123, 125–6; figs 18, 20
Bonnytown, temporary camp 126–7; fig 18
Boresti, tribe 21, 117, 120, 140; fig 18
Bothwellhaugh, fort 104
Boudica 21
Boudican revolt 21, 34–5, 37, 50, 71, 78, 80
Bowes, fort 65; fig 4
Braich-y-Ddinas, hillfort 48

Branogenium (Leintwardine) 46; fig 1
Bremenium see High Rochester
Brigantes, tribe 21, 39, 46
    economy 60
    political structure 55, 59
    territory 55–7, 91; fig 10
Brigantia, goddess 57
Brithdir, fortlet 51, 113; fig 2
brochs 90
Broomholm, fort 104, 160, 167; figs 15, 27
Brough on Humber, fort 65, 113–14; figs 4, 8
Brough-on-Noe, fort 162, fig 8
Broxmouth, native fort 168
Burnswark, native fort 91, 168; fig 10

Cadder, fort 110–11; figs 15, 17
Caer Gai, fort 51–2; fig 2
Caerhun, fort 51; fig 2
Caermote, fort 178; fig 8
Caernarvon, fort 54, 113; fig 2
Caersws, fort 113; fig 2
Caledonia 21, 56, 116
Caledonian Forest 56
Calgacus 17, 21, 129
Caligula see Gaius
Camelon, fort 30, 110–12, 121; figs 15, 17, 18, 22
    temporary camps 112, 123; fig 10, see also Lochlands
campaigns, of Agricola
    first 46–54
    second 54–68
    third 84–8, 97–8
    fourth 93, 99–104
    fifth 93–6
    sixth 115–27
    seventh 40, 127–42
Camulodunum see Colchester and Slack
Canterbury, town 74
Cappuck, fort 99, 160, 164, 167; figs 15, 27
Caratacus 21, 39
carbon-14, dating method 31, 47
Cardean, fort 149, 151, 167, 178; fig 22
    temporary camp 127; fig 18
Cardiff, fort 161
Cargill, fort and fortlet 121, 146, 153; figs 15, 22
Carlisle, fort 61, 163; figs 8, 10, 15, 27; pl 21

carnyx, native war trumpet 137; pl 14, see also Deskford
Cartimandua, queen of the Brigantes 19, 21, 38–9, 56, 59–60
Carvetii, tribe 58
Castlecary, fort 110–11, 158; figs 15, 17, 27
Castledykes, fort 103–4, 125, 158; figs 15, 16
    temporary camps 84, 103, 123; figs 10, 16
Castleford, fort 65; figs 4, 8
Castle Greg, fortlet 104; fig 15
Castleshaw, fort 57; fig 8
censitor Brittonum 168–9
chariots, native 138
Chatti, tribe 41, 152, 176
Chester, legionary fortress 26, 52–3, 152; figs 2, 8
Chew Green, fortlet 99; fig 15
    temporary camp fig 10
Chichester, town 26, 76–8
circumnavigation, of Britain 42, 140–2, 176
Cirencester, town 79
citizenship, Roman 33, 81
civil settlements (vici) 161, 162
civitas capitals 74–9
civitates 74–6
Claudius, emperor 17, 41, 81
calvicular gateways, in temporary camps 112, 123, 178
client rulers 26, 69
Cogidubnus, Ti. Claudius, client king 26, 75–7
cohors II Asturum 166
cohors I Batavorum 137
cohors II Batavorum 137, 152
cohors VIII Batavorum 137
cohors Brittonum 137
cohors I Cugernorum 166
cohors I Tungrorum 137
cohors II Tungrorum 137
coins, Roman see also asses
    circulation life 169
    commemorating victory of Domitian 42; pl 1
    from native settlements 169; fig 28
    method of dating 28–9
Colchester, Roman colony 21, 73, 81
Columella 33
congiarium 41

consulship 43
conventus 69
Corbridge, fort 30, 163, 164–5; figs 8, 27, *see also* Red House
Corionototae 57
Coritani (Corieltauvi), tribe 57
Cornelius Fuscus 152
Cornovii, tribe, 46
corruption, of Roman officials 71–2
Cramond, fort 99
crannogs 90, 116
Crawford, fort 103, 158; fig 15
cropmarks 27, 47, 106, *see also* aerial photography
Croy Hill, enclosure 108–9
cursus publicus 41, 43–4, 70

Dacians 152
Dalginross, fort 123; fig 22
   temporary camp 123; 125–6, 148, 150, 151; figs 18, 20; pl 12
Dalswinton, fort 61, 105, 158–60, 163, 164, 177; figs 4, 7, 15, 27; pl 11
   temporary camps 125; fig 10
Deceangli, tribe 22, 23, 50, 53
Demetrius of Tarsus 82
Dere Street 85, 99, 102
Deskford, carnyx from 137; fig 18; pl 14
Devona 117; fig 1
Domitia Decidiana, wife of Agricola 35
Domitian, emperor
   consulship 43
   death 183
   expansionist policy 115
   imperial acclamations 139
   jealousy of Agricola 180–7
   tyrant 18–19, 180
   war against the Chatti 41, 152, 172, 180
Doncaster, fort 65, 114; figs 4, 8
Dornock, temporary camp 127; fig 18
Doune, fort 84, 113; figs 15, 17, 18, 22
Drumlanrig, fort 106, fig 15
Drumquhassle, fort 113, 148; fig 22
Dumnonii, tribe 90–1; figs 10, 18
Dun, temporary camp 126, 167; fig 18; pl 23
   native settlement 167; pl 23
Dunblane, temporary camp 127; fig 18
Duncrub, postulated site of Mons Graupius 130
Dunning, temporary camp 84, 127, 130;

figs 10, 11, 18
duns 90
Durno, temporary camp 134–6; figs 18, 21
druids 50

Easter Gallcantray, postulated fort 97
Easter Happrew, fort 102, 104, 108, 158, 177; fig 15; pl 10
Ebchester, fort 68; fig 8
education, encouragement of 82–3
Eildon Hill North, tribal capital 91, 92–3, 167; figs 10, 13
Elginhaugh, fort 99, 108, 111, 158, 167, 177, 178; figs 15, 17, 22; pl 20
Elslack, fort 78; fig 8
epigraphy 25–6
Erglodd, fortlet 51, 113; fig 2
Exeter 79

fasti 43, 44
Fendoch, fort 148–9, 151; figs 22, 24
Finavon, temporary camp 127; fig 18
Fishbourne, palace 76
fleet 115, 126, 140, 175–6
food supplies, to forts 71–2, 169–70, 179–80
Forden Gaer, fort 161; fig 2
forest clearance 170
forts, Roman
   building of 63–5, 93, 97–9, 143–4, 177
   burning of 163–5
   demolition of 150–1, 157–8
   general disposition of 105, 149, 178–9
   glen-blocking (Highland line) 148–9
Forum Julii (Fréjus) 33, 37
Frisii, tribe 42, 169
frontier *see also* Antonine Wall, Hadrian's Wall, Stanegate
   on Forth-Clyde isthmus 107
   on Gask Ridge 153–7
   policy 112–3
frumentum emptum 71

Gabrantovices 57
Gaius, emperor 34
Galba, emperor 36, 107
Gangani, tribe 47
Gask House, watchtower 153, 156; figs 25, 26
Gask Ridge 121, 153–7; figs 25, 26; pl 19
Gatehouse of Fleet, fortlet 105, 160; fig 15

Gelligaer, fort 161
Germanicus, title taken by Domitian 41
Girvan, temporary camps 95–6; fig 10
Glenbank, fortlet 153, 156–7; figs 22, 25
Glenlochar, fort 105, 160, 164; figs 15, 27
    temporary camps 123; fig 10
Gogar, temporary camps 112
Gourdie, stone quarried from 148
Greta Bridge, fort 162; fig 8

Hadrian's Wall 108, 111–12
harbours 102, 106, 112, 162
Hartburn, native settlement 102
Hayton, fort 65, 114; fig 8
Hibernia 21; fig 1, *see also* Ireland
High Rochester, fort 90, 99, 160, 164; figs 15, 27
hillforts 47, 59, 90, 134
Huntingtower, watchtower 153
Hyndford, crannog 171
Hyperboreans 140

Iceni, tribe 21, 22, 56
imperator, imperial title 42, 107, 139
imperial cult 81
Inchtuthil, legionary fortress 143, 146–8, 151, 167; figs 22, 23
Intimilii 37
Inveresk, fort 99, 178
Inverquharity, fort 123, 149; fig 22; pl 17
    temporary camp 123, 125; fig 18
Ireland 25, 94, 176–7
Irvine, postulated Roman fort at 106
iuridicus 70, 76
ius liberorum 35

Javolenus Priscus, *iuridicus* 70
Jay Lane, fort 113
Julius Classicianus, procurator 71, 78
Julius Frontinus, governor 39, 50–1, 62, 63–5, 72, 98, 179, 180–1
Julius Graecinus, father of Agricola 33, 34

Kaims Castle, fortlet 154–5, 156; figs 25, 26
Kintore, temporary camp 134; figs 18, 21
Kirkhill, watchtower 156; fig 25
Kirkbride, fort 161–2; fig 8
Kirkintilloch, fort 109

Lancaster, fort 68; fig 8
Latin, spread of 81, 83
lead pigs 53; pl 5
Learchild, fort 102; figs 15, 27
Leicester 79
legions
    II Adiutrix 39, 152, 160
    II Augusta 79
    IX Hispana 64, 116, 176
    XIV Gemina 39
    XX Valeria Victrix 38, 49, 96, 152
Linlithgow, possible fort 112
Livy 17, 55
Llyn Cerrig Bach, hoard 40, 48; pls 2, 3
Lochlands, temporary camps 125; *see* Camelon
London 78; fig 9
Longshaws, possible fortlet 102
Loudoun Hill, fort 106, 160; figs 15, 27
Lyons ware, pottery 30
Lyne, fort 178
    temporary camp fig 10

Malling (Menteith), fort 113, 123, 178; fig 22; pl 15
    temporary camps 123, 125–6, 148; figs 18, 20; pl 15
Manchester, fort 65; figs 4, 8
Marinus of Tyre 23
Massilia (Marseilles) 33
Mediolanum (Whitchurch) 46; fig 1
Melsonby (Stanwick) hoard 60; pl 6
Middlebie hoard 91
Milton, fort 97–8, 102, 160, 178; figs 14, 15, 27
mineral resources 50
Mollins, fort 110–11; figs 15, 17, 22
Mona (Anglesey) 21
Mons Graupius, battle 17, 41, 120
    course of 137–9
    forces present at 135–8
    location of 129–37
Moss Side, watchtower 157; figs 25, 26
Mucianus 38
Muir o'Fauld, watchtower 156; fig 25; pl 19
Muiryfold, temporary camp 134, 136; figs 18, 21
Mumrills, fort 109, 111; figs 15, 17

nails, hoard of 151
native settlement 102, 117, 167–8; pl 23,

see also brochs, crannogs, duns,
hillforts, oppida, souterrains
Roman artefacts from 171–3; fig 28
Neratius Marcellus, governor 165
Nether Denton, fort 162; figs 8, 27
Newstead, fort 90, 93, 97, 158, 163, 164,
178; figs 14, 15, 27
temporary camp fig 10
Normandykes, temporary camp 134;
figs 18, 21

Oakwood, fort 104, 108, 160, 164, 178;
fig 15
temporary camp fig 10
Old Carlisle, fort 161
Old Kilpatrick, fort 109
Old Penrith, fort 161; fig 8
oppida 91
Oppius Sabinus 152
Orcades (Orkneys) 21, 141–2, 176
ordo 80–1
Ordovices, tribe 21, 46–8, 83
Ostorius Scapula, governor 49–50, 175
Otho, emperor 35, 37
outworks, attached to forts 104
Oxton, fortlet 99; fig 15

Papcastle, fort 161; fig 8
Parisi, tribe 46, 59
Parkneuk, watchtower 156–7; figs 25,
26
patrician 39, 40
pedites singulares Britannici 160
Pennal, fort 51–2; fig 2
Pen Llystyn, fort 53, 161; figs 2, 3
Pen Llwyn, fort 51; fig 2
Petilius Cerialis, governor 37, 38–9, 55,
63–5, 175
Pliny the Elder 22, 56
Pliny the Younger 15
pontificate 40
Portus Trucculensis 21, 140–1
pottery, Roman see also Lyons ware,
samian, terra nigra
dating of 29, 109
fine wares 51–2
from native settlements 171–3; fig 28
pottery, Iron age 31, 167
praefectus castrorum 177
praefectus civitatis 79
praesidia, across the Forth-Clyde
isthmus 108, 113; fig 17

praetor 35–6
Procilla, mother of Agricola 33
procurator 33, 71–2
Ptolemy, geographer 23, 25; fig 1

quaestor 33, 35

Raedykes, temporary camp 130–4; figs
18, 21
Raith, watchtower 156; fig 25
Red House, Corbridge, supply base 68,
85, 162, 178; figs 8, 10, 12, 15
Rerigonius sinus 90, 106; fig 1
Rey Cross, temporary camp 61; figs 4, 6
Rhuddlan, possible fort 51; fig 2
Ribchester, fort 65; figs 4, 8
Richborough (Rutupiae) 141
roads 99–102
romanisation 73–83
Roscius Coelius 38
Rough Castle, fort 108
Roundlaw, watchtower 156; figs 25, 26

Sallust 17, 55
Sallustius Lucullus, governor 161
Salvius Liberalis, iuridicus 70
Salvius Otho Titianus 35
samian pottery 29, 53
Sarmatian war 161
Secular games 183
Selgovae, tribe
location 90; fig 10
relationship with Rome 91–2
senate 34
Seneca 34, 80
Setantii 57
Shielhill north, watchtower 156–7; fig
25
Shielhill south, watchtower 156–7; fig
25
Silchester, town 76–8
Silures, tribe 21, 46, 50–1
Slack, fort 57; fig 8
souterrains 117, 128, 170
spacing, of forts 98–9, 111–12, 146
of watchtowers 155–7
Stanegate, frontier 108, 111–12
Stanwick, native settlement 59–61; figs
4, 5
Stracathro, fort 123, 149, 151; fig 22
group of camps 123–6, 150; fig 20
temporary camp 123, 125; figs 18, 20

Strageath, fort 121, 153, 156, 157–8, 178; figs 15, 17, 18, 22, 25
temporary camp 126–7; fig 18
Stranraer, postulated fort 106
Suetonius Paullinus, governor 34, 37, 49–50, 51, 53

Tacitus
  bias 18
  career 15, 183–4
  concern for geography 21, 55
  factual accuracy 20, 56
  hostility towards Domitian 180
  sources of information 15–16
  style 16
  textual emendation 23, 95
  use of stock characters 18, 49, 55
Taexali, tribe 117, 120; fig 18
Taus (Tay) 21, 55, 84
taxation 168–9
temporary camps 31, 84, 94, 121–7, *see also* Stracathro
  density of troops within 135–6
  design innovations 178
  Severan 131–4
  30-acre group 126–7
terra nigra, pottery 30
Tettius Julianus 152, 181
Textoverdi 57
Thomshill, postulated fort 97
Thorny Hill, watchtower 157; fig 25
Thule 21, 142
Tiberius, emperor 18
timber buildings
  speed of erection 148
  within forts 26
Titus, emperor
  colleague of Agricola 37
  consulship 43
  death 107, 115
  imperial acclamation 107
Tomen-y-Mur, fort 51–2; fig 2
Torwoodlee, broch 171
town council *see ordo*
town houses 81
Traprain Law, tribal capital 91, 171; fig 10
tribunus laticlavius 34
tribunus plebis 35
Trinovantes, tribe 22
Troutbeck, fort 161; fig 8

Tuesis (Spey) 117; fig 1
Tunnocelum 141

Ugrulentum 141
urbanisation 74–81
Usipi, cohort of 42, 176

Vacomagi, tribe 84, 117; fig 18
Valerius Paulinus 37
Venicones, tribe 117, 120, 127, 130, 157; fig 18
Venutius 21, 39, 56, 59–60
Verginius Rufus 181
Verulamium (St Albans), town 22, 74–5, 80; fig 9
  Agricolan inscription from 26, 74–5; pl 7
Vespasian, emperor 37, 42
Vettius Bolanus, governor 18, 38, 180
vexillation fortress 61–2, 64, 85
vigintivirate 34
Vindogara sinus 90, 106; fig 1
Vindolanda (Chesterholm), fort 162; figs 8, 27
vir militaris 40
Vitellius, emperor 36, 38
Votadini, tribe 90–2; fig 10

Walls Hill, native fort 91; fig 10; pl 8
Walton-le-Dale, possible fort 65; fig 4
Ward Law 95, 105; fig 15
watchtowers
  on Eildon Hill North 93
  by Fendoch 149
  along the Gask Ridge 153–7
Watercrook, fort 161; fig 8
waterpipes, lead 26, 52; pl 4
Westerton, watchtower 153, 156–7; figs 25, 26
Westerwood, fort 108
Westmuir, watchtower 156; fig 25
Winchester, town 76–8
Witch Knowe, watchtower 156; figs 25, 26
Woodhead, temporary camp 125; fig 10
Wroxeter, legionary fortress 38, 49; fig 2
  town 79

York, legionary fortress 64; fig 8
Ythan Wells (Glenmailen), temporary camps 125, 131, 134, 135; figs 18, 21